The Archaeology of War

The Archaeology of War
The History of Violence between the 20th and 21st Centuries

Private lecturer Dr paed. habil. Dr phil. habil.
Christian Wevelsiep, Bochum, Germany

ANTHEM PRESS

Anthem Press
An imprint of Wimbledon Publishing Company
www.anthempress.com

This edition first published in UK and USA 2025
by ANTHEM PRESS
75–76 Blackfriars Road, London SE1 8HA, UK
or PO Box 9779, London SW19 7ZG, UK
and
244 Madison Ave #116, New York, NY 10016, USA

First published in the UK and USA by Anthem Press in 2023

© 2025 Christian Wevelsiep

The author asserts the moral right to be identified as the author of this work.

All rights reserved. Without limiting the rights under copyright reserved above, no part of this publication may be reproduced, stored or introduced into a retrieval system, or transmitted, in any form or by any means (electronic, mechanical, photocopying, recording or otherwise), without the prior written permission of both the copyright owner and the above publisher of this book.

British Library Cataloguing-in-Publication Data
A catalogue record for this book is available from the British Library.

Library of Congress Control Number: 2024950829
A catalog record for this book has been requested.

ISBN-13: 978-1-83999-473-9 (Pbk)
ISBN-10: 1-83999-473-8 (Pbk)

This title is also available as an e-book.

The Archaeology of War
The History of Violence between the 20th and 21st Centuries

Private lecturer Dr paed. habil. Dr phil. habil.
Christian Wevelsiep, Bochum, Germany

ANTHEM PRESS

Anthem Press
An imprint of Wimbledon Publishing Company
www.anthempress.com

This edition first published in UK and USA 2025
by ANTHEM PRESS
75–76 Blackfriars Road, London SE1 8HA, UK
or PO Box 9779, London SW19 7ZG, UK
and
244 Madison Ave #116, New York, NY 10016, USA

First published in the UK and USA by Anthem Press in 2023

© 2025 Christian Wevelsiep

The author asserts the moral right to be identified as the author of this work.

All rights reserved. Without limiting the rights under copyright reserved above, no part of this publication may be reproduced, stored or introduced into a retrieval system, or transmitted, in any form or by any means (electronic, mechanical, photocopying, recording or otherwise), without the prior written permission of both the copyright owner and the above publisher of this book.

British Library Cataloguing-in-Publication Data
A catalogue record for this book is available from the British Library.

Library of Congress Control Number: 2024950829
A catalog record for this book has been requested.

ISBN-13: 978-1-83999-473-9 (Pbk)
ISBN-10: 1-83999-473-8 (Pbk)

This title is also available as an e-book.

CONTENTS

Introduction: Understanding the Violence — viii
    A Form of Critical Philosophy of History — viii
    Critical Reflection: Domination and Violence — x
    Dark Spots in History — xvi
    Reflection of Violence — xviii

PART I
VIOLENCE AND HISTORY — 1

Chapter One	War as 'Becoming': On the Ontology of Conflict	3
	History of Power	8
	History in the Space	10
	The Power of Geography	11
	Space as an Aesthetic and Cultural Dimension	13
	Violence and Order	16
	The Sense and Sensibility of Violence	19
	Between Nature and Culture	20
Chapter Two	The Embodiment of the Victim: Phenomenology of Violence Suffered	25

PART II
DARK SPOTS IN HISTORY — 31

	The Phatic Function of Cultural Memory	34
	Understanding the Century	35
	Orientation between the Centuries	35
Chapter Three	Colonial Violence: The Dark Sides of the Modern State	37
	Remembrance of Colonial Violence in 'German Southwest Africa'	37
	Violence in the Shadows: The Armenian Genocide	40
	The Colonial Gaze: Reflections on Cultural Psychology	44

Chapter Four	Hate: On the enigma of divisiveness in the age of the total	49
	The Existence of the Hate	50
	The Motif of Refusal	53
	Understanding the Ordinary and the Extraordinary	55
	Violence and Meaning	58
Chapter Five	Disastrous Violence: Ideologies	63
	The Terrible Banality	64
	The Reality of Evil	67
	Ideologies and Doctrines	68
	The War as a Noumenon	71
	The Motive of Enmity	74
	The Peculiar Emptiness of Morality	78
Chapter Six	Politics, Violence and Sacrality	81
	Religious Dark Spots	82
	What Remains? On the Sacral Dimension of the Present	86
Chapter Seven	The Frightening Love of War	95
	Violence and Philosophy	96
	The War as a Teacher	98
	Aporias of Violence	101
	The Meaning of War	104
	Under the Sign of Non-violence	107

PART III
BETWEEN THE TWENTIETH AND TWENTY-FIRST CENTURY: THE WORLDVIEW OF CONCERN — 111

Chapter Eight	The Valorative Space in Times of War	117
	Modernity and Violence	118
	Understanding the Violence	121
	Philosophy of History in the Face of Violence	122
Chapter Nine	What Does 'Learning from History' Mean? On the Implicit Pedagogy of History	127
	Introduction	127
	Philosophy of History after the Illusion of Feasibility	129
	The Power of Narration	131
	Dialogical Culture of History	135
	The Implicit Understanding of Hermeneutics	137

Chapter Ten	War Again? The Contribution of Philosophy to the Phenomenon of War	141
	Introduction	141
	The Preference of the Own	143
	Violence and Order	145
	The Challenge of Enmity	149
Chapter Eleven	From the Worldview of War to the Worldview of Concern	153
	Politics and Life	154
	The Logic of Worldviews	156
	The Worldview of War	159
	The Worldview of Concern	163
	Philosophy and History	166

Bibliography   171
Index   185

INTRODUCTION: UNDERSTANDING THE VIOLENCE

A Form of Critical Philosophy of History

Another history of violence? Has violence not been sufficiently and extensively explained? Is it not before our eyes in the countless books, so that we would only have to 'inform' ourselves accordingly? What is the point of reconstructing history if we cannot expect something fundamentally new that leads beyond the known abysses of the history of violence?

History is full of dark shades that reach into the present. The past, however, does not stand still but forces each generation to look up and take a close look. Hot and cold procedures of memory bring this history to life. In the centre of the present discussion, these procedures are to be expanded by a special approach. The dark spots of history that are being talked about here are significant – they accompany us in all present actions. In a very generalised form, it is about visualising, perceiving and coping with the violence of past times. Violence has shaped past eras, and war has shown its many faces differently in each age. However, this violence has also been perceived as an evil in the long run and has been fought with serious initiatives.

The attempts to nurture war and make peace possible lead us to a difficult point in history. It is possible that we are at a point where the relations of violence need to be reinterpreted differently. But it is also possible that violence has only changed its face, giving rise to new narratives of violence.

The preconditions of such a history of violence are not simple. First of all, we assume a uniformity and generality that conditions the frivolous talk of *a history*: an 'we' stands in this history as the subject of action and a continuous line is drawn from the past to the present. In this respect alone, the present work exposes itself to various reproaches. Humanity as a collective subject is a mere insinuation – and to the same extent history should not look beyond particular cultures. In order to counter these possible critical objections, several points need to be clarified, which at the same time leads to the methodological premises of what follows. The path from the darknesses of the past to the greyness of the present is connected with a special form of the philosophy of history, political philosophy and the doctrine of understanding, hermeneutics. These theories help to make the history of violence narratable in a simplistic way, without disregarding its complexity. Only under certain conditions can we then claim that the dark places of history have brought us to a point where violence is re-evaluated.

However, this does not mean writing a history of progress in which violence is finally defeated, nor a history of decay in which violence continues to determine the fate of the world.

The fundamental thesis is that we must perceive violence in all its shades: the present practical contexts of action must be thought of and read together with past transgressions, subconscious effects, moral burdens and legal principles. There is a call in this thesis to be aware of the ambivalences of human violence and to consider history as a whole, despite all scepticism and negative findings.

The form in which history is considered here is connected in various ways with the tradition of the philosophy of history. Philosophy of history is understood here as an approach that recognises a continuity in historical events and translates this course into a narratable and meaningful matrix. From the point of view of the philosophy of history, we can look at the rise and fall of great empires, the flowering and decline of a particular culture. This assumes the fixation of an origin and the logic of a course that, like all good stories, follows a thread that leads across time.

But one must differentiate: What kind of philosophy of history is being addressed here? The philosophy of the Enlightenment, which defines the collective subject humanity 'discovered' and wanted to advance the human path to reason? Universal history, which had progress in the consciousness of freedom in mind (Hegel) or rather the materialist variety, which pursued the perspective of the excluded and oppressed? What about the philosophy of history of power, which led to Nietzsche's distinction between the powerful and the powerless? Is the philosophy of history only possible as a negative form in the sense of critical theory or even as archaeology in the sense of Foucault?

The present perspective attempts to rehabilitate the philosophy of history to some extent in the broad field of tradition and critique and to put its motives in their proper place. Criticism of the philosophy of history does not have to be in contradiction to a critical reorientation.

The critical motif that we find in Walter Benjamin, for example, forms the basic idea that can be preserved in a critical synthesis. As is well known, Benjamin had tried to tie the concept of history to the practice of life. Neither the older historicism nor the philosophy of history of Marxism, which was virulent in his time, was sufficient for Benjamin's thinking, which was dedicated to the saving power of memory. For him, history came close to a history of meaning when it emphasised the motif of the resistant.

Walter Benjamin's philosophical worldview touched on religious allegories. His *Angel of History* was a powerful metaphor that referred to the anonymity of the course of the world. In a world where rubble was inexorably piled up, only the memory of the dead remained to piece together what was broken. The language handed down to us by this critical author with these and other metaphorical images set a standard of critical history. History was to be measured by historical suffering and injury alone. Memory was given a saving function when it saw something in these ruins that was not meant to be. The continuum that only followed the gaze of the victors would be broken. The damage that was incessantly caused by history would then be healed. To think critically about history would thus be to redeem the broken promises of the past (Benjamin, 1942, vol. 2, p. 701).

The form of the philosophy of history moves here into the vicinity of messianic thinking. At the moment when critical thinking leaves the historical time structure, we enter theological spheres that can only be interpreted at a proper distance. The only question is how far we can use the normative terms that Benjamin and others used as a matter of course in their time for the present narrative.

What principles of the philosophy of history underlie the present analyses? Various aspects can be mentioned that continue to operate subliminally and can thus be mentioned as characteristics of continuity. History, however much it breaks down into particular, scattered and sometimes fragmented individual histories, is to be understood as a continuum. Looking back, we can recognise developments in the past. These developments do not follow any preceding goal orientation and do not form a 'higher' teleology; no moral power is driven forth in them, which in the end culminates in the logic of a reasonable authority. But in history, lines of development are formed which, under certain conditions, can be connected with meaning in retrospect. These lines include the loss of religious legitimacy and progressive secularisation, the rise of the authoritative state and its decline, the emergence of cultural systems and the progress of scientific and technical action complexes.

The philosophy of history of our time receives its legitimacy from the expectations articulated in all the centuries before. Under extremely different conditions, scientific, moral or technical developments can be traced in historical cultures. But these different lines nevertheless lead to a generality that can be called universal history or world history (Rohbeck, 2004). The question is how to integrate cultural developments into a unifying generality within the framework of this grand history. The philosophy of history at issue here is concerned with wide-ranging contexts of action that can be discerned from the flight of eagles alone (Osterhammel, 2017). Its aim – as prescribed by the older conceptions – is to consider history as a whole.

Critical Reflection: Domination and Violence

Violence forces arduous reflections. Whenever violence occurs, not only is 'someone' scarred by the violence, but something is also called into question. Violence is an open question and only rarely is it answered satisfactorily.

The first and comprehensible thought is about man himself. Violence is man-made; it is the action and execution of an event that we associate with meaning in retrospect. To speak of violence is to speak of that human being of whom we know that he or she is not only capable of certain actions, but is also prepared to translate thought into action. In this respect, the human psyche is an undiscovered country, dark and remote, enigmatic and resistant. These insights have no claim to originality; they merely repeat what was formulated millennia ago. Man is the essence of violence, which should be protected from itself. The furore of violence goes back to affects that had been contained in laborious processes. Whenever the readiness for aggression becomes apparent, one fears a return of archaic violence. Have we not, writes André Glucksmann, banished collective hatred to the history books? Hasn't individual malice been delegated to psychologists (Glucksmann, 2004, p. 8)?

Modernity is in a defensive position vis-à-vis violence. One fears the return of elemental forces that are only seemingly kept in check. Knowledge about the origins of violence does not help when hatred unfolds. For hate can be denied; differentiated explanations can be invoked that relate to circumstances, situations and factors. But nothing can be done against the furore that allies itself with hatred on a large and small scale. Modernity thus remains in a situation of powerlessness: people have settled into a situation of trusting each other. But as soon as violence 'breaks into' everyday life, this trust is shaken (Reemtsma, 2008).

In the present work, a path is taken that will not initially follow this obvious reflex. The human being, who is naturally of interest as the essence of violence, moves into the background. It is the inter-existential tensions that are to be addressed in the context of violence. The themes devoted to the phenomenon of violence include human aspects: the category of domination, the relationship to religion and to a respective meaning. It is these categories that nevertheless do not suspend human beings from their responsibility.

To begin with the cause of domination is, in a sense, logical. Only in and through domination can the irrational, dark forces of violence be controlled. As we shall see, this conviction is insightful; at the same time, however, it is fraught with an eminent contradiction. For the difficulties begin at the moment when we equate domination with statehood. The following discussion takes this constellation into account. Domination and violence form a closely interwoven context that must be viewed from more than just one side.

Whatever we think we know about violence today, historically it is something we cannot get rid of. As a fundamental force, it is effective in life and permeates people's thoughts and actions. Yet its structure is contradictory. Violence permeates life, just like love or time. In doing so, it passes through all areas of life and yet remains alien, incomprehensible, insoluble in life. Phenomenologically, it is the very other of the orders in which we live (Waldenfels, 2000).

Philosophy ascribes an aporetic core to violence because it calls existing orders into question and, in a sense, finds no place anywhere. On the other hand, an objection can be raised from the point of view of history: violence has always proved to be a historically effective power in the course of time; it has shown its destructive as well as its formative side. Immanuel Kant famously opposed the tendency of contemporary war and described war as an extreme evil, but he too was aware of the effect of war. The latter was sublime in that it overrode self-interest and base interests (Kant, *Critique of the Power of Judgement*, 2005). As is well known, we find comparable statements in Hegel or Nietzsche; war still has a good reputation there because it is vitalistic, because it brings to bear the forces of life that are forgotten in times of peace. And as much as a longing for peace is spreading, a fatal finding remains to be noted: peace has less radiance; it is inconspicuous and rarely noticed. Its arrival takes place in a smoothing, calming movement; it is akin to the musical and religious language of the requiem (Waldenfels, 2019, p. 257).

This ambivalence is reflected in the relationship between domination and violence. Two theses stand in opposition to each other, without a simple mediation becoming apparent. The first thesis states that violence decreases when domination prevails; the second emphasises that domination depends on certain forms of violence. What kind of violence and what forms of domination are to be distinguished is to be asked in the following. In an abstract reading, however, we can follow this rough distinction: violence follows an existing order; it is produced and increased by it. In another view, order shows itself as a power that is superior to violence.

A look into the depths of history is instructive. Even the oldest stories that have been handed down contain motifs that can easily be transformed into contemporary meaning.

Here is an example: the famous dialogue of the 'Melians' is one of these unbreakable, ageless stories. Thucydides described it in his history of the Peloponnesian War. The Melians had resisted Athens' supremacy with good reasons and invoked their neutrality. The desire of the inhabitants on the small island in the Aegean was not to take part in the conflict between Sparta and Athens; the will of the Athenians, on the other hand, was aimed at breaking the resistance. Although Melos had no great military importance, the great power Athens faced a conflict. For if it gave in to the Melians' desire, so the argument went, it would face a development that would have fatal consequences for a great empire. As the hegemon in the region, it could not tolerate dissenters; as soon as a political unit, however small, broke away, Athens' power would crumble in no time. Countless stragglers would follow suit and the political authority of the empire would suffer incalculable damage (Münkler, 2005, pp. 30–33).

In the final analysis, the 'dialogue' ends up in a power struggle. Brute force was the reaction of the hegemonic power, which did not want or could not afford to lose face. Thus, Thucydides did not simply rewrite the history of the Peloponnesian War, but delivered a vivid lesson on power politics. The power of the factual overrode the fickle parties; Melos fell, the men were killed, women and children carried off into slavery. The downfall of the small island state was then only a prelude to further expansions by Athens – expeditions that gave the 'natural' compulsion to prey on empires and in the long run led to their downfall.

Thus, in the simplest interpretation, one could conclude: *rule is based on violence.* Even a cursory glance at history confirms this sentence. Domination is associated with a power of action that is based on physical superiority. Further historical evidence of the raw power of domination can be found.

Let us look at the Imperial Annals of 782 AD in the Empire of the Franks. Charlemagne had ordered the execution of 4,500 Saxons near the town of Verden; the gravesites suggest other numbers, but the blood court of Verden is considered a historical fact. Widukind, a Westphalian nobleman, had led the Saxon wars against Charlemagne. He was considered an adversary in the Carolingian Empire, a military leader who had been plundering and pillaging the Frankish territory since 775 AD. These were gruelling wars on both sides (Weinfurter, 2005, p. 108).

The brutalisation of war, which had found a climax in the Blood Court, seems to lend credence to the assumption that domination is in a bloody alliance with violence.

Striking images can be imagined that connect with the themes of the present. On one side is raw domination, which takes up the sword for its supremacy. On the opposite side, adversaries fight for their existence. The domination prevailed because it had the more effective means and a physical superiority; the defeated were left with nothing but the path to death or surrender.

However, one does not do justice to history with such simple images. The rule over great empires was, of course, conducted with the greatest harshness and brutality. Nevertheless, other aspects have to be taken into account that produce a different picture of rule. No rule can stand the test of time if it does not go beyond the capacity for violence; no empire would last if it relied solely on the strength of the military. It is therefore necessary to move away from the frightening picture of blood judgement and paint a broader, more open picture of rule. Or rather, the same story must be told twice, from different points of view.

State and violence form a unity in the first picture. Here one must be explicit: organised rule needs military forces that it can incorporate for its purposes. Such an abstract formulation does not yet contain a definition of the state in the narrower sense; it is merely a matter of state-like entities that were able to develop upwards over the millennia and were thereby dependent on organised violence.

The thesis of the organised violence of rule is provocative. It is not only Charlemagne's rule that would be in the twilight of this thesis, but all political organisations. In the enclosure of the state, violence is monopolised; the raison d'état becomes the ultimate certainty that justifies all violent actions. For critical thinkers, the pathology of domination lies in the means of war. War serves the ruling class to realise its essence – an essence that is fundamentally linked to violence. Only the ability to wage war makes this state an entity that has an axis and a centre, a middle and a measure.

This consideration of violence directs the gaze to the centre of politics. Some observers suspect a relation that deciphers the riddle of violence in an amazingly simple way. Statehood and war are inextricably linked. Historical observation reveals to the critical historian the compelling logic of political irrationality. When the *great men of history* feel called upon to sacrifice human lives in the name of the state, this lack of reason becomes apparent (Krippendorff, 1992).

Is this an anachronistic fallacy? Is this not a case of a form of warfare that has excelled above all in the context of state- and nation-building – and has been described many times? At the very least, it would have to be justified how the thesis of the organised violence of war could be upheld under modern circumstances. Critical publics in democratic societies at least no longer allow for simplification. The pathology of the raison d'état allows the operators of the state to use human lives for a supposedly higher cause. Not so much has changed in that regard. But both the form of war has changed and the nature of the state is undergoing permanent change.

The critical thought is to be emphasised, even if a number of shortcuts are to be criticised. Domination is associated with violence, and the state has written itself into memory over the centuries with all conceivable forms of violence. But already with the title of the state, this observation gets caught in a web of contradictions.

For the state we are dealing with in *this context is* obviously linked to a line of tradition of political rule that was founded, among others, by Machiavelli. His *Discorsi sopra la prima Deca di Tito Livio* of 1531 was characterised by a cosmic fatalism and a deep anthropological scepticism. Rome became the model for this thinker of power. The political theory of behaviour, called Machiavellianism, goes back to the dark side of human drives. Accordingly, rule requires a realistic view of the morally ordinary human being. Not religion or moral greatness secures the existing order, but patriotism alone. The 'to be or not to be' of the fatherland, still blatantly expressed in Machiavelli's late medieval Florence, was at the centre of this political thinking. The preservation of this order justified the emergency, the politics of exception and above all the ruthless violence of the ruler.

In this basic motif, numerous other philosophers have followed the thinker from the House of Medici; and here, too, the thoughts between domination and violence seem to overlap. This form of the political includes calculation as well as the generation of fear, brutal access and the awareness of one's own capacity for violence. All of this ensures the continued existence of the state without concern for the moral complications. The cards of 'moral' rule are on the table; they stem from a reassessment of the religious past. Orientation to the *here and now of* the secular order justifies political action; radically this-worldly, radically power-conscious.

Various objections can be raised against this figure of the violent state. In particular, the idea that the state is an institution without time or history must be questioned. The state is not timeless; it knows various stages of development, peaks and dwindling stages. Its shape is in a constant state of change. It is therefore not of secondary importance which state one addresses when one speaks of increased readiness for war or of de facto violence. Moreover, the thesis of the state willing to use violence can be accused of one-sidedness if only violence is taken into account and not also the ability to conclude peace.

In the following, let us try to look at the context from a different perspective. Let us first detach ourselves from the historical space of Europe. This is where the state was invented, which flourished from the eighteenth to the twentieth century and literally kept the world in suspense. The philosophers of the early modern era had seen in the state a primordial force, a moral necessity in which freedom is realised. In real history, however, this state has revealed itself as a primordial force. This path led from the detachment from church power to the totality of modernity. Constitutional law, the right of self-determination of nascent nations, colonialism and competition are among its characteristic features. This state has its advantages: the social and welfare state, democracy and the sovereign exercise of individual rights. At the same time, it has the face of the twentieth century.

It helped to shape the political system of the twentieth century, when it developed into a totalitarian state under fascism.

However, in order to do justice to the connection between domination and violence in all respects, a broad and open perspective is to be taken. The state has used war as its means, but war itself has also had a great influence on the state. If we speak of 'societies' in this context, then the thesis can be sharpened: the war has in certain respects produced state societies, larger, stronger and more secure social units than before.

Of course, this thesis is only plausible under certain conditions. War, that evil of humanity that has caused so much suffering, is not a 'value' or an 'instrument' to enable prosperity. War is a phenomenon in the human world that is difficult to grasp and appears as a permanent guest in the political world. Only archaeology, however, uncovers the functions that war has assumed in human history. Over a period of many thousands of years, developments can be shown that surprise any unbiased observer: the victors of wars have 'assimilated' the vanquished in the long term. Larger and more powerful societies emerged in the wake of these wars. Societies of a higher order were able to maintain peace in the interior and significantly increase security for each individual (Morris, 2013, p. 15).

The objection is justified: when we speak of societies, we are referring to empires and great kingdoms that conquered land, took booty and subjugated people. For archaeology and anthropology, however, it is less about political-moral facts than about long-term patterns. 'War', writes Ian Morris, 'has made humanity safer and richer' (Ibid., p. 17).

As contemporaries who remember the twentieth century with all its horrors, this thesis is admittedly ambivalent. For all the scientific distance, it is not only the function of wars that must be examined but also the phenomenology of violence. The dialectic of peace and war, security and threat, of violence and non-violence does not dissolve. Admittedly, the fundamental idea of progress cannot be dismissed out of hand. But for a comprehensive view, a phenomenology of violence is indispensable that is not reduced to the history of Leviathan alone.

These reflections should be understood in this sense: they oscillate between historical narratives that have a particular charisma. One narrative reports the violence of state rule with a wealth of historical evidence. The other is inspired by the philosophy of history; it recognises a profound progress in the history of violence from which we particularly benefit. Both positions have been thought through and varied many times; their value for intellectual history is beyond question.

However, we have to start from a different premise here. Violence as such must be thought through without starting from a strong premise – without clinging to the advantage of a peace dividend and without fixing one's gaze on the brutality of forms of rule. Violence is *in the world*, it is an explicable but also dark entity. It casts shadows that stem from the past but also from the opacity of the human psyche. The present thoughts focus on the existence of this violence, which we encounter in so many historical and contemporary situations. One should not hope for a final detachment from this violence or for a final victory; this victory would probably only have been bought with a graveyard peace. What is at stake instead is to be presented in three successive parts. The aim is to acquire an awareness of violence with all its contradictions, boundary shifts, repetitions and ruptures.

The phenomenology of violence is a form of archaeology because it uncovers the buried parts of violent conflicts; it is at the same time an explanation of the stumbling course of history, but also a confrontation with the inexplicable.

This approach can be divided into three major headings. They form a more or less dialectical connection. Dark traces of the past are to be pointed out first. We call them dark spots of history that lead a shadow-like existence in our present. These dark sides of the historical process must be opposed by forces that prove to be illuminating, luminous and consequently positive. Both parts are thus in opposition, which can be connected with a metaphor of light. Where the path of the history of violence finally leads, the closer one approaches the present in the depiction, is to be shown in the third part. The bright light of the Enlightenment and the dark shadows of the past do not dissolve; rather, they intermingle in an obscure space of the present.

Violence is, on the one hand, a form of *embodiment*, a process in which something is set aside and someone is affected. However, the lines of embodiment from the past to the present do not run in a straight line, and they can only be described today under certain conditions. Furthermore, violence as an event has acquired a specific *meaning* and has been captured as an *image*, *as* it were. This aspect is also complex and cannot be summarised in a simple chronology. Violence is enhanced, elevated or simply justified by a special meaning. But seen from the other side, this meaning is itself a moment of violence, if only because it inscribes further violence into history.

The following part, as will be shown, results from the previous insights. Under what conditions can we still speak of violence today, which has become so distant and alien to us? How can we build bridges from the past to the present in order to finally get to grips with violence or even get rid of it altogether? These legitimate questions are confronted here with some scepticism, but they would at least have to be linked to a thought that is unavoidable. We live in an *age of worry* (Part III) – this thesis will have to be justified in detail in the last part. Concern is an essential feature of human life forms, as it permeates our thinking, acting and feeling. But in the confrontation with violence, this concern stands, as it were, naked. It is not an exclusive characteristic or a noble trait that distinguishes some more and others less. It is only properly understood as a basic motif of the inter-existential form of a human world.

What exactly it means to live in a special time of concern will have to be asked explicitly in the concluding part, and as immodest as this question seems, one will be humbled by the possible answers.

Dark Spots in History

The first major part, as we shall see, determines the progress of all the following arguments. The dark spots of history are the focus of the narratives, but not in the sense of an enlightening message. What exactly can be understood under the heading must first be clarified.

The great philosopher Hannah Arendt is credited with a statement that can also be considered a diagnosis of an epoch. The only authentic form of looking into the future would be successful if one made a promise that one could keep. This insight refers to something fundamentally negative, for which various labels are ready.

The twentieth century is considered not only totalitarian, extreme and violent but also one of betrayal (Todorov, 1993). The unkept promises have shaped thinking about the twentieth century, and there is no end in sight to the efforts to understand it (Diner, 2015).

In this context, a complex psychological situation becomes apparent. It arises from the human capacity to learn from experience, to develop as a learning being and at the same time to elevate this capacity above one's own biography. This creates a claim that leads back to the dictum of the promise kept and at the same time appears as a burden of responsibility – that the events of the twentieth should not be reflected in the twenty-first century.

The difficulty, of course, does not lie solely in the capacity for action that one acquires through historical and moral awareness, but in the peculiar constellation between history and psychology. The transition from the twentieth to the twenty-first century is marked by precisely this constellation.

Can we assume that history has an impact that could contribute to a silent transmission of historical meaning? In this case, understanding what happened in the past epochs would be the prerequisite for a socially integrative context that one longs for, so to speak. However, the claim of wanting to understand also carries a certain burden. Understanding becomes the touchstone of a history from which one can expect a specific learning process. Of course, there is nothing to be said against such a learning process in principle.

And yet the hermeneutic 'ideal picture' – according to which history moves together in the medium of language – must be given a complementary view. Even if we assume with hermeneutics (Gadamer, 1971) that there is an event of meaning in the course of history, there are dark spots that cannot be completely resolved. Historical experience is not only shaped by a hermeneutically catchable meaning but also by motives of misunderstanding.

To put it simply, we are moving in a diffuse space between definiteness and indefiniteness, between unquestioning rationality and transmissions in ignorance. The twentieth and twenty-first centuries thus stand in a relationship of question and answer, whereby the structure of the answer is more complex and unfathomable than all Enlightenment intentions. The questions are open, they can be translated into legal-pragmatic, ethical and social perspectives; they aim at the indelible human dignity, at the tensions of freedom and equality and at the critique of relations of violence. The practical references are reflected in ongoing discourses on the politics of human rights in the horizon of historical experience (Brunkhorst, 2005).

The twenty-first century can thus be interpreted as a response to the experiences of the twentieth century, but the scope for questioning takes on immense dimensions.

For the tradition of hermeneutics, as mentioned before, an impact event was assumed in which the time horizons merge into one another.

What, however, would one have to consider if one did *not* unreservedly agree with this idea of an unbreakable event of meaning? History and psychology have an ambivalent relationship. In principle, everything that is historically accessible and linguistically communicable can be flushed to the surface in the medium of language. But beyond language, as is well known, there are networks of effects that are closed to the understanding of meaning. Deep hermeneutics speaks here of fractures of non-understanding (Rüsen/Straub, 1998a). It directs attention to historical and 'Findings' that do not come to light in the medium of language. Such obscurities add to the catchy image that has recently entered contemporary consciousness a little hastily: that humanity is on its way to mastering a violence that has set the tone across all historical epochs.

Reflection of Violence

The twentieth century holds many titles that emphasise the extraordinary. It was a century of totalitarianism, but also one of betrayal, an age of extremes and the incomprehensible. Betrayed, that is, at the mercy of unrestrained violence, were not only the people themselves but also, as it were, the idea of the human being. For up to a certain point, one could weigh oneself in the security of an inner connection between people. As is well known, such certainties were knocked out of hand in that century.

Many situations, many images, motifs and sources can be named for this experience of unbounded violence, which now, at the beginning of the twenty-first century, requires new forms of transmission. In an era flooded with images, however, attention is more difficult. One has to go in search of traces; not because the sources are missing, but because the form of inscription in history is problematic. This search for traces leads directly to 'what remains of Auschwitz' (Agamben, 2003), to the motif of resistance. The memories of Auschwitz show people who turned to the outside world at the lowest point of despair. How could one, although all attempts failed, give the public an idea of what was going on in the camps? How could one report on the events that would otherwise have remained without witness? In fact, there were plans of the crematoria hidden by Auschwitz camp inmates. They were finally buried in the ground, when the hopelessness of escape was realised, in a kind of message in a bottle in tinplate eating utensils (Müller, 1979, Didi-Hubermann, 2007).

Remains of history, recorded in the ground, arouse archaeological interest. Traces of the distant and near past are recorded in the historical archives; history thus becomes a clear picture with an orderly chronology. History buried in the earth, on the other hand, is silent history that is only made to speak through historiographic procedures. The indecipherable, frayed and illegible writings of the death slaves contained messages that open up a space of meaning of the historical. It is this space of meaning that is the focus of the following.

Why did people bury these documents? This question, like many others, cannot be answered definitively and it would be inappropriate to consider the individual motives of the inmates in such a hopeless situation. These experiences remain in the form of singularity. Nevertheless, the act of leaving a message in the ground touches that space of meaning that surrounds the whole century. The act embraces a resistance and an attitude that we might call concern for meaning. Far from concern for one's own existence, which probably seemed long lost at this point, it was about resistance to forgetting and negation. Numerous documents handed down the will of the perpetrators to erase the existence of the Other and, in the process, to remove even the last traces of extermination. The concept of the 'Final Solution' ultimately also betrayed motives of an unfathomable radicalism for which appropriate categories were lacking. The Others were not only to be eliminated, but to disappear, as it were, into their history. It was a matter of eliminating even the last vestige of all traces that came from the people and from the deeds.

These events are preserved in the historical space of meaning of our time. Countless documents tell of a violence that is far away and yet has an intrusive proximity. But what is the nature of the message that was conveyed there? The following reflections revolve around this as yet unanswered question. Unanswered here means: although we have accumulated immense historical knowledge, although there are high-quality treatises on the meaning and absurdity of what happened, reflecting on the violence is still a serious task. It poses itself anew for every generation and for every time. The ambition of the present study is thus by no means small. It is not just a matter of 'decoding' the violence of the twentieth century, and in particular the violence of fascism, once again. Rather, it is about finding an approach to the history of violence that helps us to shed light on violence as a phenomenon.

The means by which such an approach can be found should be shown by the present considerations. The theme of violence forces us to ascend to the heights of social theory in order to get close to the human phenomenon. In this respect, violence is a phenomenon in the social world *that counts*.

Questions about the social theory of our time remain to some extent unanswered (Pinker, 2011). The fundamental thesis of an end to violence remains controversial. The progress of human development is perceptible and, to a certain extent, 'countable' because a general tendency to renounce violence is recognisable. Overall, violence has become controllable, even if it is still present; at least it has decreased in quality and scope. According to Pinker, the present shows a decline in manifest violence that can be empirically recorded. With all the relapses, violence is now controllable; in everyday life and in major politics, in social interaction and in international relations, there is a tendency to refrain from violence.

Forces drive history forward that resist the pull of violence. Man is endowed with the capacity to reason and to weigh things up; he resists short-tempered impulses and he opposes irascibility with self-control. The empathy curbs the impulse of wounded pride; morality sets narrow limits to free forces. Non-violence may be an airy ideal to which no human order will ever perfectly correspond, but, according to Pinker, the sensible renunciation of violence nevertheless has a status in common life that must be valued. In this context, psychology recognises traditional qualities taken from the sources of the Enlightenment: a sense of morality and the power of self-control, deliberation and forbearance, empathy and morality – the catalogue is pertinent and unsurprising (Pinker, 2011, 2018).

Social theory must be measured against these statements, but above all it would have to refer to the question of countability. Steven Pinker refers to statistical statements that seem to prove that violence has been successfully combated over the centuries. Accordingly, the risk of becoming a victim of a violent act at present is far lower than in previous eras.

But this only answers part of the question of violence. The contradiction already appears in the language itself. Violence that can be counted can be translated into quantitative data, but this says nothing about the violence that counts. Violence that has meaning cannot be equated with the mere number of victims.

One of the difficulties of social theory is the ambiguity of the object of violence. Whenever we deal with phenomena of violence, we are dealing with diffuse attributions:

violence is an experience that others have had and it is at the same time a theoretical interpretation. Violence 'happens', in a context of action, between people and groups, in and with language. Violence is thus to be understood as an experience and event, although it is naturally intertwined with human action.

Another difficulty: when violence happens, it has something of an intrusion into a hitherto intact world. Reflection on violence is therefore directed towards the question of how one could restore the integrity of that world. This, however, refers to nothing other than the realm of language. And this is where the eminent difficulties of dealing with violence begin. For the hope that we could leave the zones of violence by means of the ability of language remains deceptive.

The discourse on violence thus falls into at least two parts. The older, supposedly idealistic position goes back to Hannah Arendt's thought that in the moment of dialogical encounter we are always already beyond the world of violence.

More recent approaches in social theory distance themselves from this assumption and emphasise the original entanglement of violence in linguistic contexts. A polemical structure comes to the fore in quarrels, fights or wars. Even in antiquity, people were aware of the negative trace of existence; not only vulnerability but also the power to injure characterises the social and political world.

The dark violence that was already plumbed in depth in the writings of the ancient thinkers draws a trail right into life itself. This seems to be the basic message of modern social theory. The experience of violence is its starting point. 'We' come into the world as unreservedly vulnerable beings and have to cope with the negativity of violence throughout our lives. Violence is inevitable because we are exposed to each other from the beginning and can never fully overcome the registers of violence (Butler, 2004, p. 20; Liebsch, 2018).

This way of addressing violence is uncomfortable. Violence is not to be understood as an exception that breaks through the crust of everyday life for a moment, but is omnipresent. For the present study, the difficulty thus arises in countering the contamination by violence in the theoretical account. It is necessary to search for margins of non-violence, of justified renunciation of violence, without which all reflections remain empty. In this point, the present reflections set themselves apart from conventional approaches.

The aim of the reflection was accordingly formulated as follows: phenomena of violence are to be brought up in such a way that their violent core emerges. This violence is an unavoidable component of human life that is to be transformed into a form of *comprehended violence*. At the moment of enlightenment through language, spaces of responsibility are opened up. As much as we allow ourselves to be guided by a philosophy that speaks of the motive of violation from the very beginning of natality, we must nevertheless direct our gaze towards responsible conditions of non-violence.

How, and above all with which linguistic, semantic, methodological and scientific-theoretical means this goal can be achieved is to be worked out in the further course. The focus of the analyses is, as will quickly become apparent, on the depiction of historical situations of violence. However, a connection to the violent situations of the present is always made possible. The analyses are to be understood less as systematic contributions to the discipline of historiography than as basic reflections on social theory. One of the essential aspects is to be found in the motif of conceived history.

However, the terms are more complicated than one might imply. On the surface, cosmopolitanism would be said to be close to peace, justice and equality. A cosmopolitan world would thus be characterised by liberal ideas and permeated by political relations in which individuals, groups, peoples and nations coexist in a harmonious balance.

A realistic view of conditions in the twenty-first century, however, must break away from such a simple interpretation. The question is whether the world has come closer to the ideal of the world of states that Immanuel Kant and other thinkers of the Enlightenment had in mind. Or whether we are currently dealing with a situation in which humanitarian catastrophes can and will continue to occur. Determining the gap between the idea of global law and the harsh reality is thus the primary task. The gap between cosmopolitan design and modern spaces of vulnerability is to be measured.

This task is admittedly demanding. Political ethics requires us to determine a measure of justice, security and prosperity that every individual can in principle enjoy. But under what conditions can we speak of political relations that are producible in the simplest sense? Critical theories in this context focus on relations of violence that provoke outrage. As described, critical thinking is directed against the hegemonic determinations that openly or covertly turn against life itself.

Beyond social theory, which sometimes drifts into philosophical heights, concrete questions remain. How could one move from a world of global irresponsibility to a system of collective governance that counters violence with appropriate means? How could life worth protecting be preserved without subjecting political conditions themselves to a level of violence? Of course, these are questions that have been discussed for decades in the philosophy of law and political ethics (Ruggie, 1992; Krause, 2004).

The claim of the present reflection is certainly not to provide a recipe by which the world can be healed. Theory – as always – is helpful only in that it develops a language with which we can obtain a life-serving reference to the world. The methodology must be oriented towards this language to be developed. Therefore, it would first be problematic to subject the problems of world society indicated here to a precise analysis, no matter how brilliant it may be.

Everything that is to be presented (instead) converges in a worldview of concern that is at the centre of the presentation. In this worldview, current relations and historical dynamics of concern are expressed. Before the practical question of what to do, there is the profound question of the preconditions of relating to the world and, in particular, the confrontation with that of the category of violence.

The reflections are difficult to reduce to a single point of view. Violence has many faces, diverse forms, it forms signatures and metamorphoses. In view of the complexity of human history, it seems impossible to agree on statements that are acceptable and binding for all. Historical violence is itself incomprehensible, its shape in constant change. It forms a dark and almost incomprehensible field. The questions we ask of the history of violence from a distanced standpoint are, in a sense, questions of humanity: How is violence legitimised?

What disguises serve violence in a particular epoch to mask the character of the violation? Under what circumstances does strangeness turn into hostility? The various faces of violence appear on the surface of history, only to disappear the next moment; then they return with unexpected force. So the claim cannot be to cover the entire panorama of possible situations of violence.

To provide a guide to the considerations, violence as a historical experience can be reconstructed in different narrative framings. To this end, an attempt will be made in the following to tell the story of the past century in different ways. To put it simply: the history of the twentieth century is repeatedly brought to unfoldment by choosing an alternative focus of the narrative in each case. The accent at the beginning *is on* the *phenomenon of power (first part)*. History is the history of power – with good reason we can speak of a polemic reflection. In this 'narrative', we encounter violence like a relapse. The events of violence force us to ask about the 'behind' of the story. Behind the power, as much can be asserted in advance, are unresolved conflicts, contradictions and antinomies. It therefore makes sense to consult the language of psychology with regard to the unresolved conflicts: the history of power would thus remain incomplete if it were reduced only to the raw opposition. The concepts of guilt, conscience and morality are to be integrated into the considerations.

History is then, it is hoped, more than an anonymous event, but deeply connected to the psyche of the human being.

Another reading is linked here to the concept of 'political kinetics'. History is not reduced to the functions of power. It is always to be seen 'today' also as a response to the expectations we associate with the measure of human rights. The human being is at the centre of history as an inescapable quantity. Here, another specific perspective, another point of view emerges: the history of the human being.

The history of the twentieth century is to be recounted as a historical violation, as a form of rupture *(second part)*. From the point of view of phenomenology, one must at least add here: one can only recognise the measure of the human if one adds the character of the *event* of violence. Violence *comes into the world as 'something comes into speech'* (Waldenfels, 2014, p. 136).

This is by no means a more or less original language game, but a profound, historically striking experience. In the twentieth century, as is well known, attempts were made to make others disappear from the face of the earth. This violence aimed at the complete negation of certain groups, a form of the most radical violence that was meant to destroy even the last evidence of existence. But as we know (and which is part of the heritage of our time), this performative negation failed of itself (Levinas, 1988). The claim of the Other to its own existence cannot be contested; this claim is unavailable. The violence that turned against this ethical insight as annihilating violence has written itself into history as an antinomy. The dignity of the individual has been *touchable* ever since, if we take concrete historical experience as our starting point, but it is *undeniable* and *non-negotiable* if we concede that the existence of the other is a precondition of our being. Every attempt to strike through another being is bound to this limit.

In this section, it will be important to explore the measure of human rights. A positivist reading is problematic for various reasons. Rather, we must start from a deep ambivalence in the relationship between law and morality. The example of a single violent situation can be used as a comparison: The act of violence has intentional aspects, of course, but always also supra-subjective characteristics. The dark side of violence shows itself in the excess of an event; the perpetrator is entangled in his own actions, just as all participants move in the field of violence. Furthermore, a paradox must be taken into account: A contradictory motive is inherent in an act of violence directed at the annihilation of the Other. The annihilation of the addressee is a performative contradiction; it aims at the blinding of the persona.

Dignity, it is a form of negation of the existence of the Other – and at the same time it is referred to the tacit *recognition of this existence*.

Let us transfer this surplus to the political morality of our present. Various categories must be interpreted and made accessible in a phenomenological reading: *enmity and renunciation of violence, the dignity of the victim and the right of the singular totality*. The difficulty lies precisely in leaving behind historical traditions and writing a new kind of history.

Finally, in the last part, the aim of the reflection is reduced to one essential statement. The basic idea lies in the assertion that we live in a century of concern, which produces a specific form of reflection on violence (*third part*). This reflection includes the coexistence of historical experiences, psychological constellations and political forms of judgement.

From a historical point of view, we referred to history as a teacher of life, that is, we want to learn from history and avoid certain mistakes of the past. Psychologically, we try to fight violence and counter it with something that does not itself appear as violence. And politically, we refer with good reason to the traditions of renouncing violence and to the forces of peace.

One of the signatures of our epoch, however, is that we have to realise these projects in an order that itself has an ambivalent relationship to violence. In the age of concern, the violence that is closely connected to the emergence of order shimmers through. This does not mean that literally everything is to be reduced to violence or that we are pure beings of violence; nor is our epoch to be described exclusively as violent. Rather, the genuine task is to show that situations of violence and a respective order are intertwined and that only the category of concern contributes to a deeper understanding of this constellation.

How deeply entangled in violence is our species? In antiquity, a distinction was made between wars of brotherhood and wars of subjugation. One form of violence was legitimate; against barbarians or slaves, war was morally imperative. It is only in fratricidal war that the ambivalent nature of war and the preference for peace become apparent. The idea that man lives in a permanent state of war has, of course, survived into modern times. Man lives at war with other people, his essence is confrontation. In war, the real shows itself, so the concept is more than just a loss indicator of a peaceful state.

From Thomas Hobbes to Emmanuel Levinas, such a line of polemology is drawn, and always at the centre is the question of how to exit the ontological order of war.

The category of concern is helpful in this situation. It is to be understood here as an expression of the human capacity to gather the many contradictions and fault lines of violence into a unified framework. As a philosophical category, concern defies practical, pragmatic translation. Its meaning lies rather in the fact that it brings together the abysses of violence and the ways of thinking about possible peace.

An alternative form of historiography is thus achieved. We have not reached the end of history in postmodernity, where we see each other as wiser beings.

But at least there are strong indicators of a conceivable world reason in the field of political judgement.

Thus, at the end of the reflection, we will have to ask what distinguishes the present epoch from other epochs and what elevates it at the same time. Does this epoch express a course of development, a kind of climax of human culture? Can parallels perhaps be discovered between ontogenetic and phylogenetic expressions that point to an age of political reason?

These questions obviously culminate in pure ambivalence. The regressions of political reason are too obvious, the factual political dislocations and crisis scenarios too insistent to speak of cognitive progress. Nevertheless, the present reflections aim at an idea of the course of time in which a development is emerging. This development is considered here in the worldview of worry without exaggerating it with false premises. In times of concern, both progressive and regressive dynamics are possible; the course of development of humanity follows – like all epochs before – specific cycles and different values. But, the idea of a political reason including all moral values is unavoidable in this framework. As much as reason is always threatened by the fall, as often as an achieved political level is undercut, a progress in thinking and judging can still be assumed. More than that: even if the great ideas always crash into the brutality of domination, they are still evidence of an undeniable moral grammar in common life.

For precisely those aspects of a developmental psychology of humanity (Oser, 2013), there is no evidence or empirical proof to be provided in the course of the work. Rather, a form of historical consciousness has emerged from the worldview of concern that distinguishes our epoch as a special one. It enables a consciousness of a political and moral high form – and at the same time it provides descriptions that show under which circumstances this form is subverted.

The twentieth century forms a legacy that burdens the world of the twenty-first century – for better or for worse. Under what conditions we can accept this legacy is to be asked.

PART I
Violence and History

Chapter One

WAR AS 'BECOMING': ON THE ONTOLOGY OF CONFLICT

Let us go back to the beginnings of metaphysics, to the world of Greek philosophy. From 535 to 475 BC, Heraclitus of Ephesus was active in Ionian Asia Minor. He was one of the first thinkers to pose radical philosophical questions that point to the metaphysical reasons for being and war. Here, war and existence are brought into an equally primordial context – a thesis that has occupied thought in many variants right up to modern times.

If you look into the depths of European intellectual history, you realise what role war has played for the respective culture. For Heraclitus, the phenomenon of war was a manifestation of the 'polemos' at the roots of Western thought. Heraclitus traced its inexorability and called it the *father of all things*. In early Greek thought, war was not a phenomenon to be limited morally or politically. The moral grandeur that we ascribe to the condemnation of war today was absent in early ancient thought; at that time, it was more about the concern for an underlying cosmological harmony (Heraclitus, 2007).

A culture can only develop to its full potential when it takes a closer look at the dark source of energy. Accordingly, war reveals a higher power – a conception of war that modern thinking is alienated from. War would thus be the consummation of life itself, an expression of a deeply disturbing idea.

In European thought, as is well known, other ideas about war have developed. War is not a biological dynamic, but a phenomenon that must be controlled and contained. Even Plato, Cicero and Augustine were always concerned with the moment of limiting a war through divine instruction; they hoped for a deeper insight into the justice of a community.

As is well known, it took centuries to overcome bellicose thoughts. The furore of wars had devastated the world again and again; the claim to divine justice expressed in warlike conflict had scorched the earth and eroded human morality. This alienation that stemmed from war was to be overcome; total destruction was to be avoided and the moral claim to ultimate victory to be withdrawn. Only now, in the thinking of the early modern era in Grotius, Spinoza or in Kant, was war considered in terms of its legal foundation (Stadler, 2009).

But let us remain with the idea of the ontology of war in Heraclitus (Heraclitus, 2007). The thought is ambivalent, multilayered and irritating. The knowledge of the existential dimension had quite tangible political references. The ancient Persian Achaemenid Empire had experienced a meteoric rise in the age of Heraclitus; from 550 to 525 BC it had subjugated the entire Orient with its campaigns. The Persian Wars, roughly dated between 490 and 450 BC, culminated in the Peace of Callias. The peace was followed by the Peloponnesian War, another conflict for supremacy in Greece.

These wars, and in particular the war between the Greeks and the Persians, resembled an existential confrontation. Very simplified, it was the antagonism of this age, here polytheism, there the monotheistic faith in the sense of Zarathustra's teachings. The supposed first 'despotism' stood opposite the first 'civil', political culture. The self-assured demarcation against the barbarian enemy experienced its first flowering here.

As a battle of East against West, the Persian Wars have inscribed themselves in the memory of the Occident and probably had a strong influence on Heraclitus' philosophy. In the surviving fragments, one finds the famous aphorism 53, which praises war as the father of all things. War is powerful because it makes some people gods and others slaves. War has an omnipotence that is beyond human disposal; in this motif it has a sacred seriousness.

In this philosophical horizon, life itself is characterised by conflict and opposition; the political also appears as an expression of a permanent conflict. How is life itself to be understood? As static being, as Parmenides claimed, thus in a closed cosmos in which every thing has its place? Or in the sense of permanent becoming, as dynamics and constant change? Heraclitus coined the polar basic approach of the metaphysics of that time; in the timeless movement of being, he recognised the first and last principle of action. The same applies to the essence of war; this is not to be understood (as the modern mind would counter) as a destructive, negative force, but as an expression of the Logos. World reason takes place in the becoming, in the confrontation.

It is these sentences that accompany us until the twentieth century and set the tone especially in the thinking of Martin Heidegger. His endeavour was to integrate the threat of death into the analysis of existence. Determinations of finitude led the philosopher to concepts such as fate, anxiety and fear. As is well known, this philosophy stood in an ambivalent relationship to the course of European and German history. Phenomenology remained apolitical and abstract, but in various respects the totalitarian motives of the work cannot be overlooked.

Reinhart Koselleck (Koselleck, 2000) has not only supplemented these analyses from the point of view of historicity, but has viewed it in a fundamentally different way. Accordingly, the conditions of possible history lead back to the experience of the capacity for violence (Ibid., p. 101 ff.). The need to die is an anthropological constant, but it is only through the fact that people can kill each other that history is formed. Only with this open view does one realise that it is always a historical achievement when peace is made or violence is renounced.

Behind the possibility of killing are other oppositions that can be recognised with the comprehensive view of historicity; history thus happens within the framework of inside and outside, above and below, earlier and later. As abstract as these determinations appear, they can nevertheless be related to concrete historical phenomena. The first thing that is effective in the horizon of history is the possibility of the threat of lethal violence.

Based on this simple formal condition alone, historical manifestations can be thematised that show the manifestations of possible and actual war or the art of peace. 'Stories' between 'friendship' and 'enmity' has since been told with different accentuations. Just as the constant struggle between above and below, inside and outside, has been transferred into diverse constellations, in the constant struggle between classes, nations, systems or cultures.

These narratives have a categorical claim.

The question now is how far we have moved away from this paradigm in historiography and political science today and what sense we still make of the distinctions. The twentieth century, as we know, was a century of betrayal, no longer one of formal enmity. Enmities led to sprawling or limited wars in previous eras, but as is well known, in this respect the history of the twentieth century is seen as a profound break with all that came before. In a particular diction, philosophy has authenticated this process, albeit from afar. The work of 'Sein und Zeit' (Heidegger, 1979) had shaped a specific valeur and usability for political ideologies. The basic structure of human existence was found by Heidegger in existential 'thrownness'. Man as Dasein has only his lonely death before his eyes and must therefore take on his destiny in responsibility, care and actuality, but above all in being free to die. In this specific tone (which is difficult to relate to individual, 'unmasking' passages of the text), political existentialism was able to unfold, seemingly authenticating the signatures of the extreme. Henceforth, it was necessary to distance oneself from this motif.

Reinhart Koselleck, representing many, has now shown another way of historical and semantic analysis. According to this, historicity forms a formal framework (similar to a historical painting) that reflects the change of times and the constant formal determinations between inside and outside, above and below.

What is decisive here is the extent to which this also applies to the criterion of enmity, which is arguably decisive for all normative considerations.

Constellations of enmity have filled known history. Greeks rose up against the barbarians outside Hellas, Christians fought against pagans, pagans against invaders. In modern times, enmities expanded, enemies of humanity were fought or whole groups were excluded from belonging by classifying them as subhumans. All this is part of historical knowledge.

However, what is decisive in the context of historicity is the idea of formal opposition. Only through the distinction between enmity and friendship is history made possible, and even those who invoke the value of peace have subconsciously confirmed the formal distinction. Being to death can be overtaken by being to kill at any time (Koselleck, 2000, p. 103).

*

Forms of divisiveness run through the history of violence. The idea that war is to be glorified as the father of all things has, however, as we know, always been pushed back. Its presence in the earthly world is irritating and a permanent task for thought. Neither violence nor war, neither the furore of destruction nor the relations of enmity have ultimately been removed from the world. So is Heraclitus to be proved right because he had already recognised the ontological nature of war thousands of years ago? And must contemporary philosophers and historians therefore pay respect to his work because manifold evidence of the divisiveness of man can be found? This is precisely what would have to be questioned.

Historicism leads us into a conflict-ridden area of history that one cannot and should not close oneself off to. The deep conflicts have always been about the question of how to fill up existential categories: whether others were classified as ordinary enemies or excluded as enemies of humanity. Whether units of action encountered each other as subjects and moved within the framework of a class, a nation, an ideology or whether they simply felt connected to savage violence. War, for which Thomas Hobbes (1984) famously contributed the decisive linguistic images, is always to be regarded as a present phenomenon. What was paraphrased as an ontological principle by Heraclitus becomes a transcendental category in modern times.

However, this also leads to far-reaching ethical reflections, without which what has been said so far would remain misleading. Those who confront war with holy humility have already integrated it into their relation to the world. Those who fight it, however, draw lessons from the history they know. As simple as the condemnation of war is, as complicated is the attainment of an appropriate awareness of violence. For this includes the ability to condemn war as a principle and a means, but to translate its presence into an appropriate, ethically grounded language. At this point in the argument, the possible partisan positions branch out.

On the one hand, there is a difficult apology of war. Observers who cultivate the eagle's eye view see war as a means to promote a minimum of justice. According to Michael Walzer, war is a legitimate means in justified exceptional cases, even in the absence of legality (Walzer, 1992). War also seems to have led to the higher development of societies in the long run. War has produced safer and more prosperous societies, wrote Ian Morris most recently (Morris, 2013).

On the other hand, there are motifs of thought that can only grasp war as an extreme abstraction. In the field of tension between ethics and ontology, radical existential questions are at stake that necessarily remain unresolved. The very question of the conditions under which we recognise each other and how we encounter each other requires basic ethical reflections. Is it a question of directing and disciplining the masses, who confront us anonymously and formlessly and above all must be controlled? Where can, where should the many who have lost their homes for the most diverse reasons arrive and settle down permanently?

How can we give them a voice and a face, free them from the zones of vulnerability?

Emanuel Levinas (Levinas, 1988) is considered one of the representatives of a humanistic ethics who have faced these and other challenges of the present. In the wake of a social philosophy that traces the Other (Derrida, 2000; Liebsch, 2003), Levinas drew a worldview in which we are unreservedly exposed to one another. It is precisely this – the radical exposure, the radical violence – that can be described with the author as another ontology of war. The ethical position is unambiguous: after a century in which certain groups were to be radically eradicated from the earth, a legacy of concern remains. This does not simply consist in the unconditional protection or the unconditional prevention of the worst, but this demands to consider the irrevocable alterity of the Other. This ethical ontology of war demands that we consider the coexistence of life forms in conflict.

*

An outlook on the reflections that follow is appropriate at this point. The world is a space in which we can be hurt and are thus exposed to each other – from the very beginning. This is not to paint the world as a theatre of cruelty, but to get a clear view of the basic human situation. This situation is characterised by fragility, which in reflection leads us to the need to cling more closely to ethics and anthropology.

Human practice takes place within the boundaries of constitutively fragile beings. Threats and vulnerabilities are an integral part of human practice, even if we live in peace-loving societies or if peace has to be made anew after a war. Violence is in the world; a motif of critical theory is indicated here (Adorno, 1980).

The starting point of critical thinking is the violence of raw nature. Early prehistoric man stood in a hostile, forbidding, perilous nature and had to practise the art of survival. His opportunity lay in his ability to work his way out of the menace of inscrutable nature. The animal was given instinctive security; all that remained for man was to transcend the animalistic way of life.

The violence of nature stood, as it were, against the nature of man. This success story is hauntingly dialectical and highly topical: in order to survive in the natural world, man had to escape the situation of omnipresent terror and create cultural spaces. Only the complete mastery of nature could guarantee security. Nature had lost its terror – up to the point where man had to admit to the terror of his own nature.

From this anthropological insight, a direct line leads to ethical reflection. Violence is inscribed in the human situation; violence is thus a reality that must be made present. But does this mean accepting violence as a component of social life? It would mean understanding violence as the first and last response. Every argumentation would then be traced back to the irrefutability of human relations of violence.

We want to think beyond this motif here. For it is to be asked to what extent human beings, as beings of violence, do not also have the ability to cope with violence. What critical anthropological reflection must achieve also leads to the fundamental structure of this chapter. The aim is to open up perspectives in the history of violence that have not yet been available in this way. In doing so, we will certainly not write *new chapters in human history* (a claim that some books now make, see Pinker, 2011 or Graeber/Wengrow, 2021), but perhaps scope for thinking will be uncovered.

Since the human world is characterised as constitutively fragile, it is not enough to depict violence in a formal history of events. The conditions under which we can recognise the different *faces of violence* in the *basic human situation*, on the other hand, are the primary guiding principle.

*

It is probably one of the more difficult aspects of violence that its essence not only appears dark and mysterious, but that every description is accompanied by a moment of indeterminacy. Violence knows many faces and metamorphoses; violence is an experience and an event and the act of violence itself can probably never be neatly divided into action and passion. Violence, when one attempts a theoretical description, is thus essentially abstract.

Nevertheless, the phenomenon of violence is linked to intersubjective criteria, without which any talk about violence would remain meaningless and empty. Violence takes on a form of embodiment: when violence *is done to* someone, when a violent act is *addressed in* one *direction* or when we speak of *violence suffered*. Speaking about violence only makes sense in an inter-existential form: violence is directed against the human claim to be; the form of violence denies this claim by all conceivable means (Waldenfels, 2014, p. 136 f.).

As is well known, violence already appears in language, in the performative negation of the Other, but it can just as well have an effect in symbols or in silence. The intertwining of violence with language, however, raises the question: Under what circumstances can we speak of the embodiment of violence? It is true that violence occurs in the moment of disregard, silent oppression and symbolic exclusion.

But without a moment of embodiment, one does not do justice to a comprehensive phenomenology of violence.

We will look at different forms of embodiment in the following, which are the prelude to the reflection on violence. Violence has to do with personification, which occurs beyond harmless sociology. Only with the figure of the enemy does violence receive its predicative form. Moreover, personification also means the motif of participation in the phenomenon of violence, which finds its starting point in the human body. Finally, violence is not only to be understood as a forced interaction, but as an all-encompassing event.

This motif has probably the deepest historical and philosophical dimension. If one admits the idea that the world itself exists in the form of a deep conflict, one enters the realm of an ontology that appears totalitarian from the modern point of view. But this does not absolve us from the need to think through this ontology.

This will be done in the following in the sense of a far-reaching movement of thought. The history of violence becomes comprehensible when it is brought together with the categories of space, corporeality, meaning and order. The mental flight initially takes place far above the clouds with a closed cloud cover, but all reflections receive a critical corrective through the binding to the inferior plane.

History of Power

In a now-iconic image, a crowd of European rulers gather over a map depicting the African continent: the legendary Congo Conference of 1884/1885. The image gives an approximate idea of a phase of colonialism. The leaders of the European world bend over the maps and enter into tense negotiations. The object of negotiation is the African land mass; at a round table, the remaining territories are to be divided up and specific regulations created; a 'special' right that was to put the 'effective occupation' on a basis of 'international law'.

What this was about, however, is obscured by the terms used here. The 'international law' of the nineteenth century was the means to justify land grabbing in the course of colonialist practice. Colonialism has shaped history to this day, leaving behind so many sinister stories. In the picture mentioned, however, it seems to be mainly about the dazzling phenomenon of power. The maps of Africa were 'coloured'. At the beginning of

European expansion, only the coastal strips were painted in the colours of the colonial powers; later, in the course of territorial occupation, the entire interior was to be filled in on a large scale (Stockhammer, 2005, p. 10 ff.).

Signatures of the history of power appear here. However, the picture allows for different perspectives and it is probably inadmissible to focus solely on the striking image of the highly official negotiation. The story allows a view of the supposedly great men and their entourage, but also of the structures and processes by which power and powerlessness are produced.

But the image also evokes a crucial question: How can history be told in a meaningful way? A Eurocentric position that maps all the ups and downs of colonial history has long since been adopted as obsolete (Mccarthy, 2009). A shift in historiographical attention can be noticed that is tantamount to a change in ethics. For it is necessary to write history from the peripheral location, if at all possible; the history of colonialism remains inadequate if it does not also take the position of the excluded groups and peoples.

But whichever way you turn it, the history of violence in the aforementioned constellation boils down to a metaphorical idea: history happens in a space between above and below, with Hegel speaking, between domination and servitude. For historiography, a challenge arises to orient itself between these positions. The question is how to mediate between these levels and tell the known story in a meaningful way. It would be too simple to conceive of history as an ongoing process of power relations. The integration of the inferior level must be taken into account, but here, too, a one-sided position is in danger. The philosophy of history of the present demands an integration of perspectives – and for this we need appropriate criteria of a narratable history.

*

So how can we 'imagine' the history of violence? The theory of history would be in demand as the discipline that refuses a clear answer precisely on this point. A continuous line of history with a recognisable logic is a phantasm – an idea that overlooks the peculiar *stuttering of history* (Merleau-Ponty, 1966). History can hardly be conceived as a meaningful unity, neither is it a performed drama nor a stringent idea. If one wants to express it in images, then everything accumulates in history that seems to us to be alien to meaning: the stuttering and the deviation, the chaos and the tumult. History dissolves and sometimes reassembles; in the best case, the individual events form a historical fabric whose traces we can follow (Koselleck, 2000).

Another image offers an alternative way of thinking. History has a body that can be placed in analogy to the human body. Bodies have deep traces of the past; bodies already tell of their experiences through their physiognomy. They carry history within them. The body of history has a tense relationship with language. The language of history tends to trace everything back to the diachronic, narrative aspect. History would be meaningfully narratable in this image; for example, as drama or as tragedy, but also as an irreversible process of progress. For the dress of history, language becomes a helpful instrument by enabling the linking of sentences and narratives (White, 1991).

This is how one could frame various surviving images that have found their way into the historical archive in a diachronic narrative. From the Congo Conference in the nineteenth century, one draws a mental line of geopolitics. History would thus be a succession of geopolitical conflicts due to the hunger for space. As it corresponds to nineteenth-century ideas, the world would be caught in an eternal struggle for territory.

As we shall see in the following, this image tends towards one-sidedness. The eagles' flight of fancy remains blind to the quiet inertia of history, to its wild courses and curvatures, but above all to the pre-expressive and pre-linguistic layers. Filtering out these layers must be the task of the following account. Pre-linguistic layers have equal importance to official policies and rational actions. The body of history forms an uncultivated layer. In an analogy to the psychology of the individual human being, we can start from bodily actions that reveal various mental states. To fathom them requires an interpretation that is not blinded by observable action alone. Seen in this way, history is more than just a sequence of events; it is only in the curvatures and deviations that what we only rudimentarily suspect in the horizon of language is expressed.

In other words, the history of violence will only be complete when we think beyond the obvious: there are complex motives behind the events.

History is more entangled with the psyche than we learn about it in the official narratives. For the topos of violence, this means: we must refrain from diachronic progress, as well as from the narratives of taming and civilising. The history of violence acquires an appealing form when it is set in the twilight of human orders.

In the following, this form of history will be placed in relation to the categories of *space, the human body, meaning and order.*

As we will see, violence cannot be framed in the image of origin thinking. Only philosophical anthropology provides the decisive categories. Space is the first point of view that can be spelled out in various ways.

History in the Space

Violence takes place in space. Anyone who thoroughly examines historical situations of violence will agree with this statement. However, it seems that the history of violence is an endless sequence of repetitions in which space plays the decisive role.

Anthropologically, everything boils down to the ability to act in contested spaces: in space, animals were hunted, space was colonised and fenced in; space is worked and cultivated by humans, fenced in and out.

A significant tradition of historical studies has focused entirely on the category of the spatial. This tradition entered the history textbooks as 'geopolitics', which was primarily concerned with the question of who was the master of the world. The older European geopolitics of the early twentieth century had completely surrendered to the dominant thoughts of the time and worked towards the politics of violence. Social Darwinist authors such as Mahan, Mackinder or Goblet, but also German geopoliticians, directed attention to the political and military possibilities that a respective 'natural' situation allowed. As we know today, these were unreservedly affirmative ideologies.

Meanwhile, it seems that some of the theorists who were solely committed to the spatially structured politics of power have been proven right. At the latest since the annexation of Crimea (2014) in violation of international law and Russia's subsequent invasion of Ukraine (February 2022), the suspicion seems to have been confirmed: that violence always has to do with the desire for space.

History, politics and philosophy are now the decisive disciplines that can perceive these warlike conflicts in a differentiated way and deconstruct their traditions. In doing so, however, they must adopt a distance to the contemporary history mentioned here: they should find a distance to ideology, but at the same time, they must find a distance to contemporary historical events whose expirations are not foreseeable. However, the urgency of this cannot be dismissed out of hand: What is the relationship between warlike violence and the respective spatial order? In the following, we will try to draw a wide arc that leads from the unavoidable power of geography to a modern theory of geopolitics (2). But this does not complete the relationship between violence and spatiality; for the historical category of space also contains cultural and aesthetic categories of the highest importance (3).

The Power of Geography

The example of Russia would be suitable for discussing day-to-day political aspects. In the broadest sense, however, it leads the considerations to an eminent point: world politics apparently derives from the psychology of space. The natural default structures and directs the destinies of the respective peoples and great empires, and this applies to more or less all territorial orders.

In a deliberately simple reading, the land conditions the movements and cultural traditions, the possibilities of power and domination, ultimately also the interplay of peace and war. A measure of political psychology is contained in the location of space, because space opens up scope and options for strategic action. This aspect is neither new nor surprising and has been valid since the earliest days of historiography from Thucydides to J. Burckhardt. Be it the specific location of the islands of Hellas/Greece, which explains the length of the Trojan War, be it the geographical default of the English Channel, which is one of the constant conditions of British world empire development (Koselleck, 2000, p. 86), geopolitics shows how international politics is to be understood against the background of geological and geographical factors. The elements guide the hand of historiography: mountains, deserts, rivers and proximity to the seas are the crucial aspects that determine what people can and cannot do (Marshall, 2015, p. 8, preface).

The psychological situation in space shapes action and consciousness; however, problems begin with the psychological perception of the situation. The history of Russia can be used as an example here. The vast empire, which covers an area of 17 million square kilometres, has become fixed in the collective consciousness. In the last 500 years, as we read in Tim Marshall (Marshall, 2015, p. 20 ff.), Russia has been the object of invasions several times. In 1605, the Poles crossed the North European Plain, in 1708 the Swedes. As is well known, neither Napoleon nor Hitler was able to hold their own militarily in the depths of the Russian Empire. These experiences have become fixed in the collective memory. It is also such memories of war that produce political units of action in the long term.

These experiences are not exclusive. The threat situation is a topos of war historiography; the threat of enemy invaders is a rhetorical device that is taken up courageously at times. The decisive question is therefore to what extent one can integrate the geographical specifications into a theory of history.

Natural history forms a metahistorical condition of possible human history. Trade and transport routes, land and sea, coasts and rivers, mountains and plains determine possible histories. They are to be understood as challenges to human actions. As is well known, mineral resources, climate and climate change must also be included in this equation.

Geopolitical determinism is not compatible with the contemporary theory of history. It is possible, however, to relate the metahistorical situation to the history of power. Throughout all critical theories of the past and present, the question arises as to what value we can assign to the category of space. For in the history of mankind, space has been a condition of political and military actions; only when space is overcome, when it is carved, cultivated, provided with boundary posts and others are directed to the boundaries, could domination be established. This history, if we take note of recent sociological writings, is a more or less completed past. Accordingly, modern geopolitics has long been *deterritorialised*. Various technological developments have sparked a spatial revolution; the history of power is now to be written with other theoretical stylistic devices (on this: Randeria/Eckert, 2009).

This thesis goes back to the vague insight of the loss of relevance of space. Space is not an objective default, but a social construction. The epistemology of space recognises an immeasurable variety of changes: transport and media networking, transnational linkages, social and political border crossings make for a fluctuating space. Even history, long written as the history of nation states, is now imagined as an amalgam, a confluence of different cultural experiences (Trojanow/Hoskote, 2013).

Consequently, classical geopolitics has lost its actual reason; the history of power is being continued under different conditions. One currently speaks of a global world society that is in a state of permanent change. Modernity appears in the image of a transnational, transcultural network (Löw, 2001). In this image, the struggle between ways of life replaces the old friend–foe thinking. Not the conquest of space, but the disposal of data flows, communication, trade and global infrastructures is at the centre of modern empires (Randeria/Eckert, 2009). Space is trivialised in this theoretical discourse.

This alone, however, does not adequately describe the present in which we are confronted with so many *faces of violence*. Other points of view must be considered, without us having to disregard the fundamental considerations of geopolitics. Modernity is thus a fluid, elusive phenomenon, bound neither to one place nor to one conception of time. The empire of the present forms a new architecture of power that neglects space and relies solely on the seamless structure of global capitalism (Hardt/Negri, 2000). Within this framework, forms of life collide without being able to invoke a valid narrative, a global ethic or a central authority.

In the words of Karl Schlögel (2003, p. 8 ff.), this position should be subverted to some extent. We must also mentally reclaim space and rediscover the spatiality of human history. In space we read time – this aphorism reminds us that history is first to be understood as an incessant effort to master space. Space has a veto power and we are required to read the traces in space that come with all the 'horrors', 'ruptures' and 'cataclysms' of the twentieth century (Schlögel, 2003, p. 11). After the *spatial turn*, space returns, but in a different dress than before. Postmodern talk about discourse, simulacra and virtuality is again confronted with materialist orientations.

This is not a return to a nostalgically transfigured past. It is rather about reading the horizon of history from a spatial point of view.

Space therefore has an intrinsic value, if only because it is the immediate setting for intricate stories of violence. It is important to rediscover space as an aesthetic category.

Space as an Aesthetic and Cultural Dimension

Only a philosophical and aesthetic description can meaningfully expand the previous reflections. Power manifests itself in space and can be grasped with one's hands, but a geopolitical determinism remains problematic. The category offers more starting points and it has various dimensions that will be unfolded here. In the following, we will try to approach the category from different angles. We need to ask what sensual quality space has and to what extent it is intertwined with memoria. Last but not least, we need to explain which aesthetic qualities space contains, which we should decipher especially in the face of violence.

It is easy to explain why it is so difficult to recognise space as an element of historiography. The Nazi discourse disavowed talk about space. In this context, it was about a living space over which the peoples of the planet were to war in an eternal struggle. There is no need to survey the shoals of this empty propaganda again.

If the relevance of space is emphasised on the part of the theory of history, then this is above all about a form of narrative that needs to be renewed to some extent. We come closer to the reality of war when we start from the centre of the basic human situation in which people stand – or into which they are thrown. It is true that space can be transferred into images and thus finds its way into the visual memory of the present. But as an anthropological category, it must be considered first and foremost. Everything that happens in the environment of a violent situation has its origin in spatial experience. The assertion that virtual space has long since replaced physical space, and that we could effortlessly bridge space, becomes groundless in the face of man's spatial relation to the world. The world is materially shaped; the ground on which we stand creates a friction. The human body must orient itself in a world it finds. This anthropologically significant space is a form of alienation from the world that we can only gradually overcome. Alterity in space means that we come up hard against the physical facts of geographical space and only from here can we ensure survival, form communities and social networks, become politically active. From an evolutionary point of view, man is indeed an animal that evades, flees and is in constant motion. But despite all migratory movements, it is the localisation in the real–spatial context that distinguishes every speech about history.

*

The excursus on world reference leads us back to the basic elements of philosophical anthropology, which are essential for the historicisation of violence. The diversity of human situations speaks for the importance of space. Spatial coordinates determine how we perceive the world. Are we standing inside or outside, in a spatial
centre or periphery? The place where we find ourselves opens up political, social, cultural horizons, but it also limits the respective possibilities for action. Hierarchies are also to be imagined spatially first: whether we are at the top or the bottom of a social formation is always a spatial question as well. Triviality and complexity are not mutually exclusive here: whether we, as part of a military organisation, recognise the space in front of us as a battlefield or whether we fear the attacks from above, whether we stand in the trenches, in a bunker or unprotected in the open field. Whether we hear of the war in the distance or are directly exposed to it, whether we are behind a front line or in the middle of a confrontation, whether we are finally standing in an open situation or functioning as an 'element' in a closed institution.

Triviality is not to be underestimated when we expand the situations of violence: local, cultural, national and continental determinations make a difference. The zones of violence and the landscapes of vulnerability stand abruptly next to the protected spaces of the 'first modernity'. What is non-trivial is the fact that it is first about this localisation and the spatial reference of the human being – and only in the second, third line about the exaltation with texts. Here one may recognise a quiet critique of European traditions in the humanities: these cultural approaches to history are primarily text related. We interpret, in the wake of Talmud, Maimonism or Protestantism, the world as a readable text (Sombart, 1992). The world becomes a mystery with a hidden meaning that only those who are able to read can decipher.

Here, however, it is not first about ciphers that are questioned and texts that are interpreted, but about the seriousness of the lifeworld that we encounter in its sensual concretion (Schlögel, 2003, p. 38). As an anthropological determination, space is binding both from the subject's location and for theory: we make our primary experiences as spatial experiences, in the material bodily, sensual dimension. Space is experienced as overpowering, hostile and threatening, and anyone who steps out into nature unprotected will understand this insight.

But also from a theoretical point of view, a primary dimension can be described here: as a prerequisite for human survival, space is only secondarily interpreted culturally.

The cultural and aesthetic potentials can only be hinted at in the following. While time is removed from human arbitrariness, space must be appropriated and defined. Through labour, space materialises; it becomes the product of our creations and the object of our capacity for violence. From this point, historiography can be traced back to its origins, but it is not solely about the founding event of territorial demarcation. In the basic patterns of centres and peripheries, cities and states, parcellations and border demarcations, history can be unfolded as spatial history.

Two configurations are crucial in this context: on the one hand, space can be understood as a place of encounter for cultural self-understanding. Material spaces become landscapes of memory; space is no longer solely the scene of adversity, but a context worth remembering.

On the other hand, in order not to exaggerate the history of violence, we must also look into the depths of space. For it is only there that we find humane remnants of times past for which no more theory can emerge.

*

Older geopolitics recognised space as a natural quantity that served historical–political claims. Such ways of thinking have become obsolete in the present. Contemporary cultural historiography, on the other hand, recognises in space not only land and sea, mountains and oceans. It looks into a culturally impregnated space that is significant for communities of memory. These spaces reveal themselves to the viewer with the power of their meaning; remembered space becomes a kind of counter-design to accelerated modernity. Modern contemporaneity is subject to the dictatorship of acceleration, which consumes space; the space of memoria, however, relies on persistence and permanence. The space of memory promises a hold that time can never vouch for.

Places of remembrance: this can be understood to mean a landscape that was the scene of a 'great war' in pre-modern times. It can be a memorial or a former border fence, a camp or simply an artefact taken from a special place. The cultural charge of the space is explained by the human desire to counter the irretrievable passage of time with something permanent.

Herein lies a particular peculiarity of modern memory culture: for even if space is destroyed in time in the long run, if only because it is in a constant state of change, the practice of memory seems to offer an opportunity: to stop the 'flow of time' and to 'bring the past back into the present' (Sabrow, 2014, p. 253).

Two phenomena confront each other here that go back to the human way of dealing with the history of violence: the remembered space is occupied with sacred gazes. It becomes the object of desire to charge the past violence with meaning. The space is given an aura of authenticity. However, this is contradicted by the insight that all violence is time bound and no aura of the authentic can cancel out the span between earlier and later.

Two ways of looking into space must be distinguished in this respect. Spaces of experiences of violence become places of memory, learning and remembrance. They serve pedagogical purposes and didactic considerations. Generations are supposed to learn from each other and the burden of the past is supposed to be lightened a bit. Even the 'Topographies of terror' (Buchholtz, 2010) thus become historical tourist objects. The difficulties lie in the unavoidable exaltation with sacred significance, which is supposed to vouch for a certain dignity. Because it appears unadulterated, unmediated and truthful, this space of violence is associated with claims to authenticity.

In this, one can recognise a peculiarity of cultural self-understanding. In a concrete place that can be experienced by the senses, history comes alive again by virtue of the imagination. In this respect, memory spaces go some way towards fulfilling the promise that is made.

The duty to remember is tied to the ground of primary experience. It is true that no experience can be retrieved in singular totality by subsequent generations, but memory can be transferred into a concrete, vivid, sensually mediated situation.

However, the meaning of space is to be explored in a further sense. Beyond pedagogical–didactic purposes, space also remains an expression of man's sense of foreignness. Human history is only understood in its enormity when one looks into the depths of space. The sight that test drilling in the earth would produce would be devastating for both philosophical anthropology and natural history. Nature, metaphorically speaking, becomes the compassionate observer of disaster (Blanchot, 1995). Nature would become a witness to the horror stemming from the first uses of the machine gun, the use of poison gas, serial dying and the scorched earth strategy. The history of violence is spatial history, insofar as there are legacies in the depths of the earth that provide information about the inhospitability of the world. This human world is a space of injury and devastation, a space where the human capacity for violence has pulled out all the stops for destruction. Irradiated topographies as a result of atomic destructive forces, cratered landscapes such as in Verdun, testify to a world space that radically rejects life (Liebsch, 2014, p. 243).

The view into the depths of space is disillusioning. It reveals past battlefields and war landscapes with voices that have long since faded away. These spaces contain memories that never coalesce into a coherent narrative. This makes it seem all the more urgent not to cut short the reflection of violence. In addition to spatiality, violence is interwoven with phenomena of meaning and order, as will be shown below.

Violence and Order

When violence is spoken or written about, psychology is the first instance to be turned to. Psychology helps to understand even those parts of a violent event that one actually does not understand. The human psyche is the place where violence is mentally carried out or only thought about; without this part of human affects and cognitions, evaluations and perceptions, the analysis of violence would be meaningless.

These elementary conditions suggest a psychological interpretation of the history of violence. With good reasons, a new chapter is opened in history insofar as violence – here as psychologically calculated interaction – takes on new forms. From the perspective of psychology (Pinker, 2011), the general assumption of civilisation, which is expressed in the renunciation of violence, speaks for the decline of violent relationships. According to the popular and often quoted thesis, our epoch is characterised by a degree of peaceful interaction that is unprecedented. Trend statements can be used to support the decline in violence; at the same time, we are dealing with a new worldview that allows an inkling of an emerging positive development. Progress exists despite all negativity: even if we generally fear violence against nature and living conditions, even if political conditions appear violent, there are indications of a positive development towards less violence.

There is evidence for this trend. They lead into different social and societal spheres: How are interactions within the family to be assessed; what is the extent between different groups of the population; how is the violence between regions, nations and states? There is no lasting peace in any sphere, but within each social sphere we can see positive signs (Pinker, 2011, 13). This says that progress is being made in almost every sphere of society; the actions of governments, technological innovations, the increase in knowledge and cognition, the humanisation of education and the refinement of culture – all these chapters are leading to a new history of humanity.

The following contributions on the history of violence do not contradict this assertion. They do not dispute any of the theses for which data are used and historical developments are shown. All they can do is open up another perspective that is helpful for understanding violence.

The psychology of non-violence begins in the mind. Cognitive and neuroscience can explain the extent to which our actions are associated with aggressive motives and how they have evolved evolutionarily (Pinker, 2007). But violence also needs to be thought through in a historical perspective. Non-violence is made possible in a social and societal environment characterised by relative wealth, health, education, respect, social justice and meaningful governance. It becomes positive cycles are set in motion: 'good societies' promote non-violence and non-violence promotes those very societies.

One can prove such positivist statements historically. Humanity has worked its way out of archaic, violent conditions in various steps. First in the context of early urban formations: out of an anarchy of hunter-gatherers, the first advanced civilisations emerged, which were indeed violent, but at the same time set in motion a process of pacification. Further steps were taken at the end of the Middle Ages and in the transition to modern times: Authorities and infrastructures enabled civilisation in the sense of Norbert Elias. Within the framework of the Enlightenment, moral ideas were articulated that had already circulated in antiquity but were now surpassed. The outlawing of tyranny, torture and slavery, for example, was something new in principle. As is well known, they were flanked by the development of human rights (Brunkhorst, 2005).

However, a corrective specification is indispensable. That the conditions of violence have changed in the most general sense is plausible in a broad sweep of history. We have fewer risks of becoming victims of homicide and live longer overall than our ancestors. We have established security systems and preventive means to forestall the emergence of violence. But the correction must start with the 'we' that such claims precede.

Talk of *new chapters in human history* is seductive, but not without problems. The subject of such a humanity is a multiplicity, and its world is split into different zones, spaces of violence and spheres of non-violence.

Accordingly, one quickly reaches limits of perception with the 'global' phrase. For certain historical spaces, specific conditions apply that make war unlikely – in other spaces, these conditions are to be viewed differently.

As is well known, the history of the European war of states has taken a course that today allows us to speak of a closed past. The 'old' war revolved around the conquest of territories, the possession of land and the wealth of mineral resources. The growing nation states of the past centuries entered into a competition for resources that was typical of early industrialised societies. This competition is certainly not over at present, but the social parameters have changed.

War between states has become improbable, on the one hand because a hegemony of states has been consolidated that seems like a 'natural' order to many. The fractures in world society have produced modern orders in which post-heroic mentalities have been able to develop. These societies – the West is usually referred to in this context – shun war, which produces renunciations and losses. They shun and ostracise warlike violence, which in historical retrospect has only produced massive suffering and will therefore remain forever associated with the signature of the negative. Work, barter and wealth are the integrating mechanisms at the heart of these societies (Münkler, 2006, pp. 122–148).

These perhaps irritating statements are of course not set in stone. They may seem irritating against the background of the warlike events since March 2022.

However one judges the de facto return to interstate war, the basic thesis is defensible. It describes a trend in the longue durèe, which is occasionally interrupted and takes on discontinuous courses. It should also be borne in mind that the perception of acute violence always has to do with the clash of ways of life, constructions and entire 'world views'.

From this point of view, the thesis of increasing non-violence is right. The statement goes back to a development in a part of world society for which various titles suggest themselves: in the 'first modernity', the centre of globalisation, practices of peaceful coexistence in the broadest sense were able to unfold. But the differentiation is just as compelling. For it is not about the opposition of modernity and pre-modernity, that is, the simplistic talk of the West and its rest (Hall, 1992). If, on the other hand, we assume a diversity of 'modernities', the talk of violence becomes more substantial (Eisenstadt, 2000). In some regions, war has become too expensive; in others, it is the last resort for obtaining resources. In the privileged zones, peace prevails, which yields special dividends, but also goes back to special historical constellations. In the zones of vulnerability, endemic conditions of violence prevail; there, various warlords emerge again and again who make war their business. This violence becomes a form of livelihood.

Let us summarise. One can rebel against violence with a positive basic attitude and position oneself accordingly. Accordingly, we live in times that produce something new and great: as descendants of the older violent history, we have learned to master violence. This is also true when one sharpens one's gaze and turns to those social regions that exist beyond the first modernity. The striking existence of spaces of violence in modernity is thus as scandalous as it is undeniable, but it does not diminish the persuasive power of the narrative. As a narrative of meaningful, justified non-violence, it has just as much historical relevance as the story of man in wolf form.

Nevertheless, the following reflections cannot be traced back to these plausible concepts. Non-violence will be taken up as a normative goal, but the primary consideration remains violence itself. As described, the fact of violence suggests psychological inspection.

Accordingly, violence is a social and historical context of action for which various psychological criteria are needed.

What is at stake here – not against, but beyond this tradition – is the phenomenology of violence, its shades and fractures, its dark parts and enigmatic traces, its glaring appearances and the obscure grey in the background. Violence is intertwined with human affairs, but it is also to be thought together with the existence of (humane) orders.

What aspects need to be considered in order to do justice to this phenomenology of violence? In the following, we attempt a systematic derivation of the variables from which violence emanates – the body as the a priori of human reference to the world, furthermore aspects of collectivity and singularity, finally dimensions of violent spaces and orders. The further we get in this analysis, the clearer it becomes that we can only ever understand violence in aporetic terms – as something alien and rejecting that always remains in the shadow of the existing orders.

The Sense and Sensibility of Violence

Violence begins with the body. An irritating sentence that is easy to explain. Violence, as we know, can be abstract; it nests in language or in the mind; violence has to do with interactions that are near or far. But the first clue of the phenomenology of violence is the human body.

As the interface of violence, the body functions in two ways. It is vulnerable and fragile, and at the same time it is capable of violence. The vulnerability of violence is comprehensible to everyone; it is painful and burns itself into the human body as an experience. Violence suffered is psychologically significant because it leaves a mark on the human being. But the power of the human being to hurt is perhaps of incomparably greater anthropological significance.

The physical constitution prescribes the functions of violence: the fist can become a weapon, just as the body can be imagined as a great tool. One can draw a line of progressive capacity for violence in the connection between the human body and a respective technique. In the beginnings of human history, the body was the primary instrument to arm oneself against the violence of nature, but also to defend oneself against the Other, the competitor. In order to refine defensive violence, means of violence were 'invented' to keep the injury-prone body out of the action. Already the lance created a distance to the opponent; fortifications and castles slowed down the dynamics of the attack and offered effective protective devices. This line continues through the history of violence – all the way to modern satellite and drone technologies, guided weapons and cybertechnologies.

Now the human body is seemingly removed from the action and violence becomes a long-distance duel in which, as we know, the better technology decides. This has a significant impact on the perception of violence, which loses its traditional meaning (Chamayou, 2015).

With the superficial view of physical events, one has apparently taken a first step into a materialism that claims to explain all violence. According to this, violence would be due to everything that shows itself in concrete action and physical confrontation. Violence is obviously unthinkable without the physical, is connected with the expansion of bodies and bodily injuries. And yet at this point we have to think beyond materialism, which in the final analysis leads to complete annihilation.

Let us draw on another significant category that is seemingly diametrically opposed to the physical: meaning. As is well known, violence is intertwined with language or can ally itself with it, but the specific sense of violence seems to have a contradiction to contain. Meaning and violence do not seem to fit into one context, they form a dissonant context.

It is precisely this undeniable sense of dissonance and unease that drives the thoughts here. What is the relationship between the event of violence and the respective meaning, which is not to be reduced to semantic meaning for the time being? Under certain circumstances, one tends to condemn violence as the opposite of a recognisable meaning, to deny it any meaning. But in various respects, this tends to block access to violence.

Violence is intertwined with meaning on different levels. From the victim's perspective, meaning seems to have been lost: violence breaks into everyday life, it leads to injuries that make it difficult for things to continue. One is a different person after the experience of violence and thus searches for a meaning 'behind things'. Thus, violence would be understood as an interruption by a disruptive element. The meaning that has accompanied us as an everyday, unquestioned sense of life has been permanently damaged. This sense would thus be equally fragile and as threatened as all forms of life that cannot resist violence.

But have we already covered the entire spectrum of forms of meaning with this? In a specifically human lifeworld, meaning is possible in different readings. Above all, it must be remembered that meaning has to do with communicative processes and that violence adapts to this medium.

Not every high-quality social theory can be satisfied with the close connection between language and violence. Hannah Arendt went so far as to place the capacity of language in absolute opposition to violence; according to this, violence cannot speak, it is communicatively mute. But as soon as we enter a common space embedded in language, violence is marginalised. Linguistic reason, the ability to enter into dialogue with others even under the most difficult conditions, would thus be the only hope for non-violence (Arendt, 2002).

In contrast, more recent social theory speaks of an unholy alliance between violence and language. Violence takes place in and through language, especially in silence and ignorance. In addition, there are all the conscious and unconscious dimensions of the violent actors: whoever is violent always does so with a social third party in mind. He uses his capacity for violence to show who he is or to make himself known as someone; to this end, he leaves behind a clear, ideological message, so to speak.

Or he remains silent – and relies on society recognising a presence (Reemtsma, 2008).

The connection between language, violence and meaning thus arises in every perspective. Phenomenologically to be deciphered is a space of violence that arises through the crossing of rules and intentions. The meaning of violence is to be interpreted, even if normal access to understanding is blocked. Particularly in those cases when violence appears as an intrusion of a stranger, something about what is happening is to be made comprehensible. There is no way around the embodiment of violence, no matter how blind and mute.

Between Nature and Culture

A further distinction is needed that makes violence more definable: violence moves between nature and culture. Interpretations are complicated within the framework of this distinction. They lead to a problematic tendency to associate violence with a primordial state. This state, which is imagined as natural, is archaic and raw. It is closer to the animal kingdom than to the realm of civilisation. Only when treaties are concluded, alliances made and weapons lowered do we reach the noble place of culture. Only as cultural beings, this interpretation dictates, can we leave the unsightly state of nature; only with the means of language, civil manners, diplomacy and prudence can violence be mastered. That peace is a cultural achievement is beyond question. But the historical–philosophical narrative of the exit from nature remains ultimately underdetermined.

Ancient thought already knew the difference. In Aeschylus' 'Prometheus', force and violence appear as persons ('kratos' and 'bia'). They are replaced by the 'techne', through the rational self-rule. These motifs emanated a radiance that has lost none of its potency. For it remains true: we like to locate ourselves in a realm beyond violence and regard every violent event as a regression. This historical–philosophical narrative is unbroken; progress points in only one direction. Civilisations rely on the consensus of non-violence, as violence becomes an antithesis of moral ways of life.

Various aspects can be named that show that this way of thinking is problematic. The concept of nature alone is not as unambiguous as it is often presented.

Nature-aesthetic positions raise doubts about the conceptual dualism of culture and nature. Some believe that the separation goes back to occidental violence (Descola, 2011), others see a transfiguration in the concept of nature. Rousseau, as is well known, was the first to question the idea of progress and distinguished culture as the actual place of violence.

A final position that assigns a definitive place to violence is therefore not available. Put simply, we stand on a threshold between nature and culture and must realise that violence is an unavoidable reality. It does not lead anywhere to refer violence to the initial grounds; rather, it is properly understood as a real component of social life.

These philosophical movements of thought lead to a decisive determination of relations. Violence is transferred into contexts of understanding as soon as it is brought into a relation to a respective order. Violence stands in the shadow of orders; one cannot be thought without the other (Waldenfels, 2000). In the background is the idea that the strict, hard distinction – between brute force and civilised order – cannot be maintained in the long run. Orders are not the other of violence, but they form alliances and connections with violence. No order can be justified finally and eternally, no order exists entirely without relations of power and violence. They are inevitably contingent, always differently possible and exclusive.

The people who ascribe membership to each other must agree on the conditions under which they will carry out this form of inclusion. This is of course not an argument against democratic constitutions (which will not be discussed here), but merely evidence of the irreducible interrelationship of violence and order.

Bernhard Waldenfels, who grasps violence in its depth from a phenomenological standpoint, accordingly also prefers the concept of the *violent* – an adjectival concept comparable to the *sensible and the reasonable* (Ibid., p. 23). Such violence leans on phenomena in the social world; it is not a pure substance but relies on orders. A pure substance of violence is thus a phantasm that would lead back to the 'traces of gnosis' (Ibid., p. 23).

How does violence follow order? Orders form a guide in the history of violence. How one evaluates this respective epochal order is decisive for the relations of violence that take place in the long run. Violence varies culturally and historically, but it is always carried out in view of the order presented. A few examples illustrate the connection: in antiquity, people spoke of the capacity for violence to be used against barbarian peoples, while war within a community was only corrosive and destructive. The 'holy violence' in the religious wars of the late Middle Ages served to maintain a divinely decreed order, as it followed the intimate alliance of domination and salvation. And finally, in the course of the European modern era, violence took on a tendency to dissolve its boundaries: the wars of knights and mercenaries became the war of the masses and the citizen became the soldier. The mobilisation of the masses gathered under the forming nation states steered violence in a new direction.

The orders at issue here are to be understood in the political sense: classes and strata participate in this order to varying degrees; they participate in the polity or are classical 'subjects'. Orders, however, also have to do with sacral orientations, and it is precisely in the most difficult historical moments, for example, when religious motivations fade, that strong sacral motives come to the fore. It is therefore inevitable to recognise the relational embeddedness of violence; violence is not an individualistic possession, nor is it an exception; rather, metaphorically speaking, it is woven into a respective order.

*

Finally, it would have to be asked how the principle relationship of order and violence is represented in contemporary understanding. If one simplifies it very much, the instability of orders has the greatest negative influence. Since there are fewer state wars, the violence takes place in the extra-state zones of violence. Here we are talking about protracted wars between fragmented parties, warlords and their followers, but also between

'interest groups' that do not directly belong to the respective territory. Be it in the Levant, in the regions of the Maghreb or in Middle East conflicts, these conflicts have few official titles and their ostensible characteristic lies in the fact that the respective order of the state and territory is contested and fragile.

If we ask for the faces of violence in this confusion, the following directions can be identified: violence is directed against an existing order that has established itself as a hegemonic power, among other things. Violence may be in the service of an order that is rationalised and justified. However, violence can also occur with a view to an order that is yet to be created in the future. If, for example, a non-violent order appears on the horizon, the way it is justified is, as it were, autonomous. No appeal and no instance are helpful in this situation anymore, because violence has acquired the ultimate meaning.

These distinctions are helpful in structuring the further reflections. As indicated, phenomenological social theory is at the centre of the presentation. With the help of phenomenology, we come close to understanding violence without being able to unite the many antinomies and fault lines in an Archimedean point. What is at stake, as we shall see, is first an adequate recognition of what violence is in its many figurations and embodiments, what it can be, what it encompasses and how it is effective in the social world. This procedure is not initially interested in exploring horizons of non-violence, which remain obvious and yet always far away. For the first thing is to decode the faces of violence – and only secondarily to show potentials of the analysis of violence.

We can begin to trace these faces, which we will encounter in the further course. We encounter the phenomenology of violence suffered in the figure of the victim, in real history, but also in philosophical reflection. On the other side of this spectrum is enmity – and even this social figure of the enemy does not remain with itself, but is a constant subject of political and theological debate. Finally, religion is also to be included in the considerations, insofar as it knows various forms of embodiment – forms that we encounter in history and in the present.

These exemplary studies form a special section of current research on violence. Various goals are brought together in this context. It is, of course, a matter of descriptiveness, that is, the representation of the real effects of the violent events, as long as they can be adequately reconstructed. The focus here is on the feature of narrativity, which links a specific meaning with that non-specific experience of violence. In other words, violence and meaningfulness form the two poles of an unheard-of fact – that in common life we must assume the irrevocability of human relations of violence. Nevertheless, meaning is not to be equated with the meaning we encounter in everyday life, which is helpful and orientating. What is at stake here is a more comprehensive sense that links an event that contains the absurd and perhaps even the absurd with ideas of meaning. What is decisive is not the degree of sense or nonsense we recognise in the events, but that we recognise the phenomenology of the interbody. The occurrence of violence is located in a dark in-between space, between a subjective experience and objective factors, between a normal state and an exception – in the dialectic of violence and counter-violence and not least between the own and the foreign.

Chapter Two

THE EMBODIMENT OF THE VICTIM: PHENOMENOLOGY OF VIOLENCE SUFFERED

The twentieth century holds many titles that emphasise the extraordinary. It was a century of totalitarianism, but also one of betrayal, an age of extremes and the incomprehensible. Betrayed, that is, at the mercy of unrestrained violence, were not only the people themselves but also, as it were, the idea of the human being. For up to a certain point, one could weigh oneself in an unfounded security of an inner connection between people. As is well known, such certainties were knocked out of hand in that century.

Many situations, many images, motifs and sources can be named for this experience of unbounded violence, which now, at the beginning of the twenty-first century, requires new forms of transmission.

History is like a river that carries people along. They were not allowed to shape their own history, but had to live through it as a great experience. Individual events can be taken from this stream of history that makes one think.

One of these stories leads to the so-called odyssey of the St Louis. This was an ordinary passenger ship. The route led from Hamburg to Cuba, later back to Antwerp. The passengers were all German Jews who wanted to escape the threat of the Nazi regime in May 1939. The odyssey initially took the occupants to Havana Bay, but the Cuban government did not allow the ship to dock at the pier due to changes in visa regulations. Only 29 passengers were allowed to disembark. The rest remained at the mercy of the American and Canadian authorities. Roosevelt refused to allow the ship to dock on the American coast in June 1939, and Canadian prime minister King also issued a refusal. The odyssey ended, despite all efforts to the contrary, in Europe, in Antwerp. From here, the odyssey continued to Belgium, the Netherlands, France, to areas that, as is well known, shortly afterwards became part of the National Socialists' sphere of control. Few refugees made it to Great Britain, 254 of the passengers died in the Holocaust.

The odyssey of the St Louis is one of the stories of the twentieth century that has been captured in film and literature (Ther, 2018; Ogilvie/Miller, 2006). Captain Schröder, who had unsuccessfully negotiated with various governments and even contemplated a faked accident off the coast of Britain, was honoured with the Order of Merit of the Federal Republic of Germany and was posthumously accepted by Israel into the circle of the Righteous Among the Nations. The fate of the passengers is recorded on a memorial plaque in Hamburg, on a bridge of the St Pauli Landing Bridges. The drama of the Odyssey has been put into literary form several times.

The philosophy of history comes into its own when one tries to wrest meaning from a violent episode. With Walter Benjamin, the continuum of history then becomes open when the perspective of the excluded is adopted. The angel of history Benjamin writes about is an ambivalent figure: this figure stands before the past without being able to transfer it into brighter futures. It sees the ruins, the shattered, the horror that no longer wants to be put back together. All this angel is able to do is take an unsparing look at the passions and injuries of history. As a saving idea, this historicity can only be preserved if it revives its messianic impulse (Benjamin, 1974).

What leads with Benjamin into the Jewish theological tradition has been understood as a turning away from history, a turning away from the history of victors and progress. One would like to take up these basic impulses: history is accordingly a promise that has not been kept, moreover an amalgam in which the culture of the rulers mixes with the horror. It is left to the angel of history to stop time and stand up for the rupture in history.

It is the task of a critical theory of history to pursue such impulses. In the center of history of history there is suffering, created by instrumental reason, which makes every act of self-assertion tip over into self-destruction. Only thinking that can detach itself from instrumental use keeps alive the vague hope of reconciliation (Horkheimer/Adorno, 1997, pp. 254–60).

We can take up these motifs without reaching the depth of negativist philosophy. The memory of terror, of violence and injustice is vital, as it has a right of its own. The memory of people who have fallen victim to violence is in danger of fading. We still live in a time of living contemporary history. Documents can be preserved, films can be digitally polished and literature can be edited anew. But the people involved remain in obscurity, without anyone being able to do anything about it. It is a phenomenon that historians and philosophers have devoted themselves to: How could the nameless be given a name, how could the unheard voices be given the right to be heard? History has no face, as it only knows the current of time that sweeps away everything human and everything social. The problem remains unsolved, despite all critical philosophy: people do not want to be satisfied with a history that remains anonymous. Every episode should have a face, and in that face a meaning should become recognisable.

Following on from this, it is necessary to clarify what is meant here by the meaning of history, what history 'is' in the sense meant here and what it 'is not'. First and foremost, it is not: an instance of justice. Looking back on events that we perceive as highly unjust remains in a kind of guarantorlessness. For no morality is received merely through the narrativity of the event; the experiences remain untransferable. They can be narrated and they lead to a thoughtfulness, to a pause perhaps, but not to a measure that could be called just (Koselleck, 2010, pp. 241–54).

In this respect, history is nothing more and nothing less than a narrative of the past, in which life happens and things *happen*. This does not mean that every claim to formability must be abandoned, but the desire for meaning and purpose runs into the void. In this respect, a tradition that rejects all axioms of the philosophy of history in a broad arc from Friedrich Nietzsche to Reinhart Koselleck is right. Stripped of all pretensions, history stands naked. In it, injustices intertwine with coincidences, moments of happiness and suffering for which no meaningful narrative can stand. Meanwhile, what prompted Nietzsche to reflect on the vital and the super-historical leads Reinhart Koselleck to a sceptical rejection of the impositions of meaning that conceal their theological heritage (Ibid., 9–32).

The concept of the historical must be freed from its metaphysical, theological and historical–philosophical disguises. History in itself can be told and, as is well known, it was told in all conceivable facets in view of the violent twentieth century. But this does not mean that the experiences and events coalesce into a meaningful whole that has a binding force for all subsequent historical subjects. History 'contains' the absurd and contradictory, the nonsensical and aporetic. In this respect, it cannot become better and cannot be morally enhanced afterwards (Rüsen, 2003).

In this respect, we need narratives despite everything, against our better judgement, in order to grasp the aporetic and transform it into a view. The irrational does not become more rational, but accessible. Analyses and narratives sharpen the power of judgement in order to learn to deal with senselessness. Only in open contradiction does this historicity make sense for the following arguments: the many individual experiences that others have had are vital, pluralistic, multilayered and complex. Only the linguistic processing unites them into a common reality, which is then upgraded to a 'grand' narrative.

If we take these sceptical assessments seriously and accept history in its aporetic condition, how can talk about historical spaces of meaning be justified? The thesis is that times do not pass each other by without leaving a trace, but that certain experiences are updated in new situations. The space of meaning of the twentieth century must always be considered in the twenty-first century.

In a sense, one cannot allow oneself to be suspended by history. The experiences, including all the errors and transgressions entered into, flow into the attitudes of consciousness of the present. Therefore, even if we take note of the sceptical reflections, we can speak with good reason of *a* narrative of *concern*.

Concern is directed at the many figures of violence. In the long history of violence, the victims pile up, as they become a barely comprehensible crowd. Those who deal with these stories would sooner or later resign themselves, because it seems there will always be some who remain in the shadows of history. But this resignation also gives rise to a special motif.

*

How is history to be told in a meaningful way? Of the many provisions, the connection between the objective history of violence and the perspective of being affected stands out. What is the nature of this connection and under what conditions can we give this connection do justice? From a humanistic perspective, the situation of violence is crucial: people stand in situations of violence that they have to 'cope with' or perish in. The history of violence could thus be reflected from an inferior position, as unbearable as the intensity of this narrative would be. However, this constellation is problematic if it were to claim absolute validity. The perspective of suffering is of utmost importance, especially because it corrects the tradition of *historiography from above*, but no view of events whatsoever is privileged. Perhaps it is not about the alternative of above and below, but rather about the representability of an event that does not undermine any position and does not disregard any side. Violence is an event of a power of action, exercised as action and performance. At the same time, it is *experienced as an event that* we are speechless and helpless in the face of. It is collectively mediated and affects each individual with all its harshness. Violence is experienced and embodied, suffered and enforced. It has to do with invisible authorities and at the same time with concrete people.

Beyond these ordinary statements, philosophical reflection faces the difficulty of transcending natural partiality and confronting events with abstraction and distance. Only then does a history of suffering become a narrative that allows for possibilities of design and subjective agency – however much the shock over individual suffering stands out. As we will show in the following, we can take a productive distinction from the history of violence. One side can be described as the perspective of the violence suffered, the other is the violence *itself, which* confronts the victim in various guises. In the mediation of both sides, history becomes narratable.

*

Perhaps the most extreme variant of a violent situation can be seen in the context of the Holocaust. As is well known, the prisoners of Auschwitz were forced to undergo brutal procedures. Shaving, disinfection and undressing were carried out on admission to the camps; added to this was number tattooing as, in a sense, the final act of dehumanisation.

This violence has a long shadow. That people are degraded into objects by being 'marked' is not an invention of modern times. In the Old World, slaves were treated as commodities and marked as property. Tattoos should also be seen in the context of crime prevention. In the nineteenth century, people sought to systematically record so-called anthropometric characteristics with the help of photography. Photographs of the perpetrators were supposed to provide clues to unmistakable physiognomic characteristics in order to be able to follow the traces of the 'born criminal' (Bertillon, 1895; Belting, 2014).

In Auschwitz and other camps, marking systems were applied in other respects: from 1937 onwards, the camps no longer served the purpose of 're-education' and the 'concentration' alone, they rather became forced labour and extermination camps. In these death-dealing systems, the confined people were provided with convict clothing but also with recognisable tattoos. In view of the will to extermination, at the bottom of which no language is ready, the systematic recording of inmates through archiving and card indexing is surprising. Over 400,000 persons were recorded numerically and alphabetically in the administrations of the camp statistics (Därmann, 2020, p. 268). General number series distinguished Jewish prisoners, Soviet prisoners of war, educational prisoners, Sinti and Roma, among others. A network of typing pools extended throughout the camp to monitor and direct prisoners' movements in and out of the blocks. The tattoo was a paradoxical symbol in that it placed the 'marked' in a bizarre space between life and death. The period between the registration and the issuing of the death papers was the granted period of life, which became an extended period of death for those affected. As still living, they were already marked as future corpses; as dead, they were recorded in an anonymous archive of death.

These events have been processed, must be further researched; above all, they must be made accessible to future generations. Here we are dealing solely with the question of the registry, which we encounter as perhaps the most extreme form of violence. The character of annihilation had passed into the absolute violence of meaning.

In these spaces, violence was absolute in that it negated the 'conventional' classification of a violent event. The excess of violence had erased all meaning; what had happened could no longer be captured by any sense or word. The question remains as to how definitively silence is to be understood in the face of violence. The senselessness of the violence led those affected into a zone where the power to articulate was absent. This first affected those injured in the war, the traumatised people whose world was coming apart at the seams. It also affected the following generations, the immediate environment, perhaps even an entire culture, which must regain a new form of language in order to be able to act. And the overall question is what contribution culture can make in times of crisis that have led to a deep doubt about criteria such as logos and reason, spirit and morality, self-power and autonomy.

A perhaps irritating observation should be noted in this context. The number tattoo can be read as a trace reminding us of the violence of the past. The acts of dehumanisation, meanwhile, find a resistance through empowerment and appropriation that is surprising. A film about about 50 surviving Israeli men and women shows what form life after violence can take ('Numbered' by D. Doron/U. Sinai). The survivors integrated the numbers into their self-image; some used the numbers as code for bank codes and safes. The children and grandchildren also did not want to settle into the passivity of the violence they had suffered; they sometimes had the numbers tattooed into their skin voluntarily in memory of this practice. It is, if you will, a countervailing way of reading what happened (Därmann, 2020, p. 278 ff.). For the number ultimately reminds us of the futility of the negatorial power to rule over life and to hand everything over to the disposal of power. The attempt to steal a name from the inmates and give them a number as an insignificant 'element' is, at the latest, failed when memory is linked to paradoxical effects of resistance. And so something remains in the memory of memoria that could be interpreted as a last stand against the furore of violence.

PART II
Dark Spots in History

The present reflections face a challenge: to present historical insights whose trajectories have long been known. The dark spots at issue – colonial, fascist and totalitarian violence – are preserved in historical memory and are activated on a case-by-case basis, for learning occasions or communal commemoration. So what is the point of reconstructing them in the context of a philosophical enquiry?

In the present case, the choice of viewing history is in question. Of all the questions that besiege consciousness in the face of extreme violence, one task needs to be named: Can we transfer the history of the past into a form of narration that comes close to the claim of historical meaning-making? On closer examination, the history of violence breaks down into myriads of 'small' but significant stories that are sometimes handed down and sometimes forgotten. From this ground of singular experience, an overarching structure could be conceived that does not encompass all individual episodes, but describes a horizon of the historical in which all individuals can find themselves.

This horizon brings to light something that is novel and remarkable: the narrative competence of a historically enlightened consciousness. This competence includes questions to history that every generation must ask anew: how outbreaks of violence occurred and what explanations one has at hand; how inexplicable and incomprehensible situations of violence could unfold and how they affected the psyche of contemporaries, not least the questioning desire not to repeat the transgressions of the past.

In other words, it is moral concepts of historical consciousness that give validity to the talk of narrative competence. However, one must add: the difficulty is not the complete clarification of the past, but the confrontation with the dark and unfathomable of human relations of violence. One must try to put the past into a narrative form and at the same time acknowledge that these stories are filled with voids. The entanglement in the history of violence and the stuttering of the course of history must be considered at all times.

Nevertheless, it makes sense to link the transitions between the centuries with the claim of historical meaning-making. In the same way that individuals communicate about their past and want to tell their own history, the twentieth century could be described in terms of its history.

This is an analogy for the twentieth century. One assertion precedes the following accounts: that there is a 'historical consciousness' in the midst of our present that is distinguished by a narrative competence, similar to a subject that surveys its own history and can put it into a meaningful form.

The ability to tell a story now appears at first glance to be ordinary, even insignificant in the face of disastrous violence. On closer inspection, one sees the intrinsic value: at best, we recognise the moral core of a dramatic event, we sense the humane meaning in situations of lost meaning, we follow the traces of the past lost in the darkness of history within the framework of a narrative. The competence at stake here, then, is much more than just the opportunity to grasp the past in a sequence of episodes. It is rather properly understood as a skill-consciousness, to fathom the meaning of experiences, which we can only defend to a human world as such.

In no way does the following claim to melt the twentieth century down to an insightful moral core with a grand gesture. The omissions are so conspicuous that no advocatory and universalistic claims are made. We merely extract from the history of the twentieth century a few episodes that prove to be exemplary, but by no means encompass all significant events. This 'history', like any, is location bound and particular: it obviously focuses on the perspective of Eurocentrism, which is due to the author's position. The scientific-theoretical content, on the other hand, is of greater interest: the historical consciousness we are talking about here is a form of elementary sense-making (and in this it has universal properties). To think historically means to inform oneself about the condition of the world and the relation to the past.

*

What does it mean to link the past with historical meaning? What form of narrative competence is this based on? The historical consciousness to which the following discussions are committed is located in a complex field of intersection.

Narrative competences are attributable to single individuals, but also to a larger social unit. Clarity about the past, however, is not given at all times, because whenever historical reality is spoken of, past circumstances, coincidences, actions and events are thematised in their development, not mapped. Historical meaning refers to the active construction of historical reality and primarily goes back to a 'symbolically represented world' (Straub, 1998, p. 83). Historical reality is real in the sense that we ascribe meaning and significance to our experiences; in this respect, it is based on interpretations and understandings (on the theory of history: Bruner, 1990; White, 1991; Ricouer, 1991).

A problematic thesis seems to make access difficult here. As pure constructs, historical events would be left to the perceptions of the subjects alone and thus one would be faced with the common problem of a postmodern attitude that reduces everything to arbitrariness. This is obviously unacceptable for accounts that refer to the hard causality of violence suffered. The events of violence, however, are not the arbitrarily available products of our imaginations; rather, they are to be understood as reconstructable incidents by which people were affected, touched or injured.

What is at stake here is to make it clear that history is fleeting and fragile, just as the conditions of common life are. Thinking historically means acquiring a language for this very fleetingness and transforming the lost meaning into manageable meaning and reducing the overwhelming complexity and suddenness. The historical mind *records* and *writes things down* before they are forgotten; in this respect, it goes hand in hand with objective *archival* determinations. Historical competences, on the other hand, are expressed in the ability to shape historical reality for someone through creative acts (Straub, 1998, p. 85).

Historical meaning is an object of cultural self-understanding. In a sense, cultures transcend time; they try to bring a passage of time into an understandable context. Collectives stand in their history – that is, they form culturally and socially determined expectations and experiences that are of paramount importance to them. This does not yet denote a normative view; the collective historical consciousness can rather be formally described as a three-digit relation: someone possesses a consciousness of something that is significant for a third party.

The constructive character is questionable: a past event is represented, not depicted. Traces of the past are collected and put into a narrative form that does justice to what is represented. The function of representation is crucial: in the act of historical representation, a historically 'informed' subject represents an Other for whom he or she speaks over a span of time. Speaking about, for or against others is at the centre of such historical consciousness.

As we will see, however, history is not content with the formal arrangement of events, nor with the enumeration of dates and numbers. The sequence of dates 1914, 1917, 1933–45, for example, is deeply anchored in historical memory and yet says nothing about the aspects of content. The practical sense of narrative competence is rather expressed in the sensitivity for the diversity of viewpoints, relationships and questions of power.

Let us think, for example, of the history of genocide. Ethnic groups and collectives that fell victim to colonial violence needed a long time not only to formulate their history as such, but also to receive the necessary recognition in the community of states. Let us think of the genocide in Armenia in the context of the First World War, which remained hidden in the shadows of the world community for a long time. Or let us think of the difficult debates about the 'correct' memory after 1945. It is always about the difficult questions of memory in a specific world context. Narrative acts that depict what has been experienced in a collective space enable initial orientations for the people concerned. However, the collectively significant experiences do not remain for themselves, but are taken up, intentionally or not, in a broad horizon of the general public. Only then is it decided whether this remembered and told history is given a shape, whether it can be filled with meaning and linked to interests.

Historical narrative competence must therefore balance different, conflicting forces. This includes the ability to integrate narratives into a whole of history without falling into the trap of the comparatistics of evil; for it is not a matter of comparing individual suffering and putting the monstrosity of crimes into a hierarchy. Narratively mediated history cannot be found on any objective scale and cannot be measured with any yardstick.

Instead, the value of narrative competence is shown by the extent to which a narrative functions as a stabiliser of memory, that is, the extent to which individual access to events can be transformed into an acceptable historical construct.

This claim is by no means insignificant, but of equal importance to the interest of the present reflection, which is to measure the violence of a past century in terms of its significance for the present. To this end, before we turn to the situations of violence in detail, we must clarify which competences the aforementioned historical consciousness requires.

The Phatic Function of Cultural Memory

Narrative competences are embedded in cultural orders. They denote the ability to present a narrative as meaningful to a collective. A series of events is transformed into a sequence; history becomes its own story, the corpus of history becomes visible by entering into a logic of development and being mapped in a coherent sequence.

Someone who can tell a story 'well' is characterised by a phatic ability. Someone organises a text in such a way that it creates a closeness to the listeners. In this sense, we can apply general linguistic and literary findings to history (Rosenthal, 1995; Booth, 1998).

A good story establishes closeness and familiarity; in the context of historical narratives, however, this function is very presuppositional. Regardless of the content of the event, a bond is forged between speakers and listeners through storytelling and thus a community is formed. Narratives create and deepen relationships; they can sometimes contribute to the integration of individuals. A story that deals with a disaster or an experience of violence, for example, contributes to the formation and identity of a community; in the best case, it can lift the isolation of the injured individuals. But the darker aspect of narratives must not be overlooked: in a shared society radical heterogeneity, doubt, discord and dissent can be expressed. Cultures and ways of life are in conflict. In addition to the effects of solidarity, history also expresses the experience of strangeness.

One can illustrate the function of narratives with a concrete case. The odyssey of the St Louis in the context of the Shoa, for example, could be used as a narrative that expresses precisely these social potentials. The factual events stand in the horizon of various literary and cinematic productions. Several hundred Jewish refugees were brought across the Atlantic on a former cruise ship to save them from Nazi persecution. However, they were turned away on the coasts of Cuba, Canada and the United States. The journey ended in Europe and most of the occupants were eventually led to concentration camps and murdered (Ogilvie/Miller, 2006).

It is an incident that contains many levels of meaning. One can experience a closeness to the characters if one embeds the odyssey in a narrative.

The developmental logic of the story creates a closeness to the persecuted. One reads and hears about families who, perhaps full of hope, sought their way into the distance; one follows this path with inner sympathy, although as a listener one already knows the end of the story. The phatic function consists in the interest for concrete people in the midst of their history.

But is the value of such a narrative reduced to the emotional bond? At the very least, a basic emotional quality makes itself felt that should not be disregarded. The emotional participation is significant because it is only through the embodiment that this story becomes meaningful. The political, historical and social 'circumstances' can be unfolded from this level without being misunderstood as a (supposedly less interesting) superstructure. Of particular value here are the relations of past and present that already emerge at the moment of emotional qualification: What happened then can be told in the form of a completed story. The meaning for the listener exists on different levels of validity: as valence in itself, for example, in the commemoration of the victims and their fate, but also in the comparative horizon. The stories of the past are densely connected to the stories of the present. The history of the excluded is thus never finished but continues to be written every day (Ther, 2018).

Understanding the Century

Remembering the violence of the past takes place in a medium with a constructive character. The difficulty is to be emphasised repeatedly: the individual approaches to the past are primary; memories are knowledge based and related to immediate experience. Historical consciousness, however, asks questions about the role of the construction of historical reality; *it wants to know, to question; it interprets and doubts*. It does not only want to collect information, but to confront the past in a constructive and committed attitude. In the best case, it confronts the antinomian impulse: that yesterday could be better (Rüsen, 2003; Assmann, 2018).

The difficult question of how the past relates to the present is to be brought to the point here. How does the twentieth century relate to the twenty-first century?

Obviously, we are faced with a task that can be described as monumental. The space of meaning of the twentieth century has been described in such a forceful way that any one-sense, linear understanding of the matter is not enough. In this sense, then, it is also about 'dark places', as an awareness of continuity and difference and changeability. The course of time persuades us that there is a strong connection between the centuries and that past and present interlock wonderfully – narrative competence defies this expectation. It turns to experiences of strangeness that are difficult to articulate: it asks about the unfinished and the nonsensical in history.

Orientation between the Centuries

It is difficult to reduce the function of the presentation to one outstanding aspect. The space of meaning of the twentieth century is to be represented, without any claim to completeness or finality.

Being able to take events from history is comparable to pedagogical intentions. But the orientation in time and space is misleading with the notion of *learning from history*. Every representation of history has, it should be provisionally stated, an implicit pedagogy. All action, and historical reflection in particular, stands in a valorative space (Taylor, 1994).

When we speak of historical meaning, we create orientations through acts of meaning-making. What kind of orientation we can expect in a temporal space that is so violent and enigmatic is open to question.

Linking the 'themes' with which the century has inscribed itself in consciousness is risky, however. The scope for misunderstanding and omission is probably as great as the gains in knowledge. This is not a linear linkage or a homogeneous narrative but rather attempts to explore horizons of meaning in a broad field of violence. This search encompasses first the violence of colonialism and that hostility to violence whose trace reaches into the present. It further leads us to the abysses of totalitarian violence, which we encounter anthropologically as hatred, but also in the form of ideologies.

Finally, this narratively represented history must also segue into issues that exist in the midst of our present. Here we will repeatedly come to the phenomenon that denotes a human phenomenon: *the terrifying love of war*. These insights do not bring the previous considerations to an end but to a beginning: the valorative and normative space in which we move as human beings is to be connected with at least minimal orientation. But what is the nature of the future and present actions that result from the excess of historical memory?

Chapter Three

COLONIAL VIOLENCE: THE DARK SIDES OF THE MODERN STATE

Modern societies are in a difficult situation, and not just today. Various scenarios are embellished that conjure up the creeping decline, whereby the focus is less on a concrete form of state and more on an entire culture. Cultures such as the West, whose religious powers are dwindling, are doomed in the long run because decadence and inertia, but above all a loss of meaning, have an impact within (Onfray, 2017). Such narratives, which may overemphasise politics, culture and religiosity, attract attention through their sceptical worldview alone. They are heard and applauded insofar as they give space to speculation that cannot be doubted by any logocentric strategies.

Nevertheless, there are a multitude of reasons to defend the form of modernity and, if possible, to prolong its existence. The following reflections can possibly contribute a part to this and, paradoxically, by drawing attention to the dark sides of history and the present. In this respect, the following remarks are to be understood as a specific form of defence that sharpens the eye for the shallows and negative sides of one's own.

This negativity can be seen in various dimensions. It concerns the relationship between domination and violence in general and the history of violence of the rising nation state in particular. Put simply, democracy casts a long shadow into the past, which has to do with the categories of order formation, homogenisation and the civilisation of the foreign. However, in order to avoid a one-sided presentation, the historical review must be combined with a political and a cultural–psychological reflection. Here, history, culture, psychology and politics enable an overall view of the shades of the order of modernity. And from this point of view, with an open eye on the historical conditionality of the present, progress in thinking can be hoped for in the best case.

We pick out two examples in the following. Both times, we are dealing with violent events that received little attention for a long time and were only officially recognised after long struggles. Both cases – the colonial violence on the African continent and the genocide of the Armenian people – lead our reflections to situations of suffered violence that are difficult to bear.

Remembrance of Colonial Violence in 'German Southwest Africa'

A map of the African continent in the nineteenth century depicts the military race for Africa. For uninformed observers, a peculiar mixed situation emerges. The continent is rutted by expansionist movements. Various European powers take the country and its inhabitants in the grip of their imperialist desires: French, British, Belgians, Portuguese and Germans move inland from the west; Italians and Germans from the eastern part. The Maghreb, too, becomes the 'object' of European expansions. Wars of conquest and uprisings can be observed throughout the continent, in the Algerian hinterland as well as in western Samori, in Sudan as well as at the Cape of Good Hope. The continent appears to the viewer as a snake pit of colonial politics, with overlapping lines of tension and diverse conflict zones.

Colonialism has been known to have its own language and its own morality. This morality is imbued with the belief in an inequality that seems far removed from today's standards.

Whether it can be called moral at all is questionable; but morality merely means that actions are justified and that means and ends are linked. For example, the excesses of colonial violence can be linked to a form of colonial speech. The links between violence against 'foreigners', 'barbarians' or 'savages' and violence on the European continent are obvious. The consequences of these events reach into the present (Dabag, 2004).

Colonial violence spans the event-historical horizon of the nineteenth century, but it extends into the early twentieth century. It is one of those forms of violence that will not stand still and dominates historical consciousness. In this respect, it must be at the beginning of any study of the twentieth century, because it has eminent meanings.

The phenomenon of colonialism is an intense topic for the social sciences (Mann, 1986, 1993). There are different directions to think in when trying to place colonial violence in the history of power. Colonies are linked to narrative concepts that fill space with mythological figures and enact geopolitical agency. Colonial violence is also a pattern of order that reaches deep into the history of Europe's emerging state power (Krippendorff, 1992). In the following, we pick out an example from the event horizon of colonial wars and try to extract psychological motifs of enemy production from these events.

The massacres in German Southwest Africa and East Africa in 1904/5 can be examined as examples. The focus here should not be on the event-historical horizon, but above all on perspectives of interpreting genocidal violence. However, here, as in other contexts, the phenomenon of war must be perceived in its complexity, for it is not to be understood solely as a destructive force, but also as an antinomy, that is as a creative force. This concept means: the duration of wars determined the emergence of political orders in the long run. War is – from the happy standpoint of the distanced observer – a cruel teacher and, from a certain point of view, a productive force. An ambivalent assessment that only emerges from an archaeological perspective (Morris, 2013).

Wars on the African continent were a reality even before the colonial excesses. Wars were fought over land, people, resources, rule and property. The difference to the European war order probably lies in the timing of state formation, which as we know was consolidated after 1648. One of the special features of African war history was the migratory movements of the pre-colonial states. These created dynamic military cultures, charismatic leaders, kingdoms with 'warlords' and expansionist states. The capacity to wage war was caught in a web of competition and cooperation, trade interests, fragile alliances and ever-changing power relations. War as a struggle for territory was pushed by European powers and changed the dynamics of intra-African statebuilding (Reid, 2009; Levene, 2005).

As is well known, colonial violence is a specific form of violence. It leads into the dark abysses of a violence that remains as a task of thought. Of course, it was made possible by innovations in military technology that created an imbalance. But beyond that, the form of violence also changed. In pre-colonial times, it was possible for the inferior to escape into other spaces. This violence, which seeks to remove the enemy, did not necessarily have to take excessive forms there. But after the sweeping territorialisation, the politics of disaster became reality: the first forms of total war took shape here. Tribal wars became total wars because they targeted the livelihoods of the attacked.

It is in this context that the genocide in German Southwest Africa, today's Namibia, is to be located. This genocide stands in a series of genocides, massacres and wars, but also in a symbolic relationship to the space of meaning of the twentieth century.

The events themselves can be traced back to a few sentences: Colonial societies, acting as the vanguard of the state, established so-called protection treaties with indigenous rulers. Colonial rule thus relied on various means to bring space, land and people under control. Only when the indigenous people wanted to escape the colonisers' grasp were extreme means of violence used (Langewiesche, 2019, pp. 272–400).

The German war in Southwest Africa against the Herero people began in January 1904, when more than a hundred German colonial settlers were killed by rebellious Herero. In August of the same year, the German colonial army crushed the Herero and drove them into the vastness of the Omaheke steppe. A steppe that was poor in water and thus facilitated the genocide, which has since been recognised. In the confrontation with the special forces (German: 'Schutztruppe'), 80 per cent of the Herero and a large part of the Nama fell victim.

The violence had taken the form of a punitive court, as the commander of the German troops, General v. Trotha wrote. Since they were no longer considered German subjects, every Herero, with or without a rifle, would be shot. Neither women nor children were admitted. The punitive court ended with the military's finding that the Herero had ceased to be an independent tribe.

Different approaches to these historical events are possible. The mass murder stands in a series of genocidal excesses, thus also in connection with the European Holocaust. In addition, the events take place in the context of colonialism and imperialism, of enemy constructions and power relations. In this dense field, the patterns of violent enmity are to be highlighted above all.

The empiricism of violence first directs the gaze to anthropological determinations of history. How is history possible and how can we reconstruct the conditions of possible history in retrospect? Apparently only, according to Reinhart Koselleck, if we find an existentialist language that leads back to the ultimate reasons of historical existence.

Existential categories of history are determined by fundamental experiences of violence. It is the capacity to kill that makes all known histories of violence possible. It leads to polar tensions: the capacity for violence is unavoidable and historically evident, but it also leads to the option of a temporary peace, which is to be recognised as a historical achievement.

This distinction appears formal because it denotes social differences in the field of power. But it claims to be a transcendental category of possible history. Humanity and the renunciation of violence, the prospect of peace and the settlement of disputes – all these concepts presuppose the opposition pair of friendship and enmity. They are hard existential determinations that can be filled up ideologically and existentially (Koselleck, 2000, pp. 99–110).

The anthropological-critical definition of enmity has eminent significance in this context. On one level, it is about enmities that are to be cultivated and contained. They allow for compromise and the drawing of boundaries. Only when they are existentially filled up do they create ideological distortions and radical enemy images. The Other becomes a compliant object, a 'thing' to be removed or the incarnation of evil.

Are the events in Southwest Africa just such ideological hardenings? Perspective connections between Europe and the colonised African continent are obvious. The beginnings of fascist and National Socialist violence are recognisable in the colonial policy of high imperialism. There are long lines of historical constructions that aim at the radical exclusion of the foreign and the other.

At the same time, a psychological constellation must be taken into account. Around 1900, patterns of enemy production developed in this region – as in other colonial regions.

The destruction of living space was linked to racially motivated disenfranchisement. The conditions under which wars were waged against the enemy were, of course, shaped by specific symptoms. Mark Levene, for example, recognised in this violence both the willingness to annihilate and the ambivalent fear of the Other. The belief in racially based superiority was coupled with a peculiar fear of those who were looked down upon. French and German, British or Spanish commanders ran an 'iron' regiment; they 'pacified' through massacres and repression, but not necessarily in the sense of targeted extermination (Levene, 2005, p. 265). Rather, they were overreactions towards an absolute stranger who appeared not as a hostile counterpart but as a split-off object.

Violence in the Shadows: The Armenian Genocide

Colonial violence is one of the many dark aspects of the history of violence. It casts long shadows that reach into our present. Can we make a connection here to another 'veiled' genocide of the early twentieth century?

The history of violence in the twentieth century is reconstructed here in the form of highlights. We are content with a history of events with many omissions and deliberate abridgements. What is at stake is not the historical detail, but the connection between factuality and meaning. In this sense, we can speak of a form of conceived history and its significance for the present. Colonial violence, as described, has taken on extreme forms of asymmetrical distinctions. In this respect, it is directly related to the other 'early' genocide of the twentieth century – the Armenian genocide of 1915/16. It was none other than Adolf Hitler who presumably spoke about the long-forgotten genocide of the Armenians. The annihilation of the people, the dictator said, was long forgotten after more than two decades (1939).

The ground for the readiness to physically destroy one's enemies was thus solidified and there is no doubt about Hitler's violent motives. But the ideological and cultural dimension of the events in the First World War has yet to be clarified.

It was only in the recent past that the mass murder of the Armenians was officially recognised as genocide by various states, in France in 2001 and in Germany in 2005. Turkey had refused to deal with its own past until recently. The genocide itself is part of a continuity of Turkish-Armenian conflicts. Massacres of Armenians had already taken place in 1895 and 1909; the genocide of 1915 was followed by another extermination in 1920. The genocide of 1915, however, has a special significance. The national ideology of the so-called Young Turks is central to the analyses (Dabag, 1995, 1996, 1998, 2002).

In 1908, the 'İttihat ve Terakki' (Unity and Progress) party took the lead in the emerging Turkish nation state until 1918. Although the non-Turkish minorities were given hope for legal security through the reinstatement of the 1876 constitution, Turkish national homogenisation was at the centre of the ideological orientations. It can be understood as the central element of an ideology that was intended to give the events a particular poignancy and intensity (Zimmermann, 2008, pp. 46–54).

The events must be seen in the context of the First World War. The systematic persecution of Armenians began after the devastating defeat of the Third Ottoman Army at Sarıkamış in January 1915 against Russian troops. The Armenians were blamed for the defeat, primarily by the Pan-Turkish Unity and Progress Committee. The Armenians serving in the Ottoman army were disarmed, demobilised and assembled into labour battalions. The disarmament was extended to the entire Armenian population of Eastern Anatolia, until finally deportations began from Zaitun in April 1915. The Minister of the Interior Talat Pasha had thousands of Armenian community leaders arrested and executed, as well as the Armenian notables in Istanbul and Smyrna. Finally, Armenians residing in the Eastern provinces were expelled; men were executed on the spot, while women, the elderly and children were deported on foot or by train.

The Armenian genocide is part of a larger structural context. Dan Diner sees in the processes of decay of the Ottoman Empire primarily the process of the 'Ethnification of religion' (Diner, 2001, p. 203). Religious communities of the imperial empire transformed into millets, territorial ideas of order spread, majorities and minorities became more differentiated. Bulgaria broke away from Ottoman rule in 1908, Bosnia–Herzegovina was annexed by Austria–Hungary. The Tripolitan War of 1911 against Italy and the Balkan Wars drove the process of dissolution of the Ottoman Empire. The transformation of a multinational and multi-religious empire into a homogeneous nation state, which took place over several generations, led to radical solutions – such as the alternating expulsions of Muslims and Orthodox in the course of the Greek-Turkish conflicts.

The concrete reasons for the genocide of 1915 thus lie in the murderous political dynamics of structural change, which seems like a signature of the early twentieth century.

Ethnic attributes of the 'Turkifying' individuals determined the national character; the political dynamics expressed themselves in the smouldering conflict between minorities and majorities, finally in systematic disenfranchisement.

*

Fundamental questions about history arise from these accounts. They lead us to a field of tension between anthropology, psychology and history. In general, history is referred to a dialogue, to the discursive encounter of cultures and communities. Ideally, history acquires a historical orientation function (Rüsen, 2003; Assmann, 2013a). The past is not only objectified, but it acquires meaning for *someone*. It makes people capable of reflecting on action and suffering in the respective current temporal change of life circumstances.

In addition, however, the tendency towards political closure of historical images must be considered. The decisive motif thus lies in the intersection of memory, power and morality. The visualisation of history enables individual moral interpretations, but the comprehensive morality from historical experience is far more difficult. This is because historical realities have to be conflated with different moral designs and these have to be positioned in a moral universe.

Unquestionable truths and objective validity stand abruptly next to moral descriptions of the world. These require communicative opening strategies that open up the background of specific experiences of violence.

Various indications suggest that in the case of the Armenian genocide there was a problematic instrumentalisation of history. Consider, for example, the decision of the Turkish government in 2015 to postpone the day of the commemoration, thus bringing two historical events from 1915 into competition with each other.

In view of this form of history, historians speak of memory loss, denial of reality and repression. However, these debates will not be explicitly pursued here. Rather, the question is: How can we describe the general framework of a theory of historical responsibility that encompasses traumatic experiences and victim perspectives on the one hand, and the inhibiting factors of historical politics on the other? A position that takes a universalist standpoint would have to integrate various points of view. On the one hand, it should be oriented towards a concept of human authenticity, towards the experiences of suffering and concepts of meaning in a fragile history. It would also have to take into account the fact that the survivors and descendants have had to suffer from a double trauma: from the burden of what they have suffered, which cannot be barred by the statute of limitations, and from the burden of denial.

Objectivity and partisanship are to be seen here as two aspects of one event. The historical facts point to systematic planning, social and political patterns of action that enabled the isolation of a particular group. The orientation towards the facts is interrupted by the process of historical judgement, which is then about the knowledge of the radicality of the act and the political goal of a social transformation in the shortest possible time.

This in turn forces historical research to interdisciplinary linkage with hermeneutics. For only a phenomenology of violence clarifies the forms of negative memory.

When the Armenians were told that they had to leave the cities within a very short time and leave their belongings behind, when troops entered their homes and pursued them to the last corner with drawn rifles or when they were herded together in groups, these were untransferable experiences – not to mention the death marches and shootings. For historians, this reveals forms of negative memory (Koselleck, 2013) that are unavailable in the historical depth dimension. They can be told, but never fully understood, because they reveal a past with inter-existential dimensions.

The assertion of non-transferability points to a twilight of memory politics. That which is non-transferable results from a primary inter-existential distance. This in no way means ignoring historical facts or shrugging them off. Only from the unavailable history, on the other hand, do moral perspectives emerge. The moral judgement of what happened is unquestionable. The forms of memory, however, are faced with difficult conditions. Since those affected had lost the centre of their community life through the violence, their descendants could only develop very weak forms of memory.

The vast majority of survivors were children up to the age of nine, who had been left among the corpses by chance and were eventually taken out of the death marches. In view of this, in what forms could the memoria of the experience of suffering be created? How could a binding narrative succeed in creating identity? In addition to the few official forms of preservation, rituals and commemorations in this case are dominated by oral transmission: a conversion of experience into memory and narratives, into art, film and literature.

From the perspective of hermeneutics, however, the caveat remains: there is an irrevocable gap between a past reality and its linguistic management. Events always have a different 'way of being' than the language itself that is spoken afterwards. And it is this insight that underlies the worldview of concern under which we live today.

*

The history of genocide is of a complexity that we cannot begin to grasp here. From the multitude of mass murders and genocidal violence, only two early examples have been mentioned here, although they have a high symbolic value. In both cases, recognition of the violence was withheld from the victims for a long time. These are events of violence that weigh on historical consciousness like dark spots.

Are these exemplary situations in which a dispositive of violence could have an effect? Michael Mann uses this concept of the dispositive, which was originally employed by Michel Foucault for the theory of power (Mann, 2004). This category would be helpful because it undermines the simplistic view of violence. In a universal view, we place violence on the other side of the civilisation. Accordingly, violence is raw nature, wild and unpredictable. According to the cliché, it would be the opposite of political reason. Dialogue based on reason has a power that can only be maintained in strict opposition to violence.

Theories of power have challenged this ideal and knocked all illusions of non-violence out of hand. The idea that civilised society will prevail in the long run because it no longer leaves room for violence and can relegate it to the margins fails in the face of historical events of violence. According to M. Mann, are these forms of violence not rather a violence that sees itself as part of a mission of order, that appears as a wish and desire for order? And does the reconstruction of the violent events not create a completely different image of the 'civilised' order created? Is violence not rather the (concealed) part of the laboratory of modernity that should be recognised as such (Mann, 1993, 2004, p. 113 f.)?

Michael Mann, Michel Foucault, Giorgio Agamben, to name but a few of the leading authors, have placed the dark sides of democratic orders in the glare of criticism. The greatest difficulty for social theory that wants to be guided by these thoughts is now to find a balanced position.

The dispositive of violence is a historiographical guiding category that reveals the complexity of the forms of violence. The social order itself produces this violence, so that only one interpretation is conceivable: we must think of violence as an immanent component of the order.

Up to this point, insights can be gained that correct our conventional ideas of violence. Violence knows many faces; the horror image of raw, untamed violence is only one possible variant. We find another form of violence, much more difficult to decipher, in the self-description of the civilisation.

So-called civilised nations followed a mandate of order. They placed themselves at the top of the world and forced other cultures into a strict hierarchy. The civilising mission went far beyond the establishment of their own state and reached out to supposedly backward cultures. This state power saw itself in the right: the wild violence outside civilisation was to be tamed; orders were to be established that were to be oriented towards the supremacy of the first world. As a result, this civilising spirit of difference construction followed with staying power. The world was disciplined and ordered, as it were, in order to be controllable and manageable (Mann, 2004, p. 114).

The question is, of course, to what extent this violence is a constituent moment of the modern (Western) state that is still valid today. Critical theories of violence must at least remain open to contradiction. The past trivially does not define the present, and historical learning is inevitable. This means, among other things, that one cannot transfer the events of the past to the present without circumstance. It further means that we do not stop at the historicising view of totalitarian violence alone. The critical lens must be broadened to account for the ways in which others are constructed as others. Cultural psychology gives us the intellectual tools to uncover further dimensions of colonial discourse.

The Colonial Gaze: Reflections on Cultural Psychology

In the Lexicon, encyclopedia 'Großer Brockhaus' of 1931, one reads that a Southwest African Bantu people was a freedom-loving people that was severely decimated after the Herero Uprising of 1904. In the Battle of Waterberg in August 1904, this people had been subdued and pushed into the Omaheke Desert, where about 80,000 victims were to die (Benz, 2006, p. 27). The information is factual and precise, as befits lexical forms.

Another form of narrative provides a deeper insight. Gustav Frenssen published a narrative in 1906 entitled: *Peter Moor's Journey to the Southwest* (Frenssen, 2001). The writing is in a tradition of travel narratives that enjoyed strong journalistic attention. They were printed and read in millions of copies. What was written and reported there found space in the minds of an audience; one speaks of African colonial folklore, the importance of which should not be underestimated.

Themes included accounts of campaigns, 'war adventures' and experiences on a distant continent.

The focus is on the events in the context of the war. The numerically superior enemy is overcome in individual battles and heroic virtues of the protagonists are overemphasised. Other comparable writings combined the military recollections of settler life, descriptions of nature and heroic lyricism into turgid trivial acts together (exemplary: v. Liliencron, 2014). It was about subjects, German men and women, who lose themselves in a foreign country, prove their patriotic sentiments and finally find each other as a couple. But this literature is worth mentioning above all because it shows how violence is legitimised in the forecourt of real politics. A foundation is laid that resembles an 'exercise in genocidal thinking' (Benz, 2006, p. 43) and functions here as a colonial gaze.

Violence, as we know, is physical confrontation. It goes back to the vulnerability of the human body and the human capacity for violence. But this does not represent the entire spectrum of violence. Violence has to do with disregard, with human looks or human language. Violence begins when someone is not listened to or is seen as non-existent, when their belonging is doubted or when various hierarchical gradations of groups of people are spoken of.

At the centre of the colonial texts are the representatives of a group of people who obtain their rights and take land because they believe themselves to be conscious of custom and morality. This evaluation becomes explicit in lyrical and epic forms; behind it, however, is the much more profound silence in the face of the Other. People with alleged inferiority are inherently obliged to submit. If they refuse rightful domination, they would be subjected to justified punitive actions. The war against others is thus not waged on an equal footing, but in the consciousness of ethnic and civilisational superiority. The genocidal thinking is not made explicit, but wrapped up in the common patriotic and domestic language of the time.

The psychology of history faces difficult challenges here. The historical sources are ready to be interpreted, but the psychological explanation of events is always connected with disciplinary borderline passages. This is also the case here: the motives and mental conditions of violent acts are difficult to translate into a meaningful interpretation. For one is referred to approaches of psychology that enable one to look into the abysses of violence. At the same time, such a step is necessary if one wants to find ways out of the eternal cycle of hatred and enmity.

The colonial gaze is not tied to individuals, a specific regime or even to 'the' colonialist. One example: Winston Churchill recognised in the black natives of the Sudan, who had been displaced southwards, people at the earliest stage of development, who were hardly able to 'think beyond their bodily welfare'. Remaining on a prehistoric threshold, they presented themselves to the British 'conquerors' as inherently cruel and dissolute, of low intelligence, but also of excusable moral weakness (Churchill, 1899, p. 14).

Whether one subjects Churchill's memoirs or the works of Herder, Kant or even Hannah Arendt to a revision is not relevant here. The colonial gaze is obviously not bound to the individual text or to the individually formed prejudice, but to the textures and dispositives of a time. Thus, it will come as no surprise today that colonial thinking existed before colonialism and that the colonial gaze is linked to the political imagination of society. Even before the beginning of imperial expansion, for example, one can notice unconsciously expressed colonial fantasies that – here in the case of German colonial history – amount to a profound expansive desire (Zantop, 1997). This fantasy colonialism rummaged, as it were, in the fields of power, sexuality, subjugation and self-exaltation that have been described many times. But for all that a closer analysis reveals to the viewer as a bizarre projection – it is the relationship between language and violence that takes centre stage. The colonial gaze is violent, possessive and expansive.

Let us now try to combine these insights into the past with an unbiased view of the problems of the present. The critique of colonial thought and action has long been established. The problems of violent exclusion, however, remain. In this context, are critical thinkers such as Achille Mbembe right to declare Europe an opponent on the historical stage – at least that Europe which had always insisted on being the motor and spirit of a world-historical development process? The criticism of European centrism is catchy: for the author, the 'peculiarity of European history' would consist in not allowing any 'other form of humanity' to apply, and in considering one's own form of life to be 'universally human' (Mbembe, 2016, p. 90). Europe, as a form of life that has become historical, thus defined itself through reason and universality, which is conceded to every other form of life, but also has a light core.

Only on the surface can the root of all violence be concluded from this. In depth, however – and in this respect the critical colonial view is to be defended – it is about the conditions of an emancipatory universalism, thus also the conditions of recognition and misrecognition. From the present position, the cultural–psychological backgrounds of these historical violations remain to be elucidated. Such an argument is abstract; it takes place far above historical empiricism. It is necessary to ask how we might understand the phenomenon of the foreign from an intercultural perspective, always keeping in mind the critique of colonial violence.

*

People trivially meet other people; sometimes they form new bonds and meet each other in open-mindedness, sometimes they remain strangers to each other. Both possibilities turn out to be varieties of normality. It is not the difference that is problematic, but its denial; for example, when a commonality of human beings is assumed, which is denied to specific strangers. The stranger in his otherness quickly becomes a radical stranger, a deviation from everything we assume as binding in behaviour, experience and action. This foreignness hardens and makes the own the pivot of all open or silent forms of judgement. It is the self-conception that has often enough been described as Euro- or logocentrism. In this constellation, the self becomes the absolute standard that predetermines the attitudes of our everyday consciousness (Straub, 2019, p. 26). One can go so far as to assume here a worldview that leaves no room for the worldviews of others. Or from a comprehensive picture that wants to 'unite' the different, mutually alien worldviews and yet leaves them persisting in the implied irreconcilability.

What matters, then, could be described in the words of recent intercultural psychology as follows. Not the compulsive embrace of the foreign, but an exploration of its edges would be the appropriate project. The mere suspicion that these edges between separate cultures are blurred draws attention to the unsuspected affinities, similarities, relationships and encounters in a space that is merely overwritten by foreignness. At the same time, however, that which stands between trouble-free communication, that which irritates and causes discomfort, must be inspected more closely. Recent cultural psychology speaks of the *abject* (Ibid., 36), which appears to be an apt metaphor for the defence against the foreign. The aim is therefore to delve as deeply as possible into the psychology of defence in order to get close to the phenomenon.

The form of abjection is initially an everyday as well as ordinary human act to which we are educated throughout our lives. Only when fellow human beings are turned into abjects has the boundary been crossed. Human fulfilment figures form a familiar background to our lifeworld convictions: places of residence, living spaces, neighbourhoods, the concrete living space, the home and the inhabitants living there – they are consistently inhabited orders in which one is embedded and which make being familiar possible. They are consolidated through affective references.

These quasi-universal bonds can be contrasted with abjectives, which basically comprise an essential part of human development. The abject is the dirt, the rubbish, everything that does not belong and is assigned to another side. The abject is disqualified by society as rubbish or refuse; in development, it is the moment of education towards purity.

The metaphor of abjection, that is, repulsion, has the advantage that it starts at different levels of intercultural interactions. Individual psychologically, or depth psychologically, it is about moments when we feel affective reactions and are overwhelmed by the experience of resistance. The emotional reaction to the encounter with another, accompanied by unconscious feelings of rejection, resistance or even disgust, belongs to the general spectrum of experience. Repressing it is sometimes necessary; exaggerating it is anything but helpful. As is well known, strong affects and emotions can be regulated and brought into equilibrium as soon as other psychic instances contribute their share. It becomes more difficult when social interactions are condensed, when an atmosphere is created in which we participate and by which we allow ourselves to be carried away. It is the intersubjective space that decides where the affective forces are directed: into a *life-serving constellation* that balances disgust and understanding or into a *dangerous constellation* in which dislikes harden, rigid boundaries are drawn or even tangible aggression is inspired (Ibid., p. 39).

Interculturality research puts its finger on the wound of the social. No space is probably ever free of negative affects and forces of negativity penetrate every encounter. Cultural theory frees us from the illusion of being generous and above all tolerant fellow human beings. For the psychodynamics of social relationships speaks a different language: it starts from a realm of one's own, which is determined by specific situations of the strangeness is threatened. The disquiet does not come from the stranger itself, but from the loss or threat of othering (Waldenfels, 1997; Kristeva, 1990). This disquiet by strangeness is an experience that is possible in all places and at all times; it must be emphasised, however, that abjects and abjections are relational terms that make *something* appear *as foreign to someone*. The psychodynamics of dealing with difference is thus revealing because no one can detach himself from its sources. What is crucial is the transition to the social orders in which these relations are caught.

The transition to the factual orders in which we live is by no means straightforward. As we know, we find ourselves in complex situations with political, social and intercultural dynamics by which we feel challenged or even overwhelmed. Ultimately, however, the aim must be to uncover spaces of play in the intercultural field that are obscured by the motives of power. These spaces are opened up when one frees oneself from one's own pretences, that is, when we reject the immediacy of our natural sensibilities and bring the underlying mechanisms of unease themselves to questioning.

This does not mean, however, to deny the frightening and disturbing, for it has an obstinacy and a right of its own. Especially in the semi-darkness of a violence that accompanies society like a constant shadow, a demarcation is urgent. And it can, of course, be conducted in the form of a polemical debate.

Let's try to get close to a plausible social diagnosis. At what point are modern societies confronted with the challenge of strangeness? Is it possible and, moreover, advisable to make a metric of the social that puts strategies of repulsion in a context with gestures of embrace?

At least on an abstract level, the coexistence of law and violence must be taken into account. Accordingly, the forms in which strangers are abject are complex; in the worst case, they are devalued, outsourced or locked out of the inner space of the community (Straub, 2019, p. 41). Above all, however, they, these unknown strangers, are to be kept free from the soul of the individual who has an interest in pure order.

Accordingly, intercultural psychology has a special task: it can contribute to a hermeneutics of the foreign because it makes the psychological implications of abjection comprehensible, and in this sense it could make contributions to an integrative perspective. With an interest in the elementary horizons of understanding, at the same time with a sense for the dark and abysmal sides of the psyche.

Chapter Four

HATE: ON THE ENIGMA OF DIVISIVENESS IN THE AGE OF THE TOTAL

Can violence be put into words? A question that is much more difficult than it appears at the moment of a judgement, a report or a simple narrative. As a phenomenon, violence can be depicted, it is then raw or refined, experienced directly or only in a roundabout way, it is experienced intensely or carried out at a cool distance. As an experience, however, violence is not transferable and only belongs to the person to whom it happens. Violence is therefore first of all a philosophical problem that we can approach with the help of psychological introspection, but apparently never get to its actual core.

That talking about violence presents such a difficulty is surprising given the rich body of writing that sociology and philosophy, historiography and politics have produced. Violence is a subject of the utmost seriousness and yet speaking about violence seems to face various barriers. This has not only to do with the fact that violence forms a phenomenological prism that expresses both a relational event and a structural problem. Rather, the problem goes back to the complex relationship that connects violence with the discourse about violence.

One can basically distinguish between two forms in which violence is talked about. The first possibility takes the form of a social diagnosis in which the extent of de facto violence is mapped. With the help of statistical methods, if one draws a line from the past to the present, a decrease in de facto violence could be determined. Looking at complex statistics, historical evidence and theories of civilisation, the twentieth century then receives a surprising description. This century laid the foundation for an age in which violence as a means of politics was noticeably declining, writes Steven Pinker (Pinker, 2011). The dwindling importance of violence has many sources: developmental psychology and brain physiology, education and moral theory, historical chronicles and even countable death rates all contribute to this judgement.

The other form in which we can approach violence in history and the present is the discourse on violence. While the sober analysis of historical violations relies on predictability, such as the average probability of a violent death, the discourse on violence finds itself entangled in the violence of language. It begins with the fact that it remains unclear, must remain unclear, what 'counts' as violence (Liebsch, 2014). Ultimately, the discourse on violence cannot free itself from the suspicion of complicity with violence. This is a complex, seemingly dilemmatic problem of social theory, which is intensively discussed especially in the context of phenomenology.

The relationship between language and violence is the focus of the following analyses. As we will see in the following, the approaches to violence are more difficult. For the violence of the twentieth century may – expressed in figures – already have resulted in an advance of humanity in terms of lethality compared to earlier times. But this epoch marked, as it were, a low point in human history, a rupture that cannot be healed by listing numbers.

Viewed from another angle, the question arises whether the discursive approach to violence will ever decipher the riddle of violence. Rather, it seems that recent social theory is entangled in an endless discourse that proves nothing other than the undeniability of all relations of violence.

Contemporary discourses on violence aim at entanglement in violence already at the moment of attempting to cope with it linguistically. Jacques Derrida spoke of transcendental violence, which is inherent in the opening of language (Derrida, 1967, p. 87). Judith Butler speaks of ethical violence that thwarts any prospect of violence (Butler, 2004). Merleau-Ponty or Emmanuel Levinas has varied in their works the idea that violence is already native to language, touching us and overwhelming us. Violence begins at the moment when we become aware of the unlimited responsibility that approaches us in the sense of being scrupulous (Levinas, 1988, p. 250; Liebsch, 2014, p. 362).

So how is violence to be grasped as a phenomenon, how is it to be translated into language and meaning? How can we write about violence if it is already clear from the outset that violence is embedded in our actions and that we cannot escape it? There is an aporia has no way out, which is one of its characteristics. In this respect, everything depends on the choice of a formal language with which to approach the aporetic core of violence. In order to understand the varieties and excesses of divisiveness, constellations must be shown in which the actors in the field of violence and the violence itself touch each other. And for this memorable moment of touching, we need a corresponding social theoretical framework. The search for such a framing is at the same time the goal of the following considerations.

The Existence of the Hate

Every attempt to search for the roots of violence sooner or later leads to the identification of an extreme evil, a 'malum', which was already noticed in ancient times. Is this evil rooted in the moment of hatred, which obviously unleashes enough destructive energies? And could one not simply turn to the one who carries the hatred within himself and 'free' him, as it were, so that he 'comes to his senses'?

There is probably a profound deception in phrases like this. Hate is to a certain extent unavailable; it remains withdrawn from sober analysis. However, this insight does not exempt us from the necessity to work out specific 'factors' that expose the unfolding of hatred in thought and action.

Let us take a current example of a virulent discourse. Anti-Semitism is currently – for many contemporaries with unexpected suddenness – at the centre of a global debate. Without going into detail here about the negatory 'tradition' that goes hand in hand with defamation, Judeo-phobia and stereotyping, the question today is how it can be that anti-Jewish ideas (as well as other hostilities) are once again strongly prevalent. The answers lead in different directions (Heilbronn/Rabinovici/Sznaider, 2019). The high mobilisation of affects would have to be considered in the context of new media: especially digital media and the internet lead to a faster and multiple spread of hate speech. The semantic radicalisation of anti-Semitism in word, image and sound is made easier and more seductive by the digital revolution. Entire 'digital cultures' are emerging that seem to owe their existence to a deep need for negatory violence.

The example first draws attention to the technical conditions that favour the free development of hate. As we know, Web 2.0 offers a historically completely new possibility of participation, for better or for worse. Net communication is characterised by a distinct anonymity and bodilessness that brings to light everything that leads to limitations in a confined space. Situations of speech production arise in which the thresholds of taboos are lowered. These are spaces of persuasion and provocation, of influence and polemics.

Without the corresponding regulations of a third party, 'online hate communication' can also unfold (Schwarz-Friesel 2015).

This explains the extent to which the unpleasant affects spread and how social violence unfolds. To ask what exactly exists behind the language that seems so frivolous and abysmal is the much more difficult question. For one is forced to penetrate, as it were, into the depths of the psyche and search for the hidden origin of the hatred that is driven forth in certain situations. And with that, sooner or later, one comes across the deep cause of the divisiveness that we call hatred. But what exactly is meant by this?

From a historical perspective, the questions do not become easier. The thanato policy of the National Socialists in the Second World War left the Jewish persecutees with only the slightest forms of resistance, which must be seen as a part of the history of violence. On the side of the Germans, the motive of absolute power of disposal prevailed: they wanted to determine the time, the forms and the exact place of extermination and nothing was to escape absolute control. On the side of the Jewish victims, there remained the discreet possibility of suicide, which, although it was accompanied by the risk of increased suffering, represented a quasi-spiritual form of resistance.

Moshe Szklarek, an eyewitness to such a dramatic moment, told of an old Polish Jew who confronted the armed SS henchmen, threw a handful of dust in all directions and prophesied, 'This is what will happen to your Reich. It will disappear like smoke' (Därmann, 2020, p. 106 f.).

This form of resistance turned against the radicality of hatred–enmity, which wanted to wipe the Other off the face of the earth by all means. This claim to the most radical annihilation seems to be a provisional answer to the phenomenon of hate. Sartre already recognised a self-contradictory element in the furore of violence. The Jewish collective was not only to disappear from the face of the earth, but its existence as a whole became the object of a will to annihilation. In the effort to make these others forgotten once and for all, the grotesque face of fascism was revealed. Violence was radical insofar as it extended to the existence of the Other in the past, present and future, and it betrayed its absurd shape precisely at this moment. The failure of thanato politics was thus also based on its paradoxical, unreal aspects (Sartre, 1993, p. 716).

This extreme example seems to illustrate the nature of hatred in historical reality. Hatred and enmity are in a conditional relationship. The more distant and abstract the imagined or real enemy is, the stronger this relationship can flare up in hatred. Such hatred 'works', as we know from historical experience, as long as the other is associated with evil. The problematic thing about hate is not the desire that 'something' in the world should be changed or eliminated. Rather, hatred is fundamentally personal; it requires a subject that hates and an object against which the hatred is directed. In this finality lies the totalitarian motive of hate.

If you ask yourself why someone is hated, dark spots remain. Hate emanates from ourselves and is within us – and yet it seems to overwhelm us like a disease. In a way, it takes the initiative of our actions and takes over our world relations. Hate becomes 'the subject of our lives' (Liebsch, 2018, p. 1016).

Jean-Paul Sartre recognised an aspect of the absurd and nonsensical in the radicalism of politics that had shaped the circumstances of the time. What is hateful about the Other? The furore of annihilation gives no answer to this. It only wants to get rid of the Other and erase the last traces of its existence. Hate conceals a general, universal principle that turns against the principle existence of the Other.

The paradox lies in the attempt at radical disregard, which can never succeed – we can never surrender others so completely to annihilation that all memory would be erased. Others have always been there and cannot be made forgotten. Even the most extreme hatred cannot deny their being.

This rupture – the denial of the existence of others – is connected with a task that is both a challenge and a burden. The stories of the victims must be told, the past sufferings must be remembered. What 'happened' must be made visible and audible. Is it also to be made *understandable*? This question is difficult to answer and leads to tensions in the long run. Possible answers emphasise man's ability to reason – his capacity for insight and morality. Others refer less to the psychology of the human being who is willing to learn and more to the necessity of historical learning processes. Both approaches to the history of violence are indispensable: we must think of man as a being capable of renouncing violence, and we can take 'lessons' from history that are not to be forgotten.

However, this does not yet clarify the form in which we can make the divisiveness of the human being understandable. The narrativity of the divisiveness is only insufficiently given with the means mentioned so far, because it does not succeed as simple 'enlightenment'. It also remains insufficient when it is depicted in evolutionary or functionalist images.

Learning from history is a claim that refers to the motive of understanding. However, understanding is itself a phenomenon that cannot be reduced to a concept. We can understand someone who speaks our language and yet categorically misunderstand them in the process. We can reproduce a content and in doing so miss its very essence.

Understanding is a multilayered, dynamic and also flawed, self-contradictory process. It has to do with horizons of understanding that are far removed or lead to a fusion; it is referred to categories and patterns of thought, to structures of thought and to semantic forms.

The motive of power would also have to be taken into account in the process of understanding. Those who have understood something in a definitive form may be subject to a fallacy because they have 'merely' mapped something in their categories. Those who think they have definitively understood may have only appropriated the content by force.

Understanding takes place in its own categories and is thus embedded in cultural and social worldviews. Because it is both a construction and a form of empowerment, understanding remains bound to a paradoxical form: it can only 'succeed' in the dialectic of understanding and non-understanding, of lasting strangeness and silent agreement.

These comments clarify the meaning of the following reflections. The point is to undermine the power components of understanding. Understanding is not to culminate in an ultimate form of transparency, but can only succeed in a contradictory, open form.

Layers and motifs of thought are to be uncovered, which in their interplay enable the synthesis of historical learning processes called for here.

The Motif of Refusal

In the age of the total, the very concept of understanding was affected. In order to understand what happened in the twentieth century, we must distinguish different levels of doubt before we can approach the claim of understanding. The event of the Shoa must come up here, even if only superficially. It still stands for the reproach of the rupture of civilisation that has invalidated all previous understanding. In this respect, the reflections do not initially bring anything new to light, but rather they focus on the close connection between negativity and understanding.

As is well known, the break with civilisation had to do with the loss of ontological *certainties. Certain* were the previously valid moral and civilisational limitations that restricted political action; *certain* were also the anthropological convictions.

Already the first mass wars of the modern era transformed war into a furore of annihilation, and the First World War already stands for the first transgression of boundaries. Here, the individual human being was only a statistical remnant of loss indicators in the battle of nations.

The rupture that followed the First World War was known to be deeper and more disturbing. Auschwitz bears the portent of the rupture of civilisation, because literally everything 'that bears the face of man' was called into question here (Diner, 2012, p. 461). The question of the meaning of this violence was consigned to nihilism.

However, the motive of gaining something from this historical moment that is linked to historical insight remains legitimate. Each generation that addresses the 'subject' will bring its own questions, interpretations and doubts to the events. Yet the moment of understanding remains fragile and contradictory. For one can explain the emergence of a totalitarian system that carries within itself its purpose of ultimate annihilation with various clues. Modernity has a potential that is pathological; from the beginning, sociologists write, modernisation has been accompanied by a tremendous amount of violence (Mann, 1993). Furthermore, the wars of the twentieth century are closely linked to the political structural change associated with the decline of the historical great empires

(Dabag, 2000). It is thus primarily structural aspects that are emphasised in the attempt to explain them.

In contrast, understanding in the sense meant here is not satisfied with explanations. If one encounters the cognitive core of the break in civilisation, the non-understanding is greater and more intense than the supposed understanding. This aspect of the incomprehensible has different levels of meaning. One level is tied to the historicisation of memory. In the Federal Republic of Germany, the experience of material, spiritual and ideal collapse was so strong that people initially spoke of a zero hour. It was a cipher intended to conceal a national life lie: the belief that the Nazi state was nothing more than an operational accident, a foreign domination that had settled over the Germans with diabolical power. Accordingly, starting at zero hour meant to look forward and not dwell on the past. As is well known, it took decades to realise the unity of defeat and freedom. This was associated with painful insights for generations to come to terms with the incomprehensible and inexplicable. The incomprehensible always remained a part of the specific German memoria (Hölscher, 2009).

In this respect, one could assume a learning process that gradually led to 'successes' over a long period of time and was finally integrated into the democratic self-understanding. But this alone does not comprehensively clarify the motive of understanding. Understanding and non-understanding form a complex relationship. It is generally assumed that the moment of not understanding merely falls outside the larger context of understanding. Accordingly, not understanding something would be equivalent to a failure and a deficit, just as one cannot calculate a mathematical equation, for example. But this does not properly grasp the specific position of European societies and their history in the twentieth century. The failure to understand does not go back to an ability but to a will; it has to do with self-perception and moral self-understanding. The fear that one equates oneself with evil at the moment of understanding explains to a large extent the deliberate historical refusal to understand.

Non-understanding thus means an ambivalent attitude towards a past whose core remains fundamentally alien: what happened cannot be placed in the usual context and no 'rational' or 'meaningful' explanations can be found for how it came about. There are distances between the violent twentieth century and the present century that are connected to this resistant motif. Not only silence, not only lasting strangeness, not only the faltering dialogue between the next generations has created this gap. The rift also goes back to the understandable need to draw a line between the times. For the refusal to include this part of the past in the own world of those born later prevents the morally reprehensible deeds, views and principles from being included in one's own horizon (Hölscher, 2009, p. 229).

On another, historically significant level, another form of incomprehension can be seen. Let us take the level of the people affected in the 'Bloodlands' (Snyder, 2013): here, too, a specific rupture is to be visualised. The moment of the incomprehensible, as Dan Diner writes, did not begin in the gas chambers and the death zones, but already in the threshold areas of the ghettos. There, one thought (in an interpretation that distanced itself from everything 'ordinary' about one's own life anyway) one could expect a remnant of normality. The fact that it was a place of transition into extermination, that the vast majority of the inmates of the ghettos were thus standing in a place with 'borrowed time' (Ibid., p. 463), could not enter the consciousness. The ghettos were places of simulated normality, composed of the remnants of everyday life, or so most liked to believe. But that these were only an antechamber of unprecedented horror could not be grasped.

As is well known, there are things between heaven and earth that exceed the imagination. Violence is a part of human sociality, and to that extent it is natural to integrate it into thinking. But the mass killings, as we know, reached a scale that said goodbye to any rationality and residual reason (including the self-preservation of the perpetrators).

This is precisely what the disintegration of ontological certainty means. In the context of the annihilation, nothing seemed to be based on anthropological or historical certainty. And not least for this reason we have to ask ourselves what connections can still be assumed between the centuries if all trust seems to have been lost. The hope that mistrust can be overcome, that new confidence can be gained and that the future can be placed in open horizons must of course be maintained. However, one should not expect that it is merely a matter of regaining and a kind of rehabilitation. The difficulty probably lies in the acceptance of a lasting intransparency that belongs to our world as to the world of the past.

As is well known, it is good manners in political affairs to pursue unreserved clarification and to demand transparency. In every twilight of politics, spaces of transparency should be created in which no measure and no relationship remains in the dark. Can we, however, also expect this of the history of violence?

Presumably, it is more a matter of admitting that in history we are dealing with the inevitable work on the negative, the end of which is not in sight. This in no way means undermining the seriousness of historiographical work and distrusting the evidence of historical sources. Their veto power has been undisputed since Reinhart Koselleck's famous dictum. What is at stake here, however, can only be meaningfully understood in a moral grammar that cannot recognise a residual transparency in inter-existential dimensions. Such abiding intransparency is the abiding legacy, a knowledge of the unhealed, a fractal between times.

Understanding the Ordinary and the Extraordinary

The concept of the *banality of evil* has had a peculiar career. Often quoted, it is one of the common insights from the teachings of the past. At the same time, the term stands for controversies that do not want to end because they decipher the riddle of evil so amazingly simply. Evil is presumably not allowed to be simple because it opposes man's desire for meaning and greatness (Arendt, 1963).

You can call it banality, mediocrity or ordinariness. The basic idea is aimed at people who were able to unite the most extreme contradictions and obviously held on to their convictions until their death. Whether we are talking about Adolf Eichmann or Heinrich Himmler or the 'ordinary men' of the SS henchmen and the police battalions (Browning, 2017), what we can recognise in these people is disturbing in various ways. The formulation of the banal, however, is misleading and by no means to be understood relativistically. Identification with the systematic killing agenda of National Socialist ideology was a form of extremist rationality. That it went hand in hand with bureaucracy and the ability to plan is one of the most common insights of research, which no one will doubt. However, it is still surprising to see documentaries and photographs showing the perpetrators going about their 'ordinary' activities in the surroundings of the concentration camps.

Why are these images surprising? First of all, people generally follow the widespread prejudice that the criminal and monstrous must be anchored in the very structure of the person. Those who are capable of terrible deeds are ascribed a one-dimensional personality. The traits of a criminal are therefore visible, stable, permanent and regular.

In contrast, the pictures that were presented to the world public only a few years ago were surprising. In 2007, photographs that an SS storm trooper had taken at Auschwitz went through the press. There was nothing extraordinary or frightening to be seen there, no deportations, no corpses, no killing machinery. Rather, the photos showed people doing in their free time what people usually do after work: going on excursions together, eating and laughing. The meaning of these pictures only becomes complete through the context. What was to be seen can be described as ordinary leisure time. The people in the pictures were following their natural inclinations to be together. The extraordinary is not concealed in these pictures, but tacitly assumed. For 'of course' the work in a camp must also be interrupted, the perpetrators must 'clear their heads' and relax. One can see from these statements that conventional language fails here in a peculiar way. For example, the concentration camp staff celebrated Christmas, smoked cigarettes, enjoyed themselves together. There is a cynicism in these ordinary activities that is difficult to grasp: a few kilometres away, as is well known, the transports continued to move, they were selected and murdered. How should one be able to classify the images that seem to have been taken from an ordinary operation (Welzer, 2012; the pictures can be seen in the Washington Holocaust Museum?

One must leave the question open. Evil is difficult to define because in the end it is always about people, about human affairs that are comprehensible to everyone. There is then no need for metaphysical exaggeration to classify what happened.

Nevertheless, hermeneutics must go deeper if one is not to be satisfied with a succession of 'indifferent' sentences. Understanding the past ultimately involves the complexity of witnessing, which is perhaps one of the most important issues between the centuries. Among the problems of this witnessing are, of course, the victims and those affected. Their testimonies are eminently important and must be preserved in the historical memory, but they are understandably fragile and inconsistent. Since the memory of those who were more or less directly affected by the events is linked to traumatic content, witnessing is difficult. Language, memory, the ability to synthesise and to reconstruct in a meaningful way, all this does not apply in the case of the Shoa – or only under specific conditions. One had to bear witness to events whose origin and course had to remain incomprehensible to the witnesses. The form of knowledge about the Holocaust consists in a contradictoriness of knowing something and yet not understanding it (Baer, 2000).

*

Furthermore, testimony also includes the documents and visual representations made by the perpetrators, fellow travellers and 'spectators' of the events. The hermeneutics of non-understanding is also dependent on these forms of transmission and must recognise a profound ambivalence here. The difficulty lies in differentiating the means of representation and the respective 'motivation'. What can one assume in the environment of the National Socialist perpetrators and the many fellow travellers who were simply 'there'? Which psychological motives can be assumed, which aspects must be added to obtain a complete picture?

There are images of the war of extermination that can be placed in the known history of violence. These images shock and can be read as evidence of the cruelty of war as well as the abysses of the perpetrators. Furthermore, in the context of the Shoa, a complexity of the photographs must be taken into account, which refers to the ambivalence of the image. Only through detours of reflection can this form of violence be understood.

One is forced to trace the motives of the perpetrators and 'bystanders' back to simple propositions. In the case of the mass murders, one had the possibility of refusing to accept what was happening from the outset without deserting. If necessary, one could avert one's gaze – just as those Germans had to do who were confronted with the events around Auschwitz after the liberation in 1945, for example. Other motives are conceivable, which followed the unshakeable belief in one's own ideology or even felt a desire to fear at the sight of violence.

In other words, it is about the question of sight and the visual encounter with which one transcends time. A special form of seeing comes into play when one takes into account something other than the pathological and criminal psyche of the perpetrators. What is in question is what happened at the moment the photograph was taken, when the unrepresentable and monstrous was captured photographically. In question is the position and hold of those who were able to produce these images.

The talk of 'empty seeing' leads us to the crucial point (Hüppauf, 2000). The images of naked bodies in pits are unbearable for the contemporary consciousness; at the same time, the question of the person behind the camera arises. Bernd Hüppauf recognises in the moment of the shot evidence of the emptied gaze. This way of looking at an event of violence is neither moral nor simply cruel here; it rather resembles a subjectless gaze that experiences no resonance and no response.

This emptiness of the gaze leads to other traces of the history of violence. Evidence of racism and blatant sadism has survived; the violence is central to these images. In contrast, the photography of the Holocaust is more complex and one can say more frightening because it points to a void that belongs to the actor himself and to the process as a whole. The question about the nature of this gaze leads far beyond the context of the war of extermination (Hüppauf, 2015).

Photography is to be understood here as an instance that conveys an ambivalent certainty to the actor behind the camera. The images are seen as evidence of what happened, which is subject to repression in human memory. Photographs of the war of extermination were taken, as it were, from the perspective of an invisible, disembodied subject. The gaze can no longer be equated with the recognition of the subject, but comes from a timeless and spaceless nowhere (Hüppauf, 2000, p. 227). The I is present but not involved; the emptied gaze is neutral to what is happening and secures the identity of the subject. At the end of all previous horizons of experience, ideals of ethics and humanism were subverted; all that remained in the end was the disinterested, technical apparatus. With this cold gaze, spatial relations, optics and perception were subordinated to the technical spirit.

The attempt to understand the violence of the empty gaze connects the present and the past. Furthermore, there is the question of images, which can be connected to violence in various ways. The techniques of visual representation are advanced and infinitely refined, so that the violence in the image no longer affects the subject of the view. This seems to suggest a parallel to the images of the war of extermination, yet so far removed from our present. The question of who produces which images with which intentions and purposes and feeds them into the ether of media communication leads us to the same position of extreme distance made possible by modern technical apparatuses. Of course, there are whole 'worlds' between the situations of violence. One must at least take note of the fact that there are constitutive connections between the images and the viewers that are psychologically complex. Suffice it to say that modern terror systems are aware of the power of images, while the 'other side' no longer has any understanding for this visual language of violence (Baecker et al., 2002).

Again, the question is how to deal with the domination of images, which in the worst case causes a renewed emptying of the gaze.

Violence and Meaning

As is well known, the preoccupation with violence in the age of the total has experienced various conjunctures. There have been periods of silencing and silence, of denial and repression, as well as periods of intense perception of a past that defies understanding. The question remains difficult to answer, however, whether the growth of documentaries and monographs has led to a decisive conceptual breakthrough. Are we at a point where we have crossed the final threshold of conceptualisation – where we may assume a form of history that is completely comprehended?

For research on violence, this question must be rejected or denied. The conceptual explanatory framework followed various titles that are questionable. In a first phase, violence resulted from a 'special path' of German development and could be understood as a 'derailment'. The Holocaust (which is to be read together with the Holodomor) later stood in a paradoxical connection to modernity, which in turn stands in a complex relationship to the past. Violence does not stand outside the modern order, but is part of the enigmatic 'dowry' of our time (Baumann, 2001; Habermas, 1987).

In view of this enigmatic past, for which there is no final hermeneutic conclusion, phenomenology is helpful. As a form of action and omission, violence is connected with practical aspects; only in the alliance with a respective meaning, however, does violence become embedded in a communicative grammar. At this point, a final form of understanding presents itself, which consists in the *connection between violence and meaningfulness*. For the victim, the experience of violence is the only measure, irreplaceable, singular. Only when the specific grids of regularity are related to this experience does the particular meet the general. At first, there is nothing unusual about this. Crimes are judged from a criminological or legal point of view; major events such as wars can be linked to a sense of meaning, are framed by salvation-historical pathos or modern human rights semantics.

Violence can be associated with meanings in the most diverse ways in retrospect, and this meaning of violence can assume an unbearable level. This is the case when human beings become numbers and their faces are overshadowed by the violence of meaning (Kapust, 2014). In the case of the National Socialist practice of extermination, this connection has been heightened in a way that seems absurd.

Consider the practice of tattooing the inmates of Nazi death camps. This practice involved brutal shaving, disinfection and undressing procedures. They were acts of dehumanisation that followed a historical line of appropriation through tattooing and thus a parallel in history of slavery is found. However, the process of inscription allows different aspects of the history of violence to emerge.

Basically, one can ask why tattoos were made at all in the environment of the extermination practice, who ordered them with what purpose and what sense they were subject to (in the following: Därmann, 2020). The possibility of sorting prisoners and 'criminals' according to anthropometric markings had existed since the nineteenth century. Photographic identification services were intended to serve the recognition of so-called habitual criminals. Alphonse Bertillon had created a registry in Paris in 1882 in which not only names, origin, marital status and previous convictions were recorded, but also the distinctive combination of body measurements. In this context, tattoos were considered to be the identifying mark of the born criminal.

The connection with the National Socialist practice of forced tattooing, however, is complicated (Därmann, 2020, p. 267 ff.). The orientation towards the function of criminalisation cannot be dismissed out of hand. From 1937 onwards, the camps no longer served the purpose of so-called re-education and were transformed into systematic terror, forced labour and extermination camps. The inmates were given striped suits that made them look like convicts. The number tattooing also presumably served this aspect of curbing the risk of escape (Ibid., p. 267).

However, this practice is highly contradictory at its core. It contradicted the effort to keep the genocide secret from the eyes of the world public. It also seems highly illogical in view of the murderous killing rate, in which the inmates from the cattle cars were often handed over directly to death by gassing – and thus could not be subjected to registration.

One side of this event lies in the specific order that found its sole purpose in extermination – and thus acquired an antinomic structure. The ashes of Auschwitz reveal the will for radical extermination – and yet there were identification archives, statistical thoroughness and numerical records at this place.

Was there room for resistance in this system of terror, which was run with bureaucratic thoroughness? Surprisingly, narratives of resistance to violence can be found that go directly back to the procedure of numbering.

*

Here is an example: Gal Wertman, son of one of the Holocaust survivors, artist and former creative director of an Israeli daily newspaper, is a representative of a generation that wants to remember the suffering of their relatives. In memory of his family, Wertman had a sequence of numbers tattooed on him. One suspects the background: the numbers are meaningful because they follow the Nazi practice of terror of perceiving people as numbers and subjecting them to 'treatment'. The significance of the number on Wertman's arm leads us in two directions. One direction is the one originally intended. It was about a number that also meant a number. It was engraved on 18 January 1945, nine days before the liberation of the Auschwitz concentration camp by the Red Army. Since this number was supposedly the last was stung, it is an expression of a counting and registration. At the same time, it is a symbolic number with which one feels the pain of the suffering associated with a mere number.

The tattoos, however, followed a bizarre logic. They locked the inmates in a grey zone between life and death. With the receipt of the tattoo, they became doomed to die. Death notices were already issued at a time when the persons were still alive and were to be destroyed by labour. Hannah Arendt recognised in this very early on a form of 'preparation of living corpses' (Arendt, 1948, 326). The numbers connected the realm of the living and the dead.

However, even here there was still room for resistance, which is rarely reconstructed. In order to save lives, for example, the registration of the living was exchanged with the dead as far as possible. In a few cases, prisoners were even deliberately 'mixed up' with corpses by taking over the number of the dead person and thus 'writing him off' as dead, in accordance with the cruel methodology of the National Socialists. The number of a corpse no longer had any deeper meaning for the perpetrators. Some of the inmates who succeeded in this manoeuvre became 'unknown numbers', which in this case worked to their advantage.

Covering traces by taking the number of someone who was already dead was one of the few ways of obscuring things.

The method of number tattooing is of higher significance for those born afterwards. Quite a few of the surviving Israeli men and women used the numbering for a subversive manoeuvre of self-attribution. The prisoner number served them as a secret number for the safe or a password for the credit card. Granddaughters and grandchildren had the number tattooed on their forearms to show their attachment to their relatives. The memory of the Holocaust literally goes under the skin here to be preserved.

This shows what the connection between violence and meaning is all about. Violence, as we know, can increase endlessly and lead any meaning ad absurdum. The countless attempts to give meaning to the event of Auschwitz in retrospect proved tragic and insufficient.

Apparently, violence triumphed over any meaning. What was suffered cannot be absorbed in any idea or representation that would prove adequate (Koselleck, 2000, p. 99 ff.; Primo Levi, 1993, p. 264; Didi-Huberman, 2007).

If this restriction applies to the singularity of the victims, it is overcome to a certain extent in historical commemoration. The following generations have the task of preserving the memory, which itself is linked with great significance.

The aforementioned attempts to preserve the number tattoo on one's own skin are to be understood as a form of symbolic resistance. And just as violence as excess had prevailed over any meaning, this act overcomes the permanent speechlessness.

Chapter Five

DISASTROUS VIOLENCE: IDEOLOGIES

As is well known, there is 'no language' for violence in the age of extremes. This statement means: this violence can be explained and described, its course and the conditions of its emergence can be 'deciphered', but despite everything it eludes classification in the historical horizon. The extent of the destruction and suffering is known, perhaps even quantifiable, but at the same time incomprehensible. Recognisable devastation is overshadowed by a doubt: whether the disastrous violence, which found its incalculable form in fascism, did not destroy the possibilities of seeing others. Philosophy saw itself overwhelmed, as it were, by factual history; it first had to 'find' a language again in order to be able to counter the destruction of human conditions.

Admittedly, in what framework was this language to exist when the experience of violence suffered had proved so fundamental that everything was thrown into doubt? To understand the violence of a self-destructive Europe, one needed a new beginning in thinking. T. W. Adorno, Hannah Arendt, Karl Jaspers, but also M. Merleau-Ponty, Emmanuel Levinas, Alain Finkielkraut and Maurice Blanchot translated the experience of the final unsecuring of human orders into their philosophical thoughts.

The experience of abandonment led them (as well as contemporary social theory) to a fundamental revision of the human form of life. In this form of life, the ideas that have been handed down no longer apply: that one is together in the world under the stars, that there is a lawfulness within us that makes morality and reason possible, that there are connections and meanings among people. These possibilities, he argues, were fundamentally knocked out of hand by the radical enmity that has since been headlined Auschwitz (Liebsch, 2018, p. 134). So how this violence and human forms of life would be thought together is in question. It is the question of the face of history.

A contradictoriness is decisive for this face. The disastrous violence seems to have taken place in its extreme form outside any human world, human language, human understanding. It destroyed the self-understanding with which one could view oneself and others, with which one could live together with others and found a political world. Loss had a metaphysical connotation, as it were: it appeared as a form of encroaching violence whose origin had to remain unclear. From this foreboding of loss and the fragility of all relations, a challenge for thinking can be concluded. Under what conditions is it possible to incorporate the experience of violence in the midst of the human order of life? How could one conceive of disastrous violence as belonging to the human lifeworld? The question aims at a triviality – the known story *arguably always takes place in a shared reality* – but the question of classifying and understanding what eludes remains unanswered.

The form in which this question is answered in the following aims at a polemogenic reflection. It leads back to the beginning of European intellectual history and draws lines up to the present. It finds a motif in the moment of conflict. War as a phenomenon and as a noumenon leads back to the roots of Western thought. In Heraclitus of Ephesus, we learn of a thought impulse of unrelenting hardness: that war has a sublimity in the lives of human beings because it pervades existence in a special way (Heraclitus, 2007). War thus expresses life as it actually is; it exposes the source of being – not in abstract morality, but as a conflict-ridden 'source of energy' of Western culture (Stadler, 2009, p. 10).

Law and morality, which discover an alienation in war and attempt to limit and tame evil, stand here against the unfolding of polemos. No less a figure than Heidegger had taken up this motif of polemogenic reflection (Heidegger, 1987). In the manifold manifestations of possible war, he recognised the one moment, the idea of war in its existential dimension. Conflict comes to light with all conceivable and unthinkable violence, in which something with an ontological quality is expressed: the stepping apart, the distance, the gap and the violence. Heidegger thought in hardened categories of the tragic primordiality of war and reason to which 'We' today face them with wonder and reluctance.

In this respect, everything should aim at the recovery of language in order to counter the totalitarian gaze. The power of language at stake leads to analyses that can be described as painful and unsparing. It must be clarified where the hatred comes from that has led to totalitarian excess. And it would have to be indicated at which point in the history of violence one actually stands. The analyses face the questions that other philosophies have already hesitantly answered. They confront the riddle of the extent to which hatred of others as radical hatred had extended to the principle of the existence of others and how this principle could finally unfold in the desire for radical extinction. The task of thinking would be to give this phenomenon a description that still recognises extreme hatred, absurdity and worldlessness (H. Arendt) as experiences in the inter-existential dimension. Not only that hatred was (and is) taken into the service of ideology but that it casts an irrefutable shadow on reason and enlightenment needs to be clarified.

The Terrible Banality

As the outline of the gallows loomed, A. Eichmann seized upon a language that could be described as enduring – enduring because of its peculiar characteristics. In the face of approaching death, there was no room for false sentimentality or for any kind of reckoning. Rather, it seemed that Eichmann remained completely in control of himself and wrote his own eulogy. An absurd picture drawn at this moment was the talk of faith in God, a serenity that could be explained by the insight into the finiteness of all life. And finally, there was that supercooled distance from everything in the room that is generally associated with the face of the human. Even in the last stages, that attitude was preserved which could conceal fanaticism and hatred, misanthropy and violence from the point of view of a process of purification.

As is well known, it was this attitude of amorality that led Hannah Arendt to the concept of banality, a designation that did not claim any exact characteristic, but which sprang from the moment of bewilderment (Arendt, 1963). As is well known, the banality of evil was not a formula for explaining the world, but an expression of a loss of language, a symbol of the difficulties of designating something that was considered absolutely exceptional.

The question is whether the key to understanding National Socialist ideology can be found in examining the peculiar motives of the acting National Socialists themselves. Do the individual statements and the remnants of the fascist 'idea' provide enough substance to decipher the core of this thinking? If so, then one would be referred to the level of those persons who were persecuted, convicted and tried before the court of humanity as mass murderers and criminals, as chief ideologues and executors. To do this, of course, one would have to distance oneself from a language that recognises in the atrocity an expression of a metaphysical demon.

It was probably precisely this point that had preoccupied Hannah Arendt when she was dealing with the reports from the courtroom in Jerusalem. The search for a monster who was the epitome of evil turned into an encounter with a person from whom one could only hear thoughtless last words. Whatever the trial of Adolf Eichmann between April and December 1961 brought to light, at the centre of Arendt's reflection was the realisation that what was at stake here was above all the process of demythification. At the moment of the encounter, a demonic mass murderer became an administrative mass murderer whose characteristics were average, objective and, to that extent, banal. Of course, it was not questionable that the regime, in retrospect, disguised the atrocities that had taken place as a legalistic matter. What was in question was rather the diffuse amorality of an attitude that applied both to the specific accused and to the general type of crime that made the genocide possible in the first place.

In this respect, it seems at least sensible, as a first step, to locate ideology in the correlation that conditioned part of the National Socialist force. The violence in the thinking of Eichmann, Himmler and Hitler himself has been sufficiently decoded; it leads into the shallows of destructive, necrophilic or hysterical personality profiles. But beyond such a conceivable psychology, the question remains unanswered as to whether a morality, however distorted, could be inferred from the misanthropic motives.

An apparent anecdote about conversations from the headquarter provides some insight. Nicolaus v. Brelow, long-time adjutant of the air force, quoted in the retrospective from a conversation after the failure of the Ardennes offensive Hitler's attitude in the face of impending doom: 'We will not capitulate, never. We can go down. But we will have a world' (v. Below, 1980, p. 398). Hans Blumenberg missed in this confession the usual Darwinism one encounters in comparable statements. Rather, it was a matter of specific untenability at the moment of the fall: in the delusion, world time and individual life time find a correspondence. The world is not destroyed arbitrarily, but it is abandoned as soon as the subjective possession of time seems to be lost. One can call this egomaniacal, that typical attitude of a dictator who mediates all conceivable actions, decisions and expressions of will from the horizon of the very own. For Hitler, as is well known, politics was not the ultimate destiny, but rather a surrogate for life. In this perspective, life existed only as an individual; this unconditional, radical, all-dominating idea then becomes unbearable as soon as the world (rational politics, the realities on the battlefields, even the lack of military success) turns away.

The core of this madness lay in the lack of a world horizon. 'Hitler had no world' (Blumenberg, 2001, p. 84) and that was the only reason why it was doomed. In this one recognises more than a self-destructive, simply nihilistic attitude. It is the epitome of a violence that turned against the basic conditions of existence.

A violence that tried to force the comprehensive horizon of world time to the measure of one's own lifetime.

Of course, one can call it delusion: a worldview that recognises in world time only a diabolical medium that prevents one's own all-superior will to power from unfolding. And thus the question of a morality to be deciphered would be invalid.

The analysis of Nazism, which was described as a self-chosen ideal of humanity in the midst of an eternal human struggle, therefore leads one step further. Heinrich Himmler's 'ideal' – if one wants to use these terms – aimed, as is well known, at the preservation of the peculiarity of a people and tied to these goals the virtue ideals of loyalty, obedience and honour. These are concepts that are taken from a moral universe and in a peculiar way produce a paradoxical morality: the ideal for the SS leads to an unconditionality that was directly linked to an unrestricted willingness to die. A higher bond was imposed on the individual who surrendered to the soldierly order, formally called loyalty, but whose core consisted in the suspension of the ethical.

According to the Nazi principle, Christian beliefs, religious conscience and even everyday moral ideas were considered worthless ballast. The ideal-typical soldier embodied that higher morality whose destructive force no longer needs to be emphasised today, but still causes difficulties when one tries to describe it with the help of a moral grammar (Zimmermann, 2008).

This becomes clear when looking at well-known sources such as Heinrich Himmler's address to the soldiers in Posen. Himmler spoke of a 'difficult decision', a mission that had to be carried out 'without suffering any damage to mind or soul' (Himmler, 1974, p. 169 ff.). The absurdity, of course, is only fully expressed in the imagination of having preserved a 'morality' despite all the rigorous harshness of the extermination. This moral integrity, the decency that Himmler thought he had preserved – where do these convictions come from?

For Adolf Eichmann, everything was reduced to the completion of one thing. According to him, the decision to commit genocide did not require a radical worldview, but an organisation based on rationality, expediency, order and hygiene. The criminal structure of a purification process there refers to a banal amorality, to an attitude with formalistic emptiness.

Himmler's convictions appear equally frightening when, in all seriousness, he spoke of the realisation of an ideal of humanity while asserting a 'decency'. In retrospect, a hermetic, as it were walled-off self is revealed. But to what extent could one speak of morality here at all?

The Reality of Evil

How much insight is gained by going to the level of the paradoxical moral convictions of the perpetrators? The question is relevant insofar as the short-sightedness and unsustainability of the individual worldview appear striking. To put it simply, one does not recognise a closed ideology, a worldview, but only a harshness that is covered with moral categories, motives of violence that are self-purposed, formulas that aim at nothing other than the struggle and the destruction of the other. Should such self-understanding be given more attention than it deserves? On the other hand, it is one of the convictions of violence research that in order to understand violence, one would have to take a closer look at violence, that one would also have to look at all the forms of violence from which one understandably wants to turn away.

Here, of course, it is about something else: deciphering the essence of an ideology that is to be located between distorted morality, power and politics. For this, however, we do not need psychological introspection, but a theoretical horizon that extends to the historical and moral space of meaning. Two fundamental questions therefore need to be clarified: to what extent, despite all moral indignation in the face of factual violence, we can speak of moral categories here – and with the help of which concepts we can assume the constitution of a common world. One question is aimed at the phenomenology of historical experience, the other at existential philosophical aspects.

The fact that morality is connected to power in many ways is an insight that has been valid since Nietzsche. The challenge for thinking, however, does not lie in the insight that moral self-interpretation goes hand in hand with a diffuse will to power. It is rather rooted in the motive that for a moral-theoretical and ideology-critical debate, one also considers *aloof, strange and uncomfortable* phenomena – phenomena of moral otherness and moral dissociation.

In the perspective of the philosophy of historical experience, it is not morality that stands against the lack of morality or immorality. Rather, the moral universe has never proven to be well ordered. It is true that the question of the historical place of *our morality is* answered in relation to those forms of morality that we reject with good reason. But the fact remains that there are profound conflicts 'between different moral self-understandings in history' (Zimmermann, 2008, p. 7).

When, for example, the creation of the *new* human being is proclaimed, when higher and lower categories of humanity are spoken of or when the right to life is denied to certain groups of people, then it is about perspectives of redemption and liberation, which are seen as 'extreme exaggerations' of a respective 'transformation morality' (Ibid., p. 8). Such transformations of moral categories are not to be evaluated as a relapse into pre-moral forms, as they do not even fall outside the spectrum of morality. Rather, they refer to the open historical process in which moral self-interpretations develop. These are moral standpoints that are in open opposition to each other, that can unfold value-setting and action-guiding forces and, as is well known, extend to epochal events that would have to be described as moral catastrophes.

The difficulty lies in producing a description that can be applied to those phenomena of totalitarian morality that are part of historical experience between the Holocaust and the Holodomor. Trivially, the events of violence did not arise in a world other than the human one, they did not break into the world from outside; in other words, they cannot be described with metaphysical concepts. These insights are difficult to bear insofar as one can never dismiss the rupture that was reflected in the events themselves, a rupture that can be described as a 'failure of genre' or a 'failure to understand'.

The starting point for any critique of ideology is therefore an inescapable common world in which the full validity of human intersubjectivity becomes apparent. All further reflections start from what takes place between human spaces of experience.

But this does not mean retelling the story of the excluded and oppressed. It is the basic philosophical concepts that move to the centre: *world and time, praxis and interexistence, negativity and materiality*. In the factual encounter between people, the conditions of human practice are always already embedded.

Ideologies of violence stem from a view of the world that, to put it simply, is not ours. They seem to be taken from a concept of the world that will never be able to coincide with the conventional, morally convincing approach to the world. This conviction is not a theoretical deduction, but an intuition whose value would have to be determined more precisely. Here, however, it must first be emphasised that the existence of a violence-affirming ideology is as much a part of the structure of the basic human situation as anything else. Human practice is constitutively related to the limits and possibilities, to meaning and fulfilment, to threat and endangerment of fragile beings (Rentsch, 1999). This means: within human forms of life, the features of fragile, finite life are to be envisioned; life that entails death (Heidegger), freedom that opens up the reality of evil, solidarity that carries the possibility of failure.

Ideologies that address precisely these basic features of factual life in a negatory way seem alien and inadequate to us. But they are only properly understood as extreme forms of anthropological fragility. The reference to death can go hand in hand with a readiness to die that contradicts all life-serving meaning. Without an understanding of evil that is reflected in the aforementioned generic rupture, we cannot attain any reasonable understanding of our freedom. And finally, one of the unavoidable aspects of the humane form of life is the practice of failing beings.

This, however, is precisely the point at which the misleading affirmation of an ideology must be distinguished from an inter-existential observation. Heidegger's basic political idea that one could conclude hardship from the fact of the thanatological situation appears to be a false conclusion. The concern for one's own self-being then leads in consequence to a submission to an analytics of death that is in no way contradictory to the reality of fascism (Ibid., p. 144). And it is precisely at this point that ideological perspectives would have to be deconstructed that conclude from the insight into the basic existential condition a priority of the self, the affirmation of violence and the unconditional exaltation of the struggle for existence.

Ideologies and Doctrines

The approach to the phenomenon of violence chosen here can serve as a productive contribution to decoding the ideology of fascism and National Socialism. And to do this, one must, on the one hand, look closely at ideological set pieces and, as it were, ask for the parts that make up a unified ideology. It is questionable to what extent this can be done meaningfully at all in the face of ideological constrictions. But beyond that, it must be shown that the critical analysis of ideology must establish the connections that exist between mere interests, ideas and whole worldviews.

The first question to ask is: How is the connection between the actual violence and the ideology behind it to be grasped at all? Which actions are to be read together with which ideas, conceptions or 'values'? The connections, if one were to take such a reading as a basis, are far more complex. Ideas can assume the function of a costume in the historical process. They serve to justify an action. But aren't they more than just a simple dress that individuals throw on in a summing-up? In the social world, an idea can be a reflection of what is caused by certain needs. But behind these ideas and motives, as is well known, lie material and ideal interests that directly influence the lives and actions of historical actors (Weber, 1922, p. 237). Interests that are in turn themselves enabled and supported by major worldviews. It is precisely these worldviews that should be approached in order to be able to trace the trajectories in which interests are realised.

If we assume in the following that totalitarian ideologies were able to unfold and develop in a historical culture, then this statement must be viewed in a differentiated manner. Different modes of time condition this relationship: an existing culture can provide the framework, a horizon of experience of cognitive and emotional evaluations. The actions of the actors are semantically made possible within this horizon; but to the same extent, cultural guiding concepts are available in the past to justify the *this way and not another way* of acting in retrospect. Finally, note the reference to futurity with which events proceed. These events are seen as moments in which predictions, prophecies or simple expectations are fulfilled. They are subject to the construction of a historical reality whose purpose is to achieve a goal horizon (Buc, 2015, p. 16).

In order to decipher the ideology of National Socialist doctrine, it is indispensable to consider the very horizon in which action finds justification. But the determination of this outer framework causes difficulties. For the search for the parts that make up the edifice of thought leads in different directions and it seems to quickly exhaust itself in analysis. Let us think, for example, of the formation of the early ideological foundation in Hitler's biography during his time in Vienna and Linz. The first social and cultural encounters of the young school leaver, who would only later develop into an upstart, appear beyond measure as bizarre and insubstantial. Hitler read novels and trashy tracts that fantasised about Germanic gods, races and breeding and extermination practices. Magazines and journals in which one could read about the popularisation of the Aryan ideal combined to create a more or less neurotic atmosphere. The analysis of such 'documents' does not allow the conclusion that Hitler, for example, received his ideas from the confused writings of Lanz v. Liebenfels and others. Rather, it seems that here they contributed to the colouring of a peculiar mood of the times in the person and in the surrounding culture.

Accordingly, the granite foundation of fascism stands at a contradictory distance from the dominant culture. As a subculture, it unfolded a worldview that was opposed to the dominant bourgeois world. The lessons of dime novels and newspaper cuttings seem, on closer examination, to represent a form of perversion of the traditional bourgeois world. But the peculiar dilemma one recognises in the analysis of such and similar writings points to the conflation of culture and subculture. The ideological approach did not consist in the open negation of the existing culture, but rather in an inferior image. Joachim Fest had recognised in this motif a parallelism between the peculiarities of the epoch and Hitler's biography (Fest, 1980). A fundamental need for bourgeois affiliation mixed with the sublime forms of negation of the existing. Both the mood of the times and Hitler's first orientations express this double movement: the negation of the bourgeois world and the inchoate need to belong.

But it would be misleading at this point to conflate the substance of an ideology with the views and needs of individuals. The idea is of course obvious: Hitler's personal career was initially marked by groping attempts to give an ideology a face, to let his possibly errant hatred merge into a concrete figure. In Hitler's person, there is accordingly a pathologically heightened self-esteem, the compulsion for self-aggrandisement and the fear of social relegation. In society, in turn, there were set pieces ready to give these moods a goal and strong motifs: a diffuse and 'ordinary' anti-Semitism, theories of master race and a nationalism that was becoming more intense. But it remains difficult to interpret the outline of this clearly recognisable ideology merely as a ready-made worldview that is readily taken up.

In other words, the formation of an ideology remains misunderstood if it is made up of individual parts. The thoughts of the rulers and the motives of the actors do come together, but one would have to avoid the image of psychological mechanics. As is well known, the early ideological cues were found in concise figures of the time of Georg Ritter v. Schönerer or Karl Lueger, but also in a peculiarly illuminated intermediate field of Richard Wagener. These were key figures of German-bourgeois Vienna at the turn of the century, who, in the sign of an established anti-Semitism, mixed with the yearnings of the All-Germans for affiliation and complexes of alienation.

Diffuse inclinations and resentments developed a dynamic over time; they translated moods into hermetic ideologies. Understanding this requires the abstraction of a theory of history. More precisely, it requires a framework that makes tangible the ideological turnover moments in the interactions between top and bottom.

The outer framework of the following reflection is therefore the semantics of historical times found in the work of Reinhart Koselleck and others (Koselleck, 2000). Historicism in the broadest sense is concerned with the anthropology of historical experiences of time; it is properly understood as the study of the conditions of possible history.

Event contexts are subject to specifications of history that can be deciphered in the alliance and confrontation with the existential analysis of human existence. On the shoulders of phenomenology, experiences of finitude become visible that do not become thematic from the perspective of empirical history.

In the examination of Heidegger's existential analysis, one arrives at decisive categories for all further considerations (Heidegger, 1953, 1979). The basic idea, illuminated in the pathos of the 1920s, is to be deciphered and further deepened here. The run-up to death represents the ineluctable horizon of meaning of all experience of being. As is well known, Heidegger's thanatology was clothed in a political terminology that seemed to correspond effortlessly to the political semantics of the time: one hears of the fate of a people, the inner connection of actuality, loyalty, inheritance and being free to death – concepts that could easily be usurped by fascist doctrines or adopted for their own purposes. It is not necessary to discuss here whether the philosophical semantics of the run-up to death itself already points to a proto-fascist core of Heidegger's phenomenology. Rather, it can be soberly stated that in retrospect, protective measures are no longer conceivable to justify the ideology of determination. In the feverish mood before 1933, resoluteness meant: history as destiny in alliance with being free to die. It would be absurd to grant this language a credit today that would consist in a kind of historical–philosophical legitimisation.

Instead, it makes sense to descend from the shoulders of Heidegger and climb onto the shoulders of Reinhart Koselleck, and from here to assess the categorial offer of historicity. This, as will be shown, provides a framework for placing ideological motifs in the larger context of historical experiences of time. Only with the expansion of the historical lens will it be possible to clarify the extent to which ideological constrictions can be brought together with existential modalities. In this respect, the reflections are also to be understood as an alternative in thinking in order to escape the categorical framework of thanatology. The motif of running ahead to death, which Heidegger had transferred into his political semantics, is insufficient to achieve hermeneutic depth. It puts everything down to readiness for death and experiences of finitude that *would have to be provided* by *a people*. As can be seen, this means that a critique of ideology that leads out of the semantics of being free to die is no longer conceivable. A level of cognition would have to be reached as an alternative to this, which escapes this movement of thought. One would therefore have to ask, with Koselleck, to what extent the times of history are always already interhumanly constituted and what are the external determinations that constitute man as a historical being. The determination that constituted that peculiar philosophical mood in Heidegger is full of nihilism, insofar as it means nothing other than the determined running ahead to death. A nihilism that seems dispensable insofar as it denies all further possibilities of human coexistence.

Philosophical existentialism (which, as is well known, led in completely different directions from a Camus, Sartre or even with Walter Benjamin and others) remains below its possibilities as long as it is projected exclusively onto the field of *political* existentialism and unfolds a destructiveness there. Only with the help of the less hermetic categories that lead beyond the temporality of existence can the basic structure of possible history be deciphered, in which the perspective of ideology critique is preserved.

If we categorically expand the framework with Koselleck in the following, aspects of human history come into view that are not exhausted in the determination of the analysis.

The compulsion to accept the fateful is avoided, but a thoroughly sceptical attitude towards the humane horizon of the historical remains.

The War as a Noumenon

In 1943, Thermopylae lay before Stalingrad. Here, as so often, history had become an instrument. It had been taken into the service of a military ruling class. An event of a bygone era was declared a triumph of the will to persevere. Göring famously spoke on the radio of the greatest heroic struggle in German history. 'And it will be said one day; if you come to Germany, report that you saw us lying in Stalingrad as the law, that is, the law of the security of our people, commanded' (Will, 2010, p. 117).

The Battle of Thermopylae has long been regarded as a symbol of a lost but equally awe-inspiring struggle. It was historical exemplum that served diverse interests, always when it came to a historically designated resistance. But is the ideology of National Socialism exhausted in these political interpretations that look at nothing but the struggle against foreign powers and the glorification of the will to persevere?

The history of events of past wars is always taken into the service of the next war. But the determination of that violence which becomes totalitarian does not only include the occasional propaganda. Past wars are not only to be understood as an 'argument' with which an upcoming or to-be-conquered battle could be classified. The reference to war as such is to be thematised; the world relationship is to be deciphered in which one classifies oneself to the phenomenon of war. The continuity of war in people's lives should be considered.

The difference between the propagandistic means of the past war and war as an ontological phenomenon must be pointed out. The political language of National Socialism is to be understood as an effective power: it relies on the effect and the formation of consciousness; it wants to direct, form, shape and take someone into the service of a cause. As is well known, language images, figures and myths are used for this purpose – everything that language has in store to gain followers and to arouse hatred.

It is not always easy to separate this political level from that worldview that is characteristic of the understanding of fascist ideology. What life consists of, what it is, as it were, since all origin, is an existential question. It leads back to Heraclitus. As is well known, this early thinker of antiquity did not regard war as the great evil, but as the effective power and essence of all life. At the root of Western thought is not the judgement of war, but the insight into its unfathomable existence. War is not an instrument, it has no function, as sociologists would describe it today. It can be understood neither with strict prejudgement nor with moral enlightenment. As an anthropological and historical noumenon, war is rather the creator and preserver, the simultaneous execution of an ethos and a practice. The morally sublime can only be experienced when war is considered in its ontological principle.

Thousands of years of Western cultural history lie between Heraclitus of Ephesus and Martin Heidegger. What connects the two thinkers is the moment of polemic. For Heraclitus, war was an authority, a way of being that was superior to the human world and human life. In other words, Heraclitus does not yet think of war as a phenomenon to be considered morally and tamed practically.

Neither security nor rationalisation is at the centre of early Western thought, nor theological ultimate justification or legalisation. War is nothing other than a moment of polemic – a force majeure, a priori of being. War has an immanent essence that can be hated or admired.

Independent of human judgement, however, it is about the insight into the execution of a life power, a life principle, which consists in conflict. War is a source of energy, in which the 'reality of the bios' and 'the reasonableness of the logos' united in the 'truthfulness of the polemos' (Stadler, 2009, p. 14). It is a context of meaning that is difficult to access, even though the famous aphorism is often quoted. War is the *father of all things* (Heraclitus, 2007, Aphorism 53), it shows some as gods, others as mere men – this sentence is by no means to be understood in an immediately lashing or bellicose way. It means the interplay of logos and polemos and therein lies its omnipotence – even before divine or human authority. As the dynamic principle of existence, war makes culture possible and takes place as the principle of becoming.

War is to be understood here as an expression of occidental culture, as the granite foundation of being. It is these motifs that were taken up in modern times by none other than Martin Heidegger. The gravity of this thinking only comes to the fore with a more intensive examination. After the publication of *Being and Time*, Heidegger was not concerned with the question of the human being, but with not uniting and confusing Being with the underlying Being. The reification of Being is to be criticised and radically questioned.

From the point of view of existence, everything moves towards death. Man projects into nothingness and must therefore force himself to free himself from triviality and everydayness. But this motif of Being and Time is then dropped again in Heidegger's movement of thought, in favour of an attitude that radically inquires into the powerful accomplishments of fate. It is not individual human destinies and the tragic cast that still have meaning. But exclusively the universal authority of the polemos – including the conflictuality of the human being. The polemogenic reflection, inherent in Heraclitus and forgotten over the millennia, is rehabilitated: the polemos is a dispute that is carried out before all that is 'divine and human' (Heidegger, 1987, p. 47).

However one wants to understand this unity of world and conflict, of war and reason, with Heidegger it was hidden in a dark language that makes all interpretations difficult – precisely because it was about a concept of being that remains withdrawn from the action of man.

Therefore, it would be cheap to want to extract proto-fascist vocabulary from Heidegger's language and to put its anti-human core into the light. It would be much more appropriate to ask at what point in time such philosophy proves to be a breeding ground for totalitarian decrees.

A differentiation is necessary in order not to prematurely close critical perspectives. This is not first and foremost about the process of exploitation. Of course, the set pieces of the philosophical thought movement can be exploited for ideological purposes. And of course people have been taken into the service of rule, or have willingly fitted into an order, with whatever motives. In this respect, the 'careers' of Carl Schmitt or Martin Heidegger stand for precisely this process of being taken into service under dictatorial auspices. But one has to differentiate here in the sense of the matter or the social phenomenon: there must have been a moment of change, with which the matter of philosophical existentialism increased to a political existentialism. That the fascist edifices of thought can only ever be a dwindling stage of an existentialist determination is beyond question. But how exactly the connection between individualist-existentialism and political existentialism is to be thought is open to question.

Political existentialism here means a collective movement in the horizon of totalitarian justifications (Großheim, 2003).

There have been movements at the beginning of the twentieth century for which various terms have become imprinted: people flee into a steely enclosure; they demand shelter that has been metaphysically withdrawn from them. They fear the loneliness, the bottomlessness, the nothingness that has been withheld from them not only by philosophy. They therefore erect buildings of thought that demand total surrender and the negation of the self. It is that uncanny world of absolute selflessness of which Hannah Arendt spoke. Fascist movements participate in these social processes, instrumentalising, exploiting and parasitising. And unlike all those flanking movements of the epoch, they do not serve the goal of illuminating existence, but of darkening it.

But what categories do we have at our disposal to delimit these sufficiently well-known phenomena? The question is important if one resists the reflex of denying the sting of the negative and taking as a basis a harmony in society for which there is no sufficient evidence in existence itself. What would have to be done, however, is to examine the categories with the help of which violence can be grasped as a historical phenomenon. And indeed, the basic idea of phenomenology, which cannot agree on anything other than the determined run-up to death, proves to be underdetermined. The times of history, Koselleck argues, are not identical with existential modalities of the individual being, but the human world is constituted interhumanly from the outset (Koselleck, 2000, p. 101). To understand how history is made possible, one needs categories beyond the simple fact of death. Precisely therein lies the peculiar lapse in thinking that inferred a readiness in the political from the juxtaposition of fate, destiny, people, care and fear. The run-up to death in the context of a collective that recognises its actuality in *this*? What should be the existential 'meaning' of such an initiation into fate?

In contrast, Koselleck surpasses the category of having to die with the category of being able to kill (Ibid.). This is the first category in a series of opposites that have an effect on all history. Behind the necessity of survival, the threat of being able to kill emerges as an anthropological constant. And it is only with this real and sceptical realisation that the way out of the polemogenic universe is shown: because it simultaneously enables a free view of the historical achievement of peace and the renunciation of violence.

The Motive of Enmity

That ideologies can be accompanied by forms of hostility in various ways perhaps needs no further proof. A hardened ideology accompanied by pejorative gestures is hostile per se. But the concept of enmity itself is not entirely clear. One can recognise the most diverse manifestations in history, different trajectories in which relationships of enmity could become established.

Enmity could be omnipresent as an existential social relationship, as in the medieval feudal system, or a formal relationship of impersonal war enmities. It could be inscribed in legal terms, for example, in Roman law, and delimit a realm of political enmities. In the extreme case, formal enmity even serves the recognition of an existing relationship of power and competition between states. Enmity thus excludes neither the moral criterion of national morality in the political dimension nor the historical conceptualisation of jurisprudence. All this could be inserted without problems into a historicisation of the forms of enmity and the relations of enmity (Hölscher, 2003).

Unfortunately, what speaks against such a historicisation is the fact that the National Socialist terror and the ideology behind it veered off the familiar tracks of hostility. The idea and practice of National Socialist violence knocks all the certainties out of one's hand that one wanted to believe in as a historian or as a sociologist, as an observer or as a witness. In order to fathom the nature of this form of enmity, which has been inscribed in history as unforgettable, one has to accept far-reaching detours in social theory. An examination of Carl Schmitt's political theory is one such diversions, and this in turn leads to Reinhart Koselleck's historiography. It is only with the help of the latter theory that it becomes possible at all to fathom the hardly bearable harshness and emptiness of such enmity.

On the surface, enmity appears to be a phenomenon of humanity, a constant that has been evident not only since the beginning of historiography.

Just as intensively as people have fought each other throughout their lives, of course, there have been the attempts to counter hostility, to contain it and to master it. Interestingly, Carl Schmitt's political theory is meaningful in both respects. It justifies – in a rather anachronistic way today – why enmity is considered the condition of the political, and at the same time it shows a path that excludes unbounded forms of enmity.

The political is treated by Carl Schmitt as a *fundamentum in re*; it cannot be traced back to the sphere of politics, nor to aesthetics, morality or economics. Even today, such fundamental polemics are met with sympathy (Mouffe, 1993, p. 60 ff.). For Schmitt, the political is a degree of intensity (Schmitt, 1950). It constructs an inner relationship that coalesces in demarcation from an alien outside. In order to form a 'We', strangeness must turn into enmity. This in turn means that enmity per se is not to be equated with the political – this would be a world full of anarchy, a horror image with a Hobbesian quality. Rather, it is a matter of realising enmity as a necessary political relationship and distinguishing it from misunderstood morality. For a closer definition of the political, the normal case is not enough, not that normality we talk about in everyday life. Only the state of emergency exposes the core of the facts; only in the threatening emergency situation does it become apparent who can establish and maintain rule. Only the abnormal situation, for which there is no ready-made plan and no well-rehearsed rationality, calls for a third party, for a state that does not have to justify its power any further. A rule that is based exclusively on its own ability to act and strength.

The critique is obvious and therefore does not need to be deepened: this theory thinks of the political as a warlike tension between the self and the other.

The foreign as the potentially hostile enters at the beginning of an axiomatic determination. This means: not every stranger is an enemy, but the stranger tends towards a form of enmity in external relations that makes the political possible in the first place. If one were to leave it at this abstract observation, one would probably have a blueprint for historical conflicts. But what we are dealing with here is a justification and intensification of the political. For Schmitt and others, politics is first and foremost about self-preservation, about one's own, be it the people, be it a powerful state. The self-preservation of this totality of people has absolute primacy. Preserving one's own being, defending one's own existence, all other concerns are of a moral quality that does not approach the political.

The criticism of this idea touches on the rigid distinction between inside and outside, for which there are now other, convincing narratives. In Schmitt's case, the contrast leads to a pacified policy at home and a foreign policy licensed under international law – after 1945, following a revision of his theory that was, so to speak, denazified (Schmitt, 1963, p. 27, 110). The tone of the early writings, however, probably corresponds most closely to the feverish 'Weimar' mood: according to this, a community had to prove itself in the struggle against external enemies. The political becomes a substance that is only preserved if it can renew itself in the medium of the willingness to kill and die. These are obsolete concepts, stemming from a martial philosophy of life, which seem to recognise the essence of the political in only one dimension: in the struggle for one's own being, which does not need any other or alien being (Habermas, 1996, p. 231).

But, is this the model of a *national socialist* ideology? This statement would be problematic. Rather, this theory of the political aims at a political realism of past times. In this political world, political enmities are cultivated and limited at the same time. Schmitt explicitly opposed the penalisation of aggressive war. He was concerned with the preservation of state sovereignty and its ability to use force, which is not due to any third party. This was the only way to limit the rampant acts of war and to avoid ideologically led war. Total war would also be prevented as long as one focused on the concrete enemy. Concrete enemies are enemies at eye level; they are *certain* others, *certain* groups or nations.

The worldview wars and the ideological wars, on the other hand, lead to a moral dissolution: enemies of humanity – Judaism, Bolshevism, and so on – are made absolute. For the absolute enemy, who proves to be the opponent of every human order, any means of combat would be permissible – an enmity that Schmitt wants to avoid precisely with the help of his polemical concept of the political.

This, however, is obviously the point at which a theory of the political, as much as it seems to be attached to the state world of the nineteenth century, differs from Nazi ideology. As is well known, the enemy thinking of Nazism led to a threshold of sayability at which enemies were not to be fought but, as it were, exterminated; at which it was not a matter of competition and simple power struggles but of the pursuit of a goal that no one will call political. A gap was opened between the world of the political and radicalised enmity and thus one left the ground of a rational description. In this respect, the decoding of the ideological core can only succeed if it includes essential distinctions that no other political theory deals with: the historicising distinction between humans and subhumans.

For Nietzsche, as is well known, it was the superman who was to overcome the conventional species of the democratic herd type. A higher kind of human being, a new human being who rises above the average and thus uplifts or better overcomes humanity itself. Parallel to these cultural-diagnostic moods, the antithesis was to be found in the inferior human being, which increasingly, not only in the radicalised language of

National Socialism, was able to unfold. The talk of the inferior human being has far-reaching roots. For example, Alfred Hoche and Karl Binding famously complained in 1920 that a measure of 'uselessly wasted labour, patience, expenditure of wealth' was spent on the so-called ballast existences, which called into question the existence of life unworthy of life (Binding/Hoche, 1920).

Further sources of the ideology of the subhuman lay in the psychological and biologistic determinations of the time. Widespread fears of doom were channelled biologically: one spoke of degeneration, one distinguished between sick and healthy genetic material and was thus able to transfer the determining attitude to life, the doom fear of the nineteenth century, into medical categories. Psychologically, these fears seemed to come from far away, they referred to deep-seated, religiously dressed up fear complexes of sinister evil that would destroy the vitality of the healthy (Schott, 1992, pp. 9–23).

The national economy, biology and psychology of the time found a coherent form in the ideology of Nazism. In this, both the diffuse fears of doom could gather as well as all the biologistic concepts that did not want to be stopped by moral boundaries. In the language of Nazism, one could accordingly trace a history of effects that combined various elements into a granite worldview: the substantialisation of concepts of race and species, the transfer of the Christian horizon of expectations into totalitarian figures of speech and fantasies of redemption, and finally also the distinction between the Aryan and the non-Aryan. The aforementioned asymmetry of the counter-concepts acquires the totalitarian dynamic here because and insofar as the opponent is transferred at will into the negated conceptual field.

As is well known, the non-Aryan is a hollow word, an empty concept: it serves exclusively to negate one's own position. The assignment of people to the darkened side remains at the disposal of the power holder. The indeterminacy of the non-Aryan was known to serve totalitarian linguistic politics, functionally effective for those in power, who could legitimise their actions and, as is well known, extend them to final annihilation.

As mentioned, the juxtaposition of humans and subhumans is the first step towards totalitarian furore. The basic structure of possible opposites is paradoxically thrown into doubt; one cannot now move from one side of the distinction to others. Unbelievers could become believers; parties could be changed and even barbarians might have the possibility of moving upwards from the lower levels of civilisation. The peculiar negation contained in the Nazi language regime abandoned this historical line. For now it was conceivable and thus possible for people to look at each other, as Alain Finkielkraut wrote vicariously, through the imaginary walls of an aquarium. The scrutinising, appraising gaze on the one side was directed at the usefulness and usability of the other. He, exemplarily embodied in the figure of Doctor Pannwitz, did not see dangerous or somehow inferior people, but a non-human. What Shylock in *The Merchant of Venice* could still ask with the deepest seriousness – 'hath not a Jud also hands, organs, body and limbs, senses, affections, passions?' (Shakespeare, *The Merchant of Venice*, quoted by Finkielkraut, 2000, p. 8) – this last spark of generic solidarity was destroyed.

It is not only in this respect that one should ask in conclusion whether one should not add an anthropological dimension to the historicising sequence of forms of enmity:

hatred. Not in the usual sense that hatred can have a profound share in enmity, not that hatred which is part of all human courses of conflict. Such hatred is temporary and tameable, it is one of those affects that is politically channelled or simply suppressed. This hatred flares up and burns out; it can culminate in a furore of annihilation or be captured in 'rules' as part of known history.

But there is obviously a form of hatred that represents something different and alien in its intentions and absolutism. Radical hatred tries to rid itself of the Other. But physical extinction is not enough for this hatred; it also tries to destroy any evidence of the existence of the Other. This hatred does not aim at a particular quality, at a part worthy of hatred, but at the existence of the Other. There is something absurd in the unconditionality of this negation: for it is directed at the general principle of the existence of others. 'I want to eliminate the Other par excellence – and in hatred I am thus from the outset in a radical conflict with all Others, even if I believe that I only have to permanently damage, render harmless or eliminate one of them' (Liebsch, 2018, p. 1008).

The reason for hatred lies in the mere existence of the Other; the failure of this ideology would thus lie in the impossibility of denying the transcendence of the Other. A silent victory may be understood in the social–philosophical discourse, which Sartre had recognised as a representative: even the most extreme hatred cannot subsequently deny that others exist; no programme of annihilation can change the transcendence of others (Sartre 1993, p. 716).

Another expression we recognise as returnees in the archaeological findings at the sites of the Camp Inmates of the Birkenau camp had buried a message in eating utensils hidden in the ground, with 'information' about how the camp worked. An enlightening message to the outside world – but also a silent proof of the undeniability of the existence of others, hidden in the topsoil.

The Peculiar Emptiness of Morality

Finally, a relationship is to be thematised that proves to be opaque and abstract. Ideologies are supposed to map a meaning. This meaningfulness is brought together with forms of violence, but the way in which the two areas interact turns out to be highly different.

Violence can be subordinated to a historical meaning. It can be cloaked with moral gain or framed with salvation-historical significance. In each case, it is about the relationship of a justified violence to a 'sacral' context of meaning. The violence is traced back to the meaning, but the meaning itself also evokes violence. Antje Kapust speaks of the meaning of violence in relation to the violence of meaning (Kapust, 2014, p. 51 ff.).

The violence and the meaning brought into play are, of course, not equivalent; violence always threatens to dominate the respective meaning: the victim is overwhelmed by the superiority of violence, he loses his language and ability to articulate: excessive violence 'triumphs' over meaning because the experience of the most extreme violence can never be depicted in language. Finally, violence also triumphs over any attribution of meaning.

Can the ideology of National Socialism be classified in the same sense? The outrage-provoking experience of moral otherness, which had betrayed generic solidarity seemingly without historical precedent, forces a reflection on moral self-understanding. In this respect of meaningfulness, morality still goes beyond religion.

The violence of the twentieth century and the ideological doctrines that drove that violence cast a long shadow into the past. This violence in word and deed seems to blend with religious motives. But how can one grasp this relationship between violence and religion, between totalitarian politics and the morality of redemption?

As is well known, religion acts as a factor in a complex event. Religious motives, be they diffuse or specific, thus have a part in an event; they are reduced to their functionality.

Religion is known to have an obstinacy and a notorious ambivalence with regard to violence. In the language of salvation and redemption, salvation and damnation, torments of hell and the last judgement, a potential for violence becomes visible that achieves eminent effects in social conflicts. As much as the religious consciousness can also positively grasp all the negativity experiences of finite life, it can equally bring about cruelty, fearfulness and evil (Graf/Meier, 2013, pp. 11–13).

Admittedly, this describes a context that is truncated in a psychologising and functionalist way. A historical–theoretical approach would also have to ask about the preconditions that favoured the emergence of modern political religions. But even this question could be misleading because it presupposes something that is highly controversial. Do the totalitarianisms of the twentieth century represent a substitute for historical religions (Joas, 2013)? Has politics, then, taken on a form that it has taken from religious eras and merely appears in a new guise? Would a subterranean history of the effects of religious violence thus be the key to understanding violence, right down to all Gnostic or millenarian motifs? Be it as a substitute or surrogate, as a function or compensation – in the language of functionalism we do not do justice to the peculiarity of a political religion. It is not a matter of lawful or causal connections between religious and modern epochs.

Only a historical–theoretical perspective helps at this point, leading from the dissolution of violence to the mobilisation of political power with the help of secular religion. The type of politics we encounter in the face of Nazi violence is historically novel. It could only succeed insofar as it took on religion-like features and was able to achieve mass loyalty in this way. The combination of the development of power and the expectation of salvation expressed delusional traits.

The lack of morality expressed in the language and in each individual act is not so much due to the 'absence' of religious ties. Rather, it is to be understood as a coherent and 'displaced' morality that contradicts our everyday moral convictions. In this respect, one should start with the phenomenon of historical research on perpetrators. We now know that many of the killings did not directly lead to the articulation of feelings of guilt. Many of those involved believed they were acting in the service of a cause that conformed to the established morality of killing. Himmler's Posen speech lends a bizarre aura to this assumption when he spoke of steadfastness and courage, of integrity and decency in the face of the most extreme genocidal acts.

Those involved in the murder actions during the World Wars followed an interpretation that transformed prohibitions on killing into commandments to kill, writes Harald

Welzer (Welzer, 2005, p. 16 ff.). It was not individual convictions or instances of conscience that guided actions, but an overarching framework of orientation. National Socialist ideology had so deeply penetrated language and consciousness, as well as the categories of morality, guilt and meaning, that the task of killing could be normatively integrated. It lost its original meaning of gravity and contradiction, which one would think of as anthropologically rooted. Reinhart Koselleck's basic idea that the ontological determinations of history are not to be found in having to die, but in being able to kill, comes into focus here once again in a frightening way.

The decisive driving force of Nazi ideology thus remains: it lies in the mobilisation of a willingness to use violence, which only makes the moral genre break comprehensible. The monstrous project did not lie in the ability to wage war and to mobilise forces for it, but rather in speaking the word of a new human morality.

The moral *otherness of* the profoundly anti-Semitic ideology is clearly evident today, and yet it remains unclear how the manageable circle of ruling ideologues could be expanded to include a large mass of people willing to use violence. Two insights would have to be thought together, which nevertheless appear to be irreconcilable: the moral conviction of a generic commonality and the negatory will to annihilation, which runs counter to all traditional moral concepts. What ideology and subsequent practice have proven would thus be the tragic insight that there can be no unhistorical unity of morality. The silent presupposition of a generic generality is deceptive. It is knocked out of our hands as a belief and as a conviction by historical experience.

Chapter Six

POLITICS, VIOLENCE AND SACRALITY

Another obscurity of the utmost importance: metaphysics. The category is ambivalent because it seems to be under the jurisdiction of philosophy. Metaphysical, as we know, is a world that describes an obscure *behind*; metaphysical effects are not of *this* world. Metaphysics circumscribes a realm beyond the real world and thus stands in strict opposition to everything understood under the category of politics.

Nevertheless, in the history of violence, various alliances between politics and metaphysics can be observed. These alliances encompass not only the realm of the religious but also all forms of millenarianism, the history of salvation and ultimately the ideological wars that flag themselves with sacred motifs. They are alliances that obviously point deep into the past and form a hermetic section of history.

The present age has distanced itself from the realm of the metaphysical in various ways. Power and politics depend on physical but not metaphysical grounds. The doubt one cannot shake at this point goes back to the absoluteness with which one can make this judgement. It would be all too easy for a contemporary observer to find traces of metaphysical orientations even in the present. Metaphysics is not 'historical'; it repeatedly pervades the surface of liberal structures. Such a tendency seems to be formed not only in the figure of the god-warrior but also in the forms of contemporary power politics that invoke supposedly overcome ideologies of the older war.

If we simplify these phenomena drastically, violence is justified by invoking the almighty God. God warriors invoke a higher, sacred law, absolute commandments that are disturbing to all outsiders. No less disturbing is the return of war in the first decades of the beginning millennium.

The impressions of the present (2022) are now difficult to fit into a reflection that would have to judge events from a serious distance. However, all observers seem to have the impression that the wars of the present (including above all the so-called civil wars in Syria and the wars on Ukrainian territory) are taking on anachronistic, if not metaphysical forms. In particular, the attack on the sovereign state of Ukraine in February 2022 seems to suggest such a description.

These violent confrontations are not the actual subject here, although they do enter into the reflection via detours. The disturbing nature of this violence points us to a more fundamental, extremely complex phenomenon. It is not the raw struggle for resources, land and mineral wealth alone that is decisive, albeit highly relevant, but also the orientation towards historical greatness, which alone is supposed to justify strategic action. Now this is not a problem of a single state, not a pathology that can only be found in one culture.

The orientation towards metaphysical reasons is self-evidently dangerous and notorious, but it is not a feature of past times that have been left behind once and for all. The difficulty begins with psychological inspection: metaphysical politics is not finished with the description as irrational. One comes close to things, but is dependent on further reflection.

The following reflections serve several purposes. The intention is to show ways into violence, ways that can be given a purely materialistic interpretation, but which in doing so remain inadequate in a certain sense. The gigantic and monstrous nature of the violence of the twentieth century, which we recognise in the totalitarian regimes and their capacity for violence, cannot be grasped with the conventional means of reconstruction. What is needed is a deep-psychological and hermeneutic grasp of the relationship between political religion and political violence. This connection can only be grasped here in rudimentary form. In addition, however, there is another goal that is no less complicated.

The question is whether the dark spots of political religions can be attributed to a past that is already closed. The current alliances between violence and religion, as can be observed in terrorist attacks, would then be understood as a return of religion. Another description aims at a continuity of religious and sacral dimensions that can be historicised at the same time, but would not be regarded as a closed chapter. This approach shows the conditions under which we live with quasi-religious phenomena and expectations of salvation even in modernity.

Religious Dark Spots

Religion is an ambivalent power. It shimmers, as it were, when we consider the highly contradictory forms it has taken in history. Religious motives are vital and undeniable; they outlast the times. Modern philosophers have wanted to see a secular age in modernity. They have been taught better. A variety of religious activities can still be observed. People are in search of meaning and join communities that offer them promises of salvation. The subject of religion continues to attract scientific and contemporary diagnostic interest. At the same time, the enduring vitality of religion has something disturbing about it, because religious orientations are not only absorbed in ritual and cult, they also have a well-known obstinacy that can be dangerous. In an emergency, religious certainty tends towards closure and reveals its notoriously dangerous nature. The 'theocratic temptation' (Graf/Meier, 2013, p. 8) lies in the religious and normative absoluteness that does not allow for plurality and deviation.

As is well known, this consciousness goes beyond the ordinary rationality of everyday life. Religious cults revel in images, follow myths and create order. Accordingly, they have something comforting for the individual because they transform the threatening chaos into order. In the better case, they integrate the experiences of negativity into an integrative form of life, into certainties that lead beyond despair.

But to the same extent, religion instigates the willingness to use violence against those who think differently. The connection between domination and salvation leads deep back into known history (Assmann, 2000, 2003, 2018).

Anthropology and archaeology look back to the beginnings of humans, which are also beginnings of the religious. The indications of the religious 'nature' of humans are numerous, even if they do not allow any definitive conclusions (Pettitt, 2011; Renfrew, 2016). This becomes clear when looking at significant archaeological finds: religious activity was present in human cultures from the beginning. Early human cultures used religious practices by coping with immediate experiences of negativity. Death was a constant companion and yet an enduring mystery. Where the dead went, whether they should enter a shadow realm and to what extent they continued to be in contact with the ancestors – these questions could only be transferred into religious interpretations and thus overcome. The beginning of religion was linked to magic and myth, ritual and cult; above all, however, this beginning was linked to interest in the subject of death.

The decisive question in our context, however, is not the function of religion in prehistoric times. Rather, the question is about the turning point at which the alliance of religion and violence took on a different, specific form. Even if the past of prehistory will probably always remain enigmatic and dark to some extent, even if we will never know about the stories that early people told each other in the face of the presence of death, a difference is nevertheless to be marked.

Violence changed at the moment of the turn from primary religion to secondary religion. This thesis of Egyptology (Assmann, 2000, 2003) is to be tested in various respects. It states that there are religious cultures that have created fundamentally different worldviews. In the world of primary religions, rites and sacrificial cults were cultivated as an expression of sacred moods. The world hid secrets that could be approached through religious practices. The realm of magic was like a mirror in which the upper and lower worlds, the sacred and the profane could flow together. One inserted oneself into an order of the numinous.

The religious practice of prehistory certainly had violent features, for example in the cult of sacrifice. But it was regarded as a form of intensive devotion to the world. Through the integration of human things into the divine order, a feeling of being at home in the world could be achieved.

Primary religion experienced a rupture through the change to secondary religion. Assmann calls this the 'price of monotheism' (Assmann, 2013a). This change is not to be understood as a singular moment in history. It happened in spurts and it had specific effects on the social and political world. In the old world of primary religion, there was a multiplicity of divine authorities that did not have to face any rivalry. Only the establishment of a supreme god who demanded exclusive worship brought about a change in the situation of violence. In this we recognise a trait of violence, because now unconditional obedience and the motive of truth are brought into the world, in a different form than the religions did before.

The antagonism between primary and secondary religion is crucial for the following considerations. Monotheism is at the centre of a conflict-ridden relation to the world. This problematic accompanies humanity up to the present.

Why is monotheistic faith dangerous? Monotheistic religions sharply demarcate themselves from their environment; they demand an obedience in the absolute. A spirit of preaching is introduced into the world through the observance of written laws; holy scriptures establish the one God as the sole authority. It is a religious experience that not only opposes other religions and cultures, but comes from a different worldview. In monotheistic faith, the will to truth and unconditionality is expressed (Schwartz, 1997).

Monotheism is closely intertwined with the category of truth. The comparability to the development of knowledge is obvious (Assmann, 2003, p. 23 ff.). Just as we speak of true and false knowledge, we can also assume between true and false religion. The prehistoric world of myths was gripped by wild thinking, analogies were made without causallogical claims.

Relationships between the visible and the invisible were forged by free association. People were open to the wonders of the world; they lived in the form of an affirmative attention to the world. With the introduction of new concepts of knowledge, this way of life, handed down in myths and rites, was thwarted. At the latest since the ancient concepts of knowledge, which could distinguish identity and logical contradiction, being and non-being, a negativity broke into the world of religion. Ancient philosophy, as we know, was about the strength of argument, the depth of thought and the power of dialogue; but in religion, a tremendous potential of negation was unleashed.

Decoding this potential and tracing the lines between past and present is the task of the sciences (Stark, 2001). For paradoxically, there is a deeper ambivalence in the power of discernment from which all forms of knowledge benefit: whoever speaks of truth must exclude what is misunderstood; whoever worships one God must condemn the glorification of all other greats. This interpretation is problematic for modern observers, because it blanks out the modern culture of tolerance. In a psychological and historical view of religion, however, the problem presents itself differently. The demanding One-God-Will stands for the power of intolerance, which brings with it a trail of violence.

This violence now has many shady sides, many facets and reasons; on the whole, however, it is intertwined with the new concept of faith. It is now about a knowledge of the first and last reasons that cannot be proven and yet are of the highest binding force. The revealed truth in the holy scriptures cannot be relativised, but is absolute, metaphysical and unconditional. The preceding forms of faith lived without this sharp distinction; they were matters of natural and simple evidence. They did not have to be defended or fought against. They were conducive to life.

Secondary religion, on the other hand, introduced a type of truth into the world that was the cause of intolerance and negation. From this religion springs a violence that gives rise to both new enmity and a new ethic.

The evidence for this thesis comes from historical textbooks. They tell of incidents from the archives of religious history that surprise no one. They shall be mentioned here in anecdotal brevity.

Let us look back to Clermont in the eleventh century. Here Pope Urban II gave a speech of the highest significance and historical relevance. The Council of Clermont in 1095 has gone down in history as the moment of the First Crusade. Archbishops and high clergy, but above all the ordinary faithful, listened to a speech in which dramatic appeals were made to take up arms. It took four years before the Western knights came to the walls of Jerusalem to liberate the Holy City in the name of the Christian God.

There are different versions of the speech that Pope Urban gave to the faithful. Rhetorical aspects have been handed down that defined the enemy as a people far from God, capable of the worst atrocities. The knighthood of Europe was to be mobilised to end the suffering of the Christians in the East and to expel the Muslims from the land; to this end, the highest reward of blessing was promised.

As so often in the history of violence, the language and the reality are in extreme contradiction. There was talk of a holy war and a mission of supreme consecration. Behind the carefully deployed rhetoric, brute force showed its ugly face: on its journey east, the crusade left an immense trail of blood.

'Deus vult', 'God wills it', Urban had dictated in Clermont. The masses followed him in fanatical zeal. The pope had struck a nerve. Spurred on by fanatical itinerant preachers, a popular army first set out to make its way east. But one must not overlook the momentum that turned the project into an unprecedented frenzy. On the way, which led across the Rhine, an extreme aggression was unleashed against Jews, who were defamed as Christ-killers. In addition to the religious legitimisation, there were motives of greed and lack of restraint. The towns on the way of the procession became prey. The hordes plundered in Hungary and the Balkans. Of the original 50,000–70,000 participants in the People's Army, most were eventually wiped out in battle by the Seljuks.

The procession of the knights took a different course. French and southern Italian knights set out in several groups. Thousands of knights, their escorts and horses posed an immense logistical challenge. After a difficult journey through Anatolia, the army reached Antioch.

Meanwhile, the first 'crusader state' was established in Edessa. In early July 1099, a decimated and exhausted army finally took up position at the gates of Jerusalem. Under Gottfried's leadership, the city was conquered in mid-July.

The battle had entered the annals of history. One reads about great military leaders, 'Bohemund', 'Raimund of Toulouse', 'Gottfried of Bouillon', who became known throughout Europe. The massacre of 1099 was also recorded in music, literature and art. It became a motif that fired the religious imagination; and it has been considered a prelude to the history of events ever since. The clashes between Christianity and Islam took on a clear contour here. The Holy War has here gained his form, which it was to further distinguish in further wars (Frankopan, 2012, pp. 11–27).

The thesis of monotheistic violence is forcefully confirmed here. At this point, Christianity experienced a fundamental change in its relation to the world. It had come to terms with worldly violence and made a pact that contradicted its origins. Christianity had based its ethos on non-violence. Peace in the world was the goal, but the closer the Christian community came to domination, the further it moved away from its roots. In the Sermon on the Mount, the peacemakers became sons of God; the message of salvation was first seen as redemption from worldly violence.

The history of Christianity, however, is known to be read in a special way as a history of violence. The will to peace weakened as the community moved from the margins to the centre of society. With Constantine's victory in 324, the alliance with the Roman state was complete. Subsequent church teachers such as Augustine constructed doctrines of Just War, in which injustice was punished by violence. Christianity eventually became part of the rule and created a social structure in which theology supported political authority (Metz, 2010, pp. 17–24).

*

In summary, it is not difficult to illustrate the violence of monotheism with historical situations. As is well known, this is true for all monotheistic religions, for Judaism, Christianity and also in the environment of Islam, evidence of intense violence could be found.

But this does not answer the real question for us. The alliances between violence, domination and religion exist in the past and the present, in the East and the West. It needs no elaboration that religion is an element of the history of violence, not just an episode, but an immanent part.

The aforementioned dark areas of history are now to be looked at more closely without taking up the details of the history of religion. The fundamental question arises with regard to the continuity of religious and sacral motifs. In the modern era, the sacral complex has become detached from domination. Religion and politics have been separated, at least in Western societies. But this by no means settles the 'issue' of religion.

For a comprehensive account, one must take into account the effect of religious imagination. Under what conditions can we speak of an unbroken continuity of the religious without becoming entangled in contradictions? To what extent is religion not only a function in common life, but a sustainable dimension? Has religion possibly been misunderstood precisely because it is an unavoidable force between people and between cultures?

This question will be taken up in the following. In doing so, a distinction should be made that sets it apart from other approaches. It is not a question of proving a conjuncture of religious feelings, which is sometimes stronger and sometimes weaker.

falls. The dark places referred to here are not aimed at behaviours, dispositions and strong feelings. Rather, they denote continuities, a spectrum of possibilities produced by religion. It requires a fundamental abstraction to understand this form of the sacred.

What Remains? On the Sacral Dimension of the Present

The following reflections are a challenge, perhaps also an imposition. They distance themselves from the ordinary semantics that recognise in the present a state of complete rationalisation. The language of modernity is based on a consensus that religious orientations have been pushed out of the centre of society. According to this, religion becomes a private matter and is only significant in specific niches.

This description, as can be seen, is of a Eurocentric or Western character and to that extent has a right of its own (Habermas, 1996, 2004). In a dialectical juxtaposition, this perspective is to be followed in order to subsequently place it in stark contrast. In different historical and cultural phases, an open contradictory structure is to be presented.

The difficulties already begin with the category of secularisation. As is well known, the term describes a process in which religious institutions lose their central position and acquire a rather minor influence on culture and politics. As is well known, secularisation in Western societies went hand in hand with the separation of church and state. In this context, however, different interpretations of the term must be taken into account.

An alternative reading is that religion has paved its way into modernity despite the separation. Religious traces are contained in modern ideas and ideologies that do without traditional metaphysics but achieve a comparable effect (Löwith, 1953; Schmitt, 1922). In this sense, the modern concept of progress could be derived from the linear concept of time in religion, which aimed at the promise of a better world (Buc, 2015, p. 12). In other words, qualities and characteristics of religion have been preserved that do without divine absolutism but bring other absolutist ideas into the world.

Let us try to find evidence for this thesis in the following. Admittedly, dialectical paths would have to be accepted for this. The continuity of the religious, as indicated, is evident in modern secularised societies that focus on other forms of the sacred. The sacrality of the person, of law and of diverse political beliefs is to be included in this argument. However, the sacral dimension, which is granted to modern law without reservations, is by no means saved from falling into totalitarian doom.

*

Let us look at the history of the West and its relationship to religion. For the longest time, the foundations of political rule lay in natural law and metaphysical ideas of order. Right rule was seen as the image of a cosmic harmony in antiquity; in the Middle Ages it was associated with the revelation of the Redeemer God.

The law of reason of the modern era had contributed to this centuries-long tradition being able to detach itself from its origins. Whereas in earlier epochs divine justice (as well as divine arbitrariness) was considered the pillar of legitimacy, the modern law of reason created the form of political rule that we now take so much for granted as 'legitimate'. This change, accelerated by the constitutional revolutions and the Enlightenment of the eighteenth century, promoted an abstract idea of the highest importance. Modern orders consolidate the bond between free and equal individuals who can 'say yes and no' (Habermas, 2013, p. 288).

It is a political worldview that – without divine authority – bases every decision on the political will of the participants. In this respect, the institutional separation of state and religion would be correctly described by the term secularisation. In this order, religion plays a subordinate role, if you will. It is by no means relegated to the margins or even completely obsolete. But religious convictions must fit in with the democratic consensus; their voices, like all voices, are admissible insofar as they conform to democratic principles and the rule of law. Excluded from this order, as is well known, are tendencies that are 'fundamentalist' in the literal sense of the word and contain an unacceptable potential for violence.

Faith is permissible in secularised societies as long as it does not come into sharp contradiction with constitutional principles. Accordingly, religious citizens also accept the objective primacy of political decisions; however, as soon as they radically turn away from these convictions, they move outside the applicable order. On one side of this boundary are constitutional organs, constitutional convictions and the concrete 'cover power' of the police. On the other side would be a conflict that is unacceptable because of its radical nature and which would result in police measures.

This distinction is familiar and insightful. We live in orders that go hand in hand with the power of the better argument and with rational procedures. If religious fundamentalism turns offensively against this order, it becomes a matter for the state and the police (Meier, 2013, p. 309 ff.).

This reading is sufficient for the democratic-theoretical conviction. And yet it contains a crucial blank space, a zone of unrest. Of course, one can leave it at that and refer to the demarcation of the democratic status quo. Everything that contradicts the current constitution and touches a dark area of the irrational and threatening is excluded by liberal societies with good reasons.

Nevertheless, it remains the task of the hermeneutic sciences to account for the background of religious violence. A look at history shows how quickly political judgement fails and how quickly morality descends into brutal rule.

With good reason, historians speak of *political religions* that developed in the course of modern times and unleashed a furore of violence. Where these forms of secular religions come from remains as uncertain as their trajectories in the future. The only possibility that remains is to think about parallels and constellations that follow the tendency of the return of repressed forces (Aron/Ionescu, 1968).

Quite a few theories draw a line of thought from the history of the French Revolution to the totalitarian excesses of the twentieth century (Meier, 2002).

This connection becomes comprehensible when looking at the loss of transcendence that can be recognised in the longue dureè. The historical religions have lost their power in the course of modern times, but have taken on a new form in a roundabout way. They return in political dogmas and totalitarian temptations. Behind this lies an apparent certainty of an anthropological nature: man, as a fragile and needy being, is dependent on religion. If one denies him this orientation, he falls into moral decay. This reading is based on an anthropological impossibility. Secularisation creates new patterns of order, but it does not penetrate the depths of the psyche. Quasi-religious forces push forward as soon as one retreats solely to the rationality of modern forms of life.

Violence would thus be closely linked to the loss of secularisation; political religions cloak a schizophrenic situation. They carry promises that they can only grasp in violent abstractions. They seduce the masses with messianic messages that require a related form of faith, but pervert its foundations.

*

Historiography and the social sciences are in a tense relationship at this point. History points us to a tragic situation of powerlessness. Religion is thus not only a factor but a fundamental dimension in historical existence, unavailable and unavoidable. In contrast, the social sciences remain helpless, though not speechless. They are left only with the rationality of modernity, which aims at an agreement of non-violence between people. The present studies draw added value from this constellation. This tension cannot be definitively resolved, but it can be brought to fruition.

To illustrate why the history of political religions can be observed over a period of more than 200 years, we need to look at the 'ground' of the French Revolution. The revolutionary decade from 1789 to 1799 was characterised by the fact that it had produced new emblematic condensations, solidarity and fraternity on the one hand and the face of terror on the other.

The revolution lives from the fact that it creates its own time. It generates the phantasmatic idea that violence becomes meaningful and produces a rupture in history for which it itself is responsible. Revolutionary language unfolds a horizon of expectation that is the model of all political hopes. Politics becomes a totality that eliminates all grievances and conflicts in a radical upheaval. It can only legitimise itself, even if it refers to an idealised popular will; it extends to all areas of life, even if it takes freedom as its banner.

The basic motive of the revolution lies in a reaching out to the future. This contains a religious motif that would have to be deciphered.

The change at which the violent revolutionary will aim must be total. Sacred politics in these contexts can be recognised by the compact system of convictions, dogmas and commandments. The revolutionary movement takes over the entire social world and cannot be stilled with compromises.

It would now be too easy to draw a straight line from the age of revolutions of the late eighteenth century to the epoch of totalitarianism. Historians have good reasons for refusing to fall into the trap of finalism. The events of the French Revolution cannot be understood as the 'prelude' to all subsequent revolutionary uprisings. History does not proceed along a predetermined trajectory preconceived at a particular point in time. It is misunderstood as the execution and fulfilment of a plan.

Nevertheless, one historical space contains model ideas that recur in other temporal constellations; in ideas about political action, in political semantics, in forms of fulfilment and social characters. In one case, it is the sacralisation of the moment: on a 'big night', in a collective effort, a historical moment of the oppressed masses is captured. Old orders are overthrown that night and the new order is put in its place.

The quasi-religious motives cannot be denied: distinctions between good and evil are established and given higher consecrations. Communities become sacred by invoking loyalty and devotion. This community sooner or later reaches out to the whole world with messianic messages. The telos of good fulfils the community of the elect.

At the centre are secular concepts with sacral radiance, in titles such as *nation and fatherland*, the one *party* and *united humanity*. They contain the power to represent the meaning of the whole (Koselleck, 1979; Gentile, 2002, p. 169 ff.). Morality allies itself with power, it closes itself off and becomes autistic as soon as a new political or social entity is absolutised.

Is this an easy-to-follow practice of imitating the formal language of religion? Political religions adopt motifs of dogmatics and ethics, certainly also the structure of the liturgy in which a faith community is gathered. They incorporate handed-down traditions and create a self-contained universe full of symbolism. The dark spots are well known and need not be described in detail here: they consist in the rigid exclusion of the stranger and of those who do not belong. For this negatory morality, all means of violence must be used.

*

The present interpretation of violence is not to be understood in a concretist way. One cannot reduce 'everything' to religion or religious feelings without being guilty of simplification.

The question of what remains of religion in the age of modernity has many answers. One directs attention to the emergence of totalitarian politics. This points directly back to historical epochs in which religious ultimate justification prevailed. The devastating religious wars as well as the traditions of holy war are ambivalently related to the violence of the twentieth century.

For a diagnosis of the present, this view of the ways of violence is necessary, but not sufficient. It must be flanked by a moral–philosophical view that transcends the furore of historical violence. The whole ambivalence of religion becomes visible when we focus on problems of the present in which aspects of morality, law, equality and justice are discussed. To what extent can religious forms be discerned here as well?

The question is to what extent the formal language of law emerges from the experience of violence. Can historical experiences of violence be transformed into value bonds? Can we extract an added value from the history of violence that will contain future forms of violence? Could the history of violence – deliberately expressed here in simple sentences – be placed in parallel with the history of human rights? And what role would be assigned to value bonds, which are obviously close to religious traditions? This is not about older conflicts of the reference to God in modern constitutions. Undeniably, modern democratic constitutions refer to categories of human dignity and inalienable rights, and in doing so they can go back to religious and theological traditions. However, only the aspect of the sacred is in question.

Values can acquire a sacred appearance that forms the occasion for legal–moral interventions. They can thus – varying in different historical constellations – acquire an intrinsic value that is of the highest significance in people's lives; an intrinsic value that, however, also gives rise to a turning point. Violence can also be legitimised in the name of 'values', wars can be unleashed.

The following considerations apply to this dialectic.

So let us first ask about the re-evaluation of conditions – beyond and on this side of religion. Where do our intuitions and feelings come from that we think are inscribed in our minds, as it were, from the very beginning? According to all experience, they go back to feelings of solidarity and closeness, of compassion and empathy. But they go back even deeper to the experience of the negative (Angehrn, 2015). Our attachment to values has a negativistic core: there are things that we not only consider unjustified, but that have an unacceptable quality.

These things – experiences of violence, the intrusion of the unexpected and horror – *should not be.*

Surprisingly, this fear of the negative reflects one side of religious experience. The experience of the sacred contains the enthusiastic attraction as well as the shock and terror of the very other (Otto, 1979; Joas, 2004).

We can draw a line from this motif to modern ideas of human dignity. The date 1945 forms a threshold, a turning point, which contains as many fundamentally upsetting experiences as it does the impulse for a new beginning. The German and European democracies and constitutions would of course be the first to be mentioned here, but the context is much broader. The aim is to work out a binding motif from the rubble of violent history that anticipates and counteracts future events. The reference to the actual tyranny of National Socialism and fascism is, as it were, self-evident; modern constitutions mention the shock of barbarism and tyranny.

But historical experience is not only inscribed in the declarations and legal texts; it forms a broad context of consciousness due to historical education.

The latter point is possibly the decisive one. It goes back to traumatisation that has penetrated the body of those affected, but at the same time has an indirect reference to the development of human rights. The declaration of human rights thus has an 'epistemic' reason (Morsink, 1999, p. 36). The orientation towards human rights is rooted in religious language and humane dignity, but also in the unavoidable experience of negatory violence. The efforts after 1945 to create a 'security' after all the experiences of de-securing testify to this awareness.

With the help of a sharp conceptual distinction, one can decipher these connections. The experience of the sacred (Joas, 2013) points beyond religion. Sacred moments are like cultural forms that link historical contexts in the form of a particular narrative. The sacred would thus be the historically older source of human communities. The emergence of the sacred is a fundamental anthropological phenomenon that has probably preoccupied people at all times. At the moment of self-transcendence, we experience a power that transcends our own will and self; the sacred is ascribed qualities that set it apart from all everyday 'business'.

Such transcendent experiences are of strong cultural value. People form cultural traditions and forge strong bonds in the form of ideals. These ideals embody ideas about good and evil. They form a foundation of certainty that contains specific attractions.

It would be misleading to imagine these ideal formations on a straight line (Joas, 2004). As is well known, the arrow of time in history has different vectors. The time of secular ideals is just as truncated as the 'return of religion'. We have to start from different forms of sacred ideals that are of high importance in people's lives, past and present. If we now link to the contexts of violence and trauma, then corresponding idealisations can be observed.

The historical events that entail sacred values are naturally familiar to us. They resemble entries in the cultural archive of humanity that should be maintained. The trauma of the Holocaust, for example, is regarded as a negative founding myth of a new Europe, but events going back further have also been formative for cultural self-questioning, for example, the slavery of Africans taken to North America or the expulsion and extermination of the indigenous American population. History thus has enough motifs of suffering in store that give rise to the moral universalism of the present.

As is well known, there have been intense disputes about the validity of suffering. Here, a sensitive point of the history of violence is to be noted: the traumatic violence has to be transferred into a liveable present; experiences have to be transferred into texts and narratives without thereby 'healing' the past. At this moment, however, a diffuse conflict arises between the specific suffering and the generalisable recognition. The conflict is complex and irritating; for every suffering trivially deserves recognition. No experience of violence whatsoever can be excluded. However, the psychological situation that arises in the context of experiences of disregard must be taken into account. For what 'consequences' and what forms of action, what values and what conclusions are to be drawn from the simple fact of human vulnerability, which has existed at all times? The reference to suffering alone does not provide satisfactory orientation values.

In other words, we are at a turning point after 1945, which has been reflected at least in language and texts. But what, more precisely, is this moment of 'moral' and 'political' new beginning about? A reorientation in the face of utter horror, of course, but also a shift in a horizon of values. The idea that there is a *right to human rights* has since been an undeniable certainty. It is true that the specific validity of concrete rights, such as cultural rights, is disputed and fought over. But the core area of fundamental rights, which results from the facticity of human vulnerability, is now inscribed in the moral grammar of the present.

However, this is connected to another form of conflict. We are living today in an era of universalisable rights, but by no means on a ground of stable self-evidence. Various unresolved conflicts and deeper ambivalences are evident in relations within and between states. The fundamental question is how to classify the relationship between politics and human rights in the global and international context.

Human rights have a sacred ring. However, and this is what constitutes their conflict structure, they must be viewed in a relationship between a specific social order and the applicable normative orientation. The fact that they are considered sacred values does not make them any less susceptible to conflict. As is well known, these rights are not equally pronounced in every social sphere; to put it simply, they are subject to the profane interests and selective strategies of those in power.

Can we speak at all today of a human rights policy worthy of the name (Deitelhoff, 2006; Brunkhorst, 2005; Butler, 2004)? The practical content of human rights is revealed as the result of an interaction between normative intentions and social orders. This seemingly abstract connection has serious consequences at the level of application. As is well known, the international order is contested; an arena of divergent interests, filled with power and relations of violence. Nevertheless, in the broadest sense, we speak of a world domestic policy, that is, of a world in which legal and moral claims can be articulated at any place and at any time (Kohler, 1996). However, the moment human rights are disregarded, the question arises to what extent this world domestic politics describes a factual situation. Has the world of international relations transformed itself into a domestic space of law or at least come closer to it? On closer examination of contemporary wars, such an assertion would be nonsensical.

Different assessments are possible in this context, just as differentiation of the conflict structures would be called for. A sceptical assessment cannot be dismissed out of hand.

The strongest contradictions of our time are formed in the interplay of sacred values and factual power relations. By no means do historical events amount to the establishment of a cosmopolitan order, of which philosophy has spoken since Kant. The hoped-for state of peace is sometimes realised in scenarios of containment, sometimes this leads to the opposite in situations of unbounded violence. In the confusing labyrinth of civil wars, no order of law seems to emerge that would correspond to the sacred semblance of human rights in the long run. Rather, dynamics of decomposition take hold, in tough struggles for hegemony, in world civil wars and geopolitical wars. All this had been projected onto past historical times when world disorder still prevailed. In this panorama of violence, the endemic instability that prevents a secure rule of law is a cause for concern. Equally worrying, however, is the way in which military and strategic interest politics are enforced under modern conditions.

The philosophy of law puts its finger in the wound of the world conscience: increasingly, the complex continuum of human rights, popular sovereignty and peace is being suspended (Maus, 1999, 2011). Under the title of humanitarian interventions, achievements are being destroyed that actually form the sacred content of modern law.

For over 200 years, a fundamental democratic connection has been formed that could be the brightest core of modern order: the ability to mediate the freedom of individuals with cultural traditions. The dignity of democracy is revealed in the preference of sovereignty. Individual subjective legal claims form that quasi-sacred core of modern societies, but they are in a contested situation as soon as the principle of peace is undermined – by all sides of contemporary world politics (McCarthy, 2009).

Thus, the dark side of sacred values is revealed in the context of world politics: with military interventions that, in the name of sacred values, betray the original context of democratic self-determination. Some observers fear a bleak future scenario here: the emergence of a world state in which freedom rights are redefined as norms of self-empowerment (Brunkhorst/ Köhler/ Lutz-Bachmann, 1999). The sceptical view of the current world political agenda thus itself has an ambivalent core. One cannot smoothly enforce human rights; these are not 'material of realisation', but inalienable rights for which no secular and no religious monopoly of force can arise.

Chapter Seven

THE FRIGHTENING LOVE OF WAR

War again? The phenomenon that is as old as humanity and whose pathology has long been uncovered is once again at the centre, yesterday as today. Wars irritate the consciousness of a respective generation, and the necessity of writing about war leads back to antiquity. Even Thucydides, the chronicler of the Peloponnesian War, was shocked by the pathology of human destructiveness. War, in this view, 'has always' plunged people into an abyss 'which is itself and in which no one awaits it, no god, no civitas either, to lead it home to peace' (Metz, 2012, p. 45).

War needs to be rethought. As many concepts and theories about its existence are ready, many questions remain unanswered (Geis, 2006). But as soon as war breaks into everyday life as a reality and it can no longer be ignored, the questions become more urgent.

Two decades ago, a consensus of modernity was questioned in this context. If possible, so the criticised agreement read, war should be kept completely out of the present household. But, 'those who no longer wage war [...] wrote Herfried Münkler, for example, in view of the wars in the Balkans in 1999, 'must also no longer think war' (Münkler, 1999, p. 678).

The ambivalence remains unresolved to this day: war is considered unacceptable, an extreme evil. However, the refusal to think of it as a phenomenon and to outlaw it as a means of war leads to a moral dead end.

The accusation leads the present reflection into a broad field in which a loss of orientation threatens. For all the uncertainties in the field of geopolitics, which cannot be resolved here, a particular cognitive interest stands in the foreground. In which categories is war to be grasped as an object if one wants to understand it? What contribution can we expect from philosophy and hermeneutics if we place war at the centre of reflection – and always presuppose its necessary ostracism in social orders?

The interest is thus less aimed at a normative justification, but rather at a determination of a relationship with indeterminate consequences. One might assume that this task is associated with clear answers. In the simplest terms, war exposes the brute force of man, his bestiality and unreasonableness. The quest for power, booty, honour, territory and possession forms the basic pattern of the *terrifying love of war* (Hillman, 2005; Münkler, 2002). Understanding war would thus be a didactic task that combines the political actions of a given era with the psychological determinations. In this respect, the attempt at understanding observation leads to the certainty of the Hobbesian world.

However, the phenomena of war and violence cannot be translated into simple equations. Their complexity complicates philosophical reflection: violence must always be considered in the light of a particular purpose and is thus incomplete. And one step further it must be remembered that even philosophy cannot do without violence, that in the extreme case violence and philosophy enter into an unholy alliance.

Thus, if one wants to think through war down to its philosophical basis, it is necessary to clarify the position of philosophy from which all further views, concepts and narratives are presented. Understanding war means clarifying philosophy in relation to violence (Violence and Philosophy) as well as deciphering the possibility of the human relationship to the world (The War as a Teacher) and therein the possibility of war (Aporias of Violence). Understanding war is, after all, a task with various dimensions (The Meaning of War).

Violence and Philosophy

Philosophy's relationship to violence is exceedingly complex. This goes back to the irritating insight that even still the philosophical movement of thought allies itself with violence or cannot sufficiently distance itself from the claim of non-violence. For violence, simplified, already begins at the moment of linguistic empowerment, simplification, generalisation and even at the moment when we try to bring events down to a common denominator. The philosophies devoted to this aporetic relationship are numerous (Derrida, 1967, 2000; Waldenfels, 2000; Kapust, 2014; Butler, 2005).

For contemporary reflection, the legacy of the twentieth century is at the centre, whereby it is not only about the historical events, but also about the aberrations of social theory. The violence of this century was also the violence of culture and thus also of philosophy. The accusation weighs heavily: philosophy, reduced to a sentence, turns to violence and in the course of this thinking becomes the philosophy of violence (Wood, 2000). This constellation leads into the depths of philosophical traditions and finally ends in a fork in the road. One path is the path of violence, which is paved by philosophy through concepts and thus becomes part of a destructive power; the other path is properly understood as a form of distancing. It is not a matter of getting rid of violence for good, but of clarifying its preconditions and formal characteristics.

The first path seems to correspond to the thought movement of Martin Heidegger's phenomenology. In the footsteps of Heraclitus and Nietzsche, violence is transferred into an ontological determination. In everyday understanding, we assume that violence exists as an intentional structure between people and is thus referred to agreement, renunciation, peace or even reconciliation. In the ontological dimension, on the other hand, the world relationship as a whole becomes thematic; violence becomes a topos, a quantity to which people must relate. It should be emphasised that these are two completely different ways of thinking about violence.

Violence in the sense of Heidegger's existential philosophy (Heidegger, 1953, 1979) is as original as it is inescapable and cannot be overridden by formal oppositions. Man himself is violent already in the sense 'that he needs violence because of and in his violence-activity against the overwhelming' (Heidegger, 1953, p. 115). The world is violent in itself because it shows itself to man as something overpowering.

Various starting points can now be thought of to clarify this philosophical construction in relation to political reality (starting from Heidegger's biography: Farias, 1989;

Faye, 2005). What is obvious, however, is that philosophy opens itself up to violence: in every historical situation, a conflict arises between the human capacity for violence and a superior power. And it is this dark conflict that supposedly brings out man's capacity for violence in the first place (Heidegger, 1953, p. 119).

It is difficult to see anything in this other than an unconditional affirmation of violence – and it is precisely on this point that the present discussions should offer an alternative. Violence appears in this theoretical universe as a challenge that is not simply to be understood in negative terms as a disturbance, but which demands the human being as the 'agent of violence' (Ibid., p. 115).

The ambivalence of social theory by no means lies solely in the past. 'Whoever before 1933', wrote Reinhart Koselleck, 'spoke of determination (leading to death) could no longer escape ideologisation after 1945 at the latest' (Koselleck, 2000, p. 100). The pathos of the 1920s has long since faded, however, and the political categories of *the people, loyalty, actuality and freedom from death* no longer have the same meaning today.

If one makes it simple, one could therefore ascribe these semantics to the moods of the times before 1945 and place them in a historical constellation that would be closed. One could thus distance oneself from this past and keep the political categories away from oneself, since they appear as the expression of a fundamental aberration. But what about the specific social theory that has, as it were, witnessed and accompanied the violence of the epoch, that has, as it were, lent it a subsequent legitimacy? The question leads us back to the basic distinctions of the phenomenological movement of thought. The first point of view of critical reflection is to clarify these distinctions and their misalignments.

The assertion that violence is the overwhelming and at the same time the undeniable in a human world is to be problematised. The irreconcilability, which is sometimes openly expressed, sometimes implied in sombre images, contradicts the basic determinations of a moral world. In the context of existential analytics, it is a 'thanatological' determination of temporal concern. In *Being and Time* (Heidegger, 1979), concern for one's being was defended against philosophical traditions. As is well known, it was an attempt to abandon traditional metaphysics and radically place the human being in the open. According to this, man has only an empty future before him and determines himself as a subject in severe loneliness. Death as the outermost limit and the actual being-capable result in a worldview that can be described as political thanatology – a worldview that radicalises the call of concern and, as is well known, could not distance itself from the historical eruptions of violence.

The existential concept of the world proves to be problematic in many respects. At the centre of our reflection is above all the *instrumental point of view of care*. Dasein, which amounts to death, is oriented towards nothing other than concern for one's own self-being. The structure of care remains walled off monologically.

In contrast, it must be emphasised that in the analysis of human relations of care, being with others must be systematically taken into account. What is missing is the formulation of a moral grammar that addresses inter-existential relations.

A theoretical decision is indispensable for the theme of violence. In radical isolation, individual existence confronts its mortality – and draws from it the power of being-capable. The totalisation of the relations of violence must be problematised in this respect.

The alternative now by no means lies in a mild gesture of reconciliation, which would not be theoretically tenable. Rather, we have to describe the basic determinations of existence in a different form. Philosophical anthropology asks with equal radicalism about the conditions of possibility of a common practice. There we encounter first and foremost the moral grammar of human designs of meaning. Human concern, the overcoming of violence and the acquisition of a moral attitude first take place in a communicative horizon (on this: Rentsch, 1999, 2000).

This philosophical orientation is of eminent importance for understanding violence. Reduced to a strong thesis, it could be said that the analysis of interexistence preserves the basic idea of phenomenology without falling into thanatology. As we shall see, we can transfer the irritating love of war into a philosophical worldview. The possibilities of renouncing violence and solidarity enter into this worldview just as much as the dislocations of violence. Both aspects are to be considered in an existential analysis.

As described at the beginning, the following considerations are intended to contribute to an understanding of historical violence. For this purpose, the basic ideas of hermeneutics are used. Here, understanding does not function according to the pattern of making texts and sources accessible. Rather, it is to be understood as an achievement of the practical relationship to the world. The human ability to understand belongs to a horizon that opens up the reality of the whole to the one who understands. In view of violence, however, this process of understanding is highly problematic – as shown, it must not go back to the unconditional affirmation of human relations of violence.

The errors lie, as indicated, in the narrow focus on death analysis. In the worst case, the analysis falls prey to a longing for death and becomes nihilistic. In contrast, the basic question must be considered, which addresses the possibility of a human world and then gradually incorporates the reality of evil and the fact of violence into the considerations.

The War as a Teacher

History has aspects that suggest a learning process. The phrase 'Historia Magistra Vitae' appears in older texts; it famously said that history itself is effective as a teacher of life. History teaches us something – and with good reason, the same could be said of historical wars.

Wars also have a teaching and ordering function. They shape the human world relationship for better or for worse. They flow into myths and narratives that form a certain image of the world.

But can we go so far as to recognise in war a teacher who has taught us lessons that can never be forgotten – and by which one henceforth acts? Is this exceedingly strict, violent teacher helpful in gaining orientation in history? Or is it not rather the case that historiography stands before a stream of history and one merely pulls out individual debris without directing or stopping the stream in any way?

Understanding the history of violence may be a false expectation. Perhaps it would be wiser to follow tradition and ask *questions of history that* always allow only provisional answers. As is well known, it depends on which points of view, which times of war and which forms of violence are brought into focus. Is it about the nation in its historical function of order, which had developed into a comprehensive promise since the eighteenth century? Is it about the history of revolutions and the promise of history-making? Or is it about the violence of taking possession of foreign spaces and foreign peoples? Do we learn something from history when we look at events from the height of the eagles and contemplate the eternal dance of power and geopolitics? Or if we look at events from the centre of the basic humane situation?

It may be difficult to derive a universal claim from the diversity of perspectives. The location-boundness of the observer is decisive. For example, we can trace Europe's wars since the eighteenth century and reconstruct their path into world history. Accordingly, one could reconstruct the regional wars, the wars of the cabinets and the colonial conquests, for which the term European 'Theatrum Belli' has become common. And one would be referred to follow this theatre of war in its further course, which extended across the entire globe in the twentieth century. It is therefore 'world history', if only because the theatres of war went beyond Europe. However, this narrative would be quite Eurocentric. European states had the power to plunge the world into war. At the same time, they accelerated the decline of the great empires and thus undermined global hegemony (Langewiesche, 2019, p. 34).

Thus, we are faced with the challenge of transforming the history of war into a form that is binding for all. However, this is an exaggeration that is inappropriate and carries the danger of using history as an instrument. This danger comes from various directions. There is, for example, a fatal 'liaison dangereuse' between the politics of history, the perspective of the contemporary witness and historiography, which is rarely brought to our attention. Even when history is taken into the service of a popular pedagogical purpose, its dignity and autonomy are endangered. Master narratives emerge that, while grounded in historical knowledge, can lead to rigid repetition. No matter how one turns it and which particular position one takes, there is a danger of self-reference. History then becomes the object of extra-historical purposes (Sabrow, 2014, pp. 13–26).

The contradictions, on the other hand, must be made clear: the pedagogical aspects are fundamental and the reappraisal of a violent epoch is deeply serious.

Only the claim of enforcing historical narratives remains problematic.

The realisation of the history of violence is an immense challenge. It 'succeeds' only if one traces the reflections back to elementary determinations. It touches on older impulses in the philosophy of history, as we shall see, and yet it comes with reservations.

The motives, which we can only hint at here, are ambivalent: the narrative perspective remains tied to the location of the suffering people, without being able to grasp a telos of these experiences. That which is suffered can be portrayed retrospectively and grasped in its course; it can also be linked to individual meaning. But an overarching horizon of purposeful history is not meant by this; there is simply no *telos of* a third party, no *cunning of reason* as in Hegel, no *providence* and no *intentions of nature*. In this respect, history is blind and autonomous; people are largely exposed to history. The 'nonsense' of history only becomes apparent from a higher vantage point (Koselleck, 2010). Individual people cannot know what results their actions will lead to (except for those subjects who want to rape history as well as people with all their might). The intentions and plans remain singular and unconnected; at least no large historical subject can stand out that would direct history from a higher place.

Nevertheless, objections with normative stubbornness remain. People look at their history and interpret it with a view to future events. They not only act as if they could direct their history towards a goal, they also act purposefully and rationally. Against all irrationality they encounter, they align their actions with their evaluations and narratives. In this attitude, we recognise what is, if you will, an ultimate historical–philosophical claim. According to this, a human world is something other than merely an evolutionary development that remains completely beyond the will of human beings. The contradictions are to be kept conscious: there is indeed no *final standpoint of history as such*; *but* man's capacity for narrative synthesis and for reconstructing 'their own history' is undisputed. One can derive from this dialectic a type of historical–philosophical thinking that combines the critique of universal history with underlying normative patterns of thought (Rohbeck, 2004, 2013).

The idea of the saving critique, as it was conceived by Walter Benjamin, can only be read in deeper layers. It can only be understood as a weak version of the older messianic impulses.

*

The following reflections show with fundamental intent under which conditions we can speak meaningfully of violence in human existence. The first meaningful question is not how we can tame violence and get rid of it once and for all, whether this has already succeeded or failed. What is binding, on the other hand, is the philosophical question of the possibility of a human world. To what extent can we understand ourselves as human beings and understand the violence in this world?

Philosophical anthropology *according to* Heidegger (Rentsch, 2000) first recognises the full structure of the basic human situation. It consists of the practical life situation in which individuals can relate to themselves. This basic situation includes irreversible temporality, which determines all history as irretrievable. The gradient towards death determines the uniqueness of existential life, but unlike Heidegger, insights of *common life* can be derived from it.

In the primary world, people orient themselves with practical concepts of meaning and with forms of fulfilment and failure (Rentsch, 1999, p. 192). Human life consists of active engagement and shaping, from which arise the perspectives of responsibility, guilt, meaning, unjustifiability and identity. The features of the human situation are furthermore characterised by fragility, threateningness, power and dominance, asymmetry and neediness, violent distortions, but also moral claims (Ibid., p. 194).

This results in a perspective with contradictory categories. Violence and non-violence must be thought of together in the context of the situation indicated. There is a systematic connection between non-violence and the constitution of the human world; there is the constant possibility of violence, which we experience as exposure, fragility and vulnerability. Fragility arises from the constitutive insecurity and defencelessness of all our actions. We are unprotected from all the adversities of everyday life, we live without guarantees and securities, even if the modern way of life plays us precisely this. To speak of a lack of guarantees in human circumstances is the first step towards a comprehended history.

History has never been consistently non-violent. This means that we must first consider historical existence in its irrevocable fragility before we can even speak meaningfully of the idea of non-violence. This, in turn, does not at all mean viewing the world as an eternal battleground and ascribing all meaning to our actions to conflict, divisiveness and confrontation. Bellicism has no 'meaning' for existential philosophy. Rather, the interplay of the pervasive violence and the forms of non-violence is to be considered.

Fragility means evil is a reality; violence is always possible. From the very beginning of our existence, we are dependent on each other and must rely on others. Exposed to one another, we are required to form a communication in solidarity.

Where does violence begin? And how can forms of non-violence be distinguished? Violence begins in the moment of forgetting and denial. We live not 'because' we owe our lives to others, but by experiencing meaning together, which we owe to no one. Morality is the realm of remembering the conditions of meaning in common life; this becomes explicit in the truthfulness of common language, in the importance of cooperation in realising common life and in the constitutive importance of unconditional openness. If these universal forms of practice are undermined, 'violence' is at play, in all historical forms of which the story tells. The pursuit of non-violence remains bound to these and other criteria. No instance, however, vouches for this claim.

From this moral-philosophical position, determinations of violence can now be specified in more detail. The practical foundation of life is set; it consists in the implicit call to understand communicative solidarity and to orient one's own actions and designs towards interexistence (Rentsch, 1999, p. 264). However, violence is thus not relegated to the margins of a 'higher', morally perfect form of life, but is to be made legible in the realm of common life. It 'shows itself' in a plethora of distorted modes, in strategies and omissions, in forms of language and laws. This immeasurable magnitude of possible violence is to be systematically decoded here and finally interrogated in the large-scale form of war. We proceed as follows: violence is first presented from a phenomenological perspective. The concept of war is thus described in the context of European philosophy as an existential topos. The dismaying love of war is here held in an unusual light: it can only be understood in a dialectical movement of thought.

Aporias of Violence

If, in accordance with social theory, we understand violence as an unconditional component of our existence, what would we need to consider beyond this admission? Does violence remain an intangible, abstract, unthinkable quantity that we never really comprehend, as a majority of philosophical viewpoints suggest?

At the very least, we should insist that the more precisely we spell out the criteria of meaning, the closer we come to violence as a phenomenon. Already with the presentation of scientific criteria that have lifeworld relevance, we leave the problematic traditions of positivism. As is well known, there are patterns of thought that do not let us go because of their suggestive power: the world would be non-violent if only the achievements of civilisation were preserved. The world would become more just, harmonious and thus non-violent as long as only the evil natural impulses were suppressed. The state of nature would thus become 'history' and the present would shine in the splendour of the promises of the philosophy of history. We would thus have relegated violence to a dark corner of history and any real violence that penetrates our present would be nothing more than an unpleasant relapse into past times.

There is much that is questionable about these motifs, much that also corresponds to a real development. For our presentation, however, we need a different approach to violence without disregarding the value of progress. In principle, violence stands in the middle of our world relations, it forms manifold alliances in and with language, violence stands between and within our orders. Its symbolic character shows up in rituals and practices, in interpretations and even in our dreams. It is thus no small decision *not to* attribute violence to a past state of nature.

Another distinction has to be made. We are used to looking at violence from a psychological point of view. That is, violence is something we observe from afar, in various encounters and confrontations. Sometimes we ourselves are affected and perhaps even scarred by the violence, sometimes we can see the violence far away from the violence.

They are consistently individual psychological approaches to events in which the motives of the actors drive the actions. We are then faced with violence, as if we only had to decipher the psychological dispositions to understand everything.

In contrast, from the point of view of philosophy, violence requires a supra-individual perspective. It is to be seen above all as an aporetic relationship and in mediation with meaning.

Violence is to be understood as an aporetic relationship. The conventional approach sees violence as a break with a *rule*, the disregard of an expectation. The core of violence, however, seems to lie in the moment of *violation*. Violence and violation are intimately connected. This does not mean, however, that all violence should be related to the position of the victim. Any reduction undermines the complex event, which is to be located between diverse spheres (hereafter: Waldenfels, 2000, 2014; Delhom, 2014; Kapust, 2014).

Linguistic distinctions are indispensable: things and objects can be *damaged*, people and persons *are injured*. The violation presupposes a self-reference: one turns against the integrity of the person and against the integrity. In addition, a violation is also connected with the perception of a rule. But here, too, the shift in meaning is possible and exceptions must always be taken into account. Not every violent act breaks the law, not every transgression of a rule is illegal. In principle, an act of violence goes beyond the damage of property and the disregard of a rule (Waldenfels, 2000, p. 13).

Thus, the perspective of the victim of violence must be addressed first and foremost. Reduced to a sentence, in the moment of violence *something* is *done to someone*. This moment contains a distinct truthfulness. The sphere of the body is central. The body as a sphere of vulnerability is at the beginning of the philosophical reflection on violence

(Derrida, 2000; Levinas, 1997, Merleau-Ponty, 1994). The body is visible, touchable and threatened; it is a form of territory that can become the site of violence (Waldenfels, 2000, p. 15). The history of violence can be told, as it were, as a history of bodily experiences: from forced flight to degrading clothing, burglary, expulsion from one's home – it is always about links with the human body.

From the point of view of experience, questions need to be asked that explore the quality and form of the suffering (Delhom, 2014). The field of violation can be central or peripheral and the nature of the suffering can be direct or indirect. In current violation and structural violence, it is evident that it does not have to be directly about a single target. In many cases, violence permeates the lifeworld and can hardly be kept out of habits and orders.

However, the further one moves away from the sphere of corporeality, the more complicated become the analyses that identify violence as a meaningful event. For example, one can recognise an anonymous event in a situation of war, in which the responsibilities become blurred. In the broad field of violence, collectivity, individuality and anonymity go hand in hand. If one brings things to a head and asks about the individual imputability that exists despite all anonymity, one is pointed to a further antinomy. For phenomenology, the moment of violence reveals an interplay between speech and counter-speech, violence and counter-violence, action and counteraction. The individual stands in his or her individuality in a social space that is a field of violence (Waldenfels, 2000, p. 17).

It is the interconnections that suggest the original strangeness of violence: victims stand next to other victims, perpetrators next to accomplices, accomplices next to recipients of orders, powerless people next to actors. Saints and heroes can be found on other linguistic levels; the primary focus here is on a space of violence in which the forces are distributed in certain ways. These spaces open up a spectrum of perpetration and complicity, of positions of powerlessness and suffering, closely intertwined.

This raises the question of how we can get out of these confusing circumstances by virtue of philosophical reflection and whether we can extract meaning from things. Violence 'happens' and is thus free of meaning. However, as we know, the human psyche demands interpretations of meaning and exaggerations in order to gain something from what cannot be grasped, beyond fatalism and nihilism. Moreover, we have to consider violence as an episode in a specific relationship to a respective order.

Violence varies according to the orders in which it appears (Ibid.). As revolution, it is directed against a particular order whose time has passed. As a legitimate struggle, on the other hand, violence is taken into the service of order when the cause of justice or even a 'fatherland' is to be defended.

But beyond that, violence also occurs in the shadow of orders – and this facet still seems closest to the present. We know the long-lasting devastating civil wars in history and the present that cast a long shadow. The political backgrounds are complex, but on the surface the lack of a recognisable order seems destructive. The zones of state and rule are furrowed and only residually present, but also the target horizon of an order to be achieved remains in the dark. This distinguishes the wars of the present from the wars of the past. In the context of European history, for example, one spoke of state-building wars, which were full of sacrifices and losses, but which in the long run brought about the order of nation states.

This draws our attention to what is perhaps the decisive relationship. Violence is formed in connection with a particular meaning. Violence becomes meaning and the meaning itself acquires the character of the violent. The connection seems abstract, but it can be applied to various historical situations.

In a human world, the phenomena of war and violence must be placed in relation to a symbolic, linguistic and moral perspective. The experience of violence does not remain with itself; it has to be classified, rationalised and 'processed'. Plans are made on how to anticipate future events. Its reasons are explored as to how the events could occur. Violence becomes significant in the horizon of the general: wars are made great, violence is described as serving and expedient. The particular – which is only recognisable from the singular standpoint of the individual – is assigned to the general. Recent philosophical contributions already recognise the motif of the violent in this (Kapust, 2014; Baumann, 2001; Butler, 2004). Meaning itself is violent because it does not let the subject rest. Violence is transferred into grids, transformed into legal procedures, framed with a halo. The narrative of violence becomes a *history of salvation, a sacred violence, a culture war or a struggle for recognition*.

The Meaning of War

This philosophical consideration is helpful if we want to transfer the irritating love of war into a historicising perspective. In a philosophical and historical perspective, war has a deep structure with various dimensions. Its roots go back to antiquity. Even then, war was ascribed a meaning that was supposed to elevate it above conventional practice.

However, we can draw a line from this past to the modern age: War, then as now, is thought of as a mode of appearance of the 'polemos'; it is ascribed the greatest possible significance. Philosophically, it must be remembered that the realm of thought is never completely detached from the realm of practice. Rather, acts of action and cognition flow into one another; Dasein, which thinks, is always already Being, which is performed.

The connection between war and meaning is demanding because it cannot simply be controlled by moral intuitions. The moral condemnation of war is necessary and urgent, but this leads to an unpleasant reduction. Only when the essence of war is *thought* – this is perhaps how one can summarise the borderline of philosophy – is a position of moral sublimity avoided.

The dialectic of the polemic (hereafter Stadler, 2009, pp. 7–15) should be noted. This follows the original antagonism, the divisiveness, the conflict, which is given a universal form.

Plato, Cicero and Augustine gave war a specific form: war was thought of as ethics, as law, as a form of faith. The categories can be traced up to the present day; at that time, however, the assumption of an original cosmic, transcendental harmony was working in the background. The justice that is established through war is anthropologically mediated. It has its origin in external spheres, which people never come close to. Accordingly, war would always also be an expression of a way of being that has its origin far from human actions.

In the age of rationalism, a different image of war came into focus. War was seen primarily as an instrumental means of man, it served to enforce a will, became a means of power, exemplified by Machiavelli (1965). But modern legal thinking was also founded in the Western European Middle Ages. The School of Salamanca shaped the legalisation of war (Grice-Hutchinson, 1952). War was legitimate when a just cause (*ius ad bellum*), a state authority (*ius belli*) was combined with the appropriate conduct (*ius in bello*).

This construction is still relevant today and has produced a specific way of reflection: wars are thus accessible to an interpretation that recognises them as 'just' and 'morally legitimate' (Walzer, 1992). The contradictoriness, however, will never be resolved: if we grasp war as a legal act, we are already in a field of violence in which the air for moral concepts becomes thin. Occasions, motives, good reasons, categories such as justice, authority and legal processes – all this will not be found in pure form in the reality of war.

However, let us remain at the level of the meanings attributed to the essence of war. The phase of change from the Middle Ages to the modern era is to be appreciated. The primary issue here was the legalisation of violence. Ways out of unrestrained morality in the form of religious wars had to be found. As is well known, the form of the rational state rose above the devastating wars derived from transcendence in the early modern period. Early state power was no less violent and bellicose, but it was a profound change in thinking. The religious ultimate justification became the argument of the state's will. The absoluteness of religious struggle was overcome; the formal state created a new mediation. Wars were transferred into the purpose rationality of the state (Grotius, 2003; Hobbes, 2010).

Finally, in the nineteenth century, war returned to the realm of 'polemics'. This means that war is not subject to contractual thinking alone; it cannot be understood with rationality and calculation alone. Rather, it is linked to cultural morality, which is recalled in the age of emerging nations. Philosophy confirms this turn towards the culture of war (v. Bredow/Neitzel, 1992). According to Clausewitz, war reveals the essence of the political; in Fichte we read of a transcendent duty to fight for moral freedom. Nietzsche, too, sees in the phenomenon of war a form of cultural self-assertion – war may not be redemption, but it is a therapeutic means. The decline of a culture would only be prevented as soon as the warlike impulses are seized again. These are aspects of a philosophical worldview that is far removed from contemporary motifs and yet is discussed again and again (Bohrer, 2007).

An examination of the phenomenon of war, as we can see, always comes up against the basic antinomy of violence. An immediate taking of sides seems impossible; every reflection is required to work its way towards the contradictions of the object. The assumption of ancient thought that warlike violence is not a characteristic of the psyche but an ontological quality is probably the most difficult thesis here. Modern social theory has translated this suspicion into various terms and thus indirectly confirmed it: in Heraclitus, Western thought was set in motion by stylising war as the 'father of all things'. In Heidegger, this idea is taken up again; war thus proves to be a force majeure that compels us to take a stand (Heidegger, 1953, p. 47).

The existential task of human culture is revealed in the overcoming of the original violence, which one cannot escape. The existence of war thus reveals a communal dimension of life (Stadler, 2009, p. 11).

These thoughts can only be explained in a perspective that proves to be open to contradiction. Already in Kant, one finds the contradiction that war, on the one hand, is to be regarded as the ultimate evil, as a scourge of humanity that is to be controlled. And yet the Königsberg philosopher expressed himself with polemical stylistic devices that war advances civilisation (Kant, 1795).

War awakens people's passions, which resemble anthropological tensions: Sigmund Freud saw in the First World War an expression of the unfolding of love life in alliance with all hostile impulses. Thanatos and Eros find each other and combine to form a theatre of cruelty (Freud, 1924).

These contradictions can also be seen in contemporary theories. The challenge lies in understanding death as naturalness and war as normality (Hillman, 2005, p. 52 ff.). War penetrates the crust of superficial thinking. For Foucault, war becomes the basis of all social orders (Foucault, 2000). History takes place in the form of war, not in the form of language. At this point, at the greatest distance from thinkers like Hannah Arendt, the capacity for language is degraded, obscured by the strategies of power.

*

Let us try to translate this constellation into an 'equation'. Different levels are to be distinguished. The connection between violence and meaning proves to be outstanding. Ethics must be oriented towards this distinction.

The discourse of the third is superimposed on the simple facticity of violence. It is a form of inversion (hereafter: Kapust, 2014, p. 55 ff.). The violence becomes significant and the experience itself is given over to a 'higher logic'. That is, violence becomes the centre of attention, while the unavailability of the unique experience is overlooked. In the excess of violence, any 'higher' meaning is undermined. The violence suffered can hardly be captured in words; what always remains is a diffuse speechlessness and the withdrawal of meaning. In this respect, violence is 'only' pure experience; it remains walled up in a singular horizon.

Attempts to articulate it, to make sense of it, remain in vain; the overwhelming power of violence leaves the subject helpless. There is no language left to link experience with criteria of meaning.

This forlornness of violence, which has become paradigmatic for twentieth-century philosophy, nevertheless stands in a tense relationship to the discourses of the present. The semantics are pertinent: some invoke a theodicy under post-metaphysical conditions, some see the end of known history approaching. The experience of violence can take on a salvation–historical, social–psychological, political or historical–philosophical meaning. In the form of attribution however, the *meaning of the violence is* reversed; the *violence of the meaning* overlaps the original context.

The ethics we recognise in this antinomy lies in the realm of the singular. Brought to a common denominator, ethics is required to break through the forms of violence by recalling the reconnection to the 'singularity of the victim' (Ibid., p. 51).

It is an ethical position with a far-reaching tradition. It takes reflection into more difficult terrain as it leaves the conventional paths of moral reasoning. Can the individual find a moral foothold in concepts of logocentrism and subject philosophy? Emmanuel Levinas doubted this in his work and left a provocative philosophy for modern thought (Levinas, 2022). What is decisive, he argues, is the moment of coming into the world – a moment that already carries all ethical answers within it. From the beginning, we find ourselves in the world as exposed – as dependent on one another (Liebsch, 2018). The encounter with others is the immediate challenge of being, which can never be decoded rationally. Guilt and responsibility, being with others, are antecedent qualities of human life.

Levinas left behind a wealth of thoughts that are directed against philosophy's claim to absolute truth and remind us of an eminent relation to the world. Violence is in being itself. Every moral intervention is therefore a risk. In the end, it is not a matter of fixing and determining, but of becoming aware of an unavailable basic situation of suspension. We must confess to this situation without already knowing where this ethics will lead us.

Ethics as First Philosophy promotes the standpoint of the philosophy of the singular. The vulnerability of the other reveals a claim to truth that we can only guess at. This level of the singular must be defended against all the violence that is visible in so many faces.

Under the Sign of Non-violence

What can we hold on to if we agree with these reflections? What room for manoeuvre would be conceivable at all if we assume an ontological doom in which violence plays an unavoidable role? Different categories must be systematically related to each other: anthropologically, man as a violent being stands in a basic situation; historically, his existence in spaces of violence must be considered. Only the ability of language, however, allows further criteria to emerge under the sign of non-violence, including the ability to trust. Finally, time is perhaps the most important dimension that comes close to the longing for peace.

The most difficult exercise remains first of all to comprehend the violence of the human being as such. The psychology of insight into the violent nature of man is fragile. The evil in man is difficult to bear – we only bear the thought by keeping evil away from us. In relation to the inconceivable violence of National Socialist extermination, the mechanics are pertinent: *monstrous violence can only be performed by monsters*; the cruelty of the deeds evokes the image of an *extraordinary, 'inhuman' being*. The image of violence becomes bearable, as it were, when the image of the man of violence is simplified. The Nazi perpetrator is metaphysically exaggerated.

Recent research has worked towards a different image of the human being. This image encompasses harmlessness and routine, sociability and the normality of all human activities. In the context of Holocaust research, not only the ordinariness of evil in the sense of Hannah Arendt has become thematic (Arendt, 1963).

The possibility of killing is also integrated into the scope of modern societies as an 'acceptable' act. This exercise in thought is painful, however, because the abyss of the deeds in Auschwitz cannot be equated with the monstrosity of the perpetrators. Rather, parallels with the modern world of work should be noted. Judging by the semantics, *work in war is* related to *work in factories*. Sources from wiretap transcripts, field post letters and diaries prove that the actors were able to analogise their actions with forms of work: work that was arduous but honourable; work that was invested with conscience, pride and ethos (Lüdtke, 2003; Welzer, 2012, 2005; Browning, 2011; Neitzel/Welzer, 2011).

Different psychological motives have to be taken into account. Contexts and frames of reference are the primary criteria. The social situation of war provides the shift of the frame, even the moral concepts are 'adapted' in this specific situation. By no means is it sufficient to state that people lose or forget their morality and morality in war, rather a shift in references can be seen. Work at the front becomes a compulsory exercise; the social group in which one fights forms its own norms. The social near-world becomes decisive; each member sees himself as he believes he is seen by the group (Welzer, 2012, p. 516).

*

Which image of the human being is generated in war is the one question that gives rise to scepticism. No particular ideological influence is needed to create a specific situation of violence. More important than ideological or political motives is the placement in the social context in the shadow of war. Anthropology must take note here that humans acquire a special attitude in special situations.

Therefore, the inspection of the human being as the essence of violence is not sufficient. One needs diverse criteria of the situation of violence: of space, of times, of signatures.

Historiography puts its finger in the wound of historical situations of violence in which space is the decisive factor. Whenever frames shift and individual safeguards are suspended, an intensification of violent relations becomes apparent. The violence in the 'bloodlands' during the Second World War is one of these (Snyder, 2013), but spaces of total dissolution of boundaries were already created at the beginning of the century, especially during the First World War. In the vastness of Eastern Europe, especially in Ukraine, the short-term absence of state authority enabled a particular dynamics (Baberowski/Metzler, 2012; Schnell, 2012). In the spaces that emerged between the respective warring parties, different actors used their potential for violence. The view into these spaces is naturally disturbing. Both in the situation of the camp (Sofsky, 1993) and in the context of new wars (Münkler, 2002), the cruel face of war is revealed. Humans, the observers conclude, are in principle capable of deeds that speak against the narrative of the process of civilisation.

The decisive question would therefore not be: What can prevent people from committing such acts?

But rather, what criteria must be observed in order to come close to the idea of non-violence and the renunciation of violence. Philosophy and anthropology have the advantage that they can distance themselves from concrete historical situations and engage in abstract thoughts. If special rules of permitted and commanded violence apply in times of war, what principles apply in other, more peaceful times? Where does the violence that prevails in orders of violence 'take refuge'? The logic of enabling and empowerment alone cannot explain these phenomena. Any mechanics that assume an execution of a rule remains undercomplex (Ortmann, 2002).

As a first instance, we can refer to the human capacity of language. It is true that language cannot deal with violence; language is inferior to physical violence in close proximity. But from the distance of abstraction, we can ascribe to language an incomparably greater power of action. This first requires an illusionless consideration of its polemical quality, which it can assume. Beyond that, however, language is the predominant means of offering lasting resistance to violence.

In doing so, a subtle dialectic must be taken into account: for language, in the form of rhetoric, is also a means of violence – but it is indispensable in order to sound out the scope for non-violence.

Language is linked to violence: by virtue of language we can exclude others, disregard them and define them down to an object. The ability to draw others into the circle of violence through language should also be noted. This dazzling power of language has preoccupied philosophy basically since its inception. Language is capable of subtle rhetoric and violent persuasion, of demagogy and manipulation. With the chains of language, allegiance is established. It is the means that completes violence only when physical threat alone is no longer sufficient. If you like, language is the first gateway for enmities. Passions are first heated up by language; word and deed can form a deadly unity. Conversely, silencing is also a subtle form of violence, when we erase others from our collective memory by remaining silent (Liebsch, 2018, Vol. I., p. 392 ff.).

But this by no means exhausts the potential of language in the context of human relations. For language can just as well generate trust, put compassion into terms and, above all, create scope for the renunciation of violence. A form of resistance is present in language that cannot itself be reduced to violence. The philosophical tradition refers to this peaceful motif of language, in different, sometimes controversial variants.

Hannah Arendt's thought seems almost classic in this context. According to this, the capacity for linguistic understanding stands in stark contrast to brute violence (Arendt, 2002). Only the communicative grammar of an argumentative assembly helps against violence. The ethos of the political community is formed through the language with which we encounter others, take them seriously as counterparts, as co-players or even as opponents.

Finally, this refers the reflections to an existential dimension. The described love of war is not the last word and not the last thought. The telos of understanding, the tradition that is, as it were, sacred to modern philosophy, is also an 'igniting' thought in the context of a polemical consideration. What scope is opened up by linguistic understanding is thus the last question to be asked.

Across history, philosophy draws an alternative line of resistance. As indicated, from Heraclitus to twentieth-century phenomenology, an idea was spelt out that in Dasein itself the form of war was inherent. In this Dasein, however, and this takes us beyond the conventional praises of peace, is also contained the resistance of language. The resistance in language thus goes deeper than assumed. The lack of unity is by no means temporary, but permanent.

Dissent cannot be removed like an obstacle, but is at the centre of our linguistic disputes. Every speech is therefore threatened by misunderstanding and failure. It is this insight that allows us to justify the ethos of resistance (Ranciere, 2002; Liebsch, 2003; Lyotard, 2002).

What are the consequences of this worldview for dealing with violence? The political discussions cannot be delved into here without oversimplifying the realities. The philosophical perspective endows an abstract sense of the relationship between the capacity for violence and linguisticity. The ethos of resistance in language is grounded in categories of concern for the Other. Every conflict, every violent confrontation has to do with the violated claims of the Other. Making these claims perceptible, the voices audible and the violations visible are the basis of the idiosyncratic pathos of language. No harmonious unity can be consolidated with it, but at least a claim to resistive speech can be raised (Liebsch, 2018, Vol. I., p. 402 ff.).

One might object that this is a clever play on language: Isn't this merely adding the subtle power of words to physical violence? Is it not a continuation of war by other means? And to what extent is the position of the victim affected by this, when it is now additionally about *speaking against others*?

Everything depends on whether one can keep things in balance. Adversity can be dealt with without existential hostility as long as negatory violence is excluded. Conflict within communities is acceptable and can sometimes be used productively. What must be prevented and what we must recognise in the framework indicated: violence must not become blindly violent.

Modern orders have accordingly created safeguards that enable dissent to be aired.

The difference to past times is philosophically concise: it consists in the establishment of a linguistic field with contradictions that are close to democratic thought.

The position of the existentialist philosophy of the early twentieth century indicated before has become historical at best, if we are to draw a provisional conclusion. For it remained within the walls of a philosophy of the subject that allowed only self-preservation and self-enhancement to apply. This position accompanied de facto violence and inspired the culture of self-aggrandisement. Contemporary thought, on the other hand, has been enabled to remember alterity: this assumes the original alienation of people from the world and the necessary hospitality that is demanded in the face of foreignness that cannot be erased (Ricoeur, 2015).

PART III
Between the Twentieth and Twenty-First Century: The Worldview of Concern

Does the twentieth century lie before our eyes like a book? Is history readable and left to our interpretation? In such talk lies an error in thinking that leads to problematic consequences. The history of violence breaks down into episodes that can be integrated into a whole. The individual events can be framed in a narrative and arranged according to a certain logic. How one thinks together the aspects of colonialism, imperialism and fascism, for example, how one connects the eruption of violence with the disintegration of the great empires – all this can be determined narratively. To these patterns of interpretation, however, we must add a perspective that cannot be reduced to a concise motif. In this sense, the talk of dark places emphasises that the past century has not been opened up in every respect and that the events of violence are still a cause for heightened reflections that may well turn out to be gruelling and agonising.

But what is the point of presenting it in essay form if the insights from a certain point of view are few? The claim of the present discussions goes back to the idea that we live with a world reference in which the past century enters in various ways. In order to stabilise this world reference, a coping strategy is needed in which historical narratives can and should make a contribution. Not by reconstructing the harrowing experiences of violence over and over again, but by linking them as strategies of self-assurance.

Historical constructions fulfil psychic effects, which cannot be disposed of at will, but which produce a specific cultural meaning. The century of violence evokes the psychological reflex of justification and self-protection (hereafter: Straub 1998, p. 138 ff.). The culpable involvement in violence must be cleared up, without finally being able to 'clear the air'. Who was involved in the situation of violence under what circumstances and with what intentions can no longer be meaningfully resolved. Henceforth, it is more a matter of the complex relationships between past and present temporalities. From a phenomenological point of view, it should be considered that our own self is directly entangled with the determinations of the foreign. The idea of entanglement with violence, then as now, in concrete space and in abstract height, near and far, has a special validity.

This results first of all in a rejection of a diagnosis that serves self-aggrandisement, as if we had long since left violence behind. The century of violence is certainly not juxtaposed with a century of non-violence, nor has violence simply continued. Rather, it is a matter of legacies that remain indistinct, of shadows that do not fade. To conclude that only the extreme behaviours help further would be fatal: accusations, self-accusations, humiliations as well as self-aggrandisement do not lead anywhere. The only thing that makes sense from the present point of view is to process what has happened through cultural reorganisation. The past holds horrors that can and must be confronted through a difficult search for traces.

*

In this respect, it is worth asking repeatedly what actually happened in the twentieth century. Obviously, the twentieth century inscribed itself in history in a special way – unlike other epochs before it. Obviously, it left something behind that was left to the interpretations of contemporaries. That a special space of experience was created in the twentieth century is beyond question. But what meanings can be taken from it?

Older historical–philosophical motifs push themselves into the foreground. The Marxist 'Narrative' spoke of a collective subject of the working class that had a special task. It was to fulfil its world-historical mission and take responsibility for human history. As is well known, this history took a different course and the optimism of the philosophy of history was permanently weakened. Nevertheless, the idea remains undeniable that there must be a collective responsibility within the framework of a comprehended history that resembles an overarching context. The search for the standard that unites moral universalism with a subject capable of action thus remains. A metaphysical attribution would answer this question with an objective measure that would apply to all cultures and every individuality, but this answer would be problematic for various reasons. Does an ontological principle prevail in history from which human beings are not 'allowed' to escape? Philosophies that recognise the absolute value of human life operate with these terms. But the search for a supreme authority that ensures the preservation of this historical subject is only properly understood in the form of a reflection. No metaphysical subject can assume this responsibility. Only in the form of a historically centred mediation can the philosophy of history be thought (Zimmermann, 2008).

The thesis of the present reflection states in this respect that historical space is filled with a contradiction that results in an ongoing process of effects. One can no longer go back behind the experiences of the violence suffered, just as one might have forgiven each other after a quarrel. Forgetting, which was an important dimension of dispute resolution in older conflicts, had its own right historiographically. But after the deepest divisiveness, the possibility of peace will remain permanently bound to the claim of remembering (Meier 2010).

This is about memory practice but also about more. For there is a dichotomy in the aforementioned historical space of meaning that must be theoretically disentangled.

On the one hand, there is the desire for meaning and subjectivity in this communicative space: it is directed towards a historical actor who rises above all previous history. The theoretical desire means here: an awareness is assumed for one's own role in the process of history – henceforth, no one other than man himself must take responsibility for man's history. But such a philosophy of history is meanwhile inscribed with doubt. It seems to be a metaphysical construction, with an instance of responsibility that rises above all concrete, bound and fallible existence.

On the other hand, there is the insight into the location-bound nature of all historical beings. Even the moral standard that one thinks one can take from the past is embedded in a moral context of mediation. Accordingly, the moral universe has not proven to be well ordered, but rather a dynamic event with value-setting forces. Human moral self-interpretation is in an open historical process (Zimmermann, 2008, 177–185).

This polar tension reveals the current worldview of concern. It aims at an order in a concrete historical situation with an unquestionable claim. It binds all communication and judgements to the standard of universalisable ethics. And yet it remains referred to a context of mediation in which counter-concepts, asymmetries and forms of contradiction are to be balanced or overcome.

There are thus good reasons to doubt the idea of a *unified substance of responsibility*. *What* is hoped for is a historical subject that rises above all descent or affiliation and creates a common space of meaning in which all subjective aspirations gather. Such a space would be filled, as it were, with a historical responsibility from which man cannot escape.

Such a metaphysical subject is difficult to imagine. What is questionable, however, is the elementary orientation towards a standard that proves to be responsible and historically mediated. It would make sense to construct it with a view to the value of human life and its preservation. It would only be misunderstood as absolute if it were described as the ultimate certainty or objective authority.

The question of when a century began and over what period of time it extended, however, cannot be answered unequivocally. Dates that shape a century extend far beyond their time. Chronology gives the impression of a clarity that cannot be described as objective. It has been said of the nineteenth century that it was a long one and that its significance arose above all from the preceding horizon of events that was stretched open in 1789. At the same time, it extends into the twentieth century to the critical date of 1914, when the world imagined itself on the brink of an abyss. Of the twentieth century, on the other hand, a shorter time span is readily taken as a basis; it begins with the world conflagration of 1914 and ends in the collapse of the old order in 1989. Thus, it becomes at least understandable that the chronology is narrowed by the century deadline and that the counting appears arbitrary. The numerical designation of a century is merely coincidental; it is, on the other hand, the historical contexts of events that are momentous and thus significant.

At the same time, it should be asked what title a century deserves that encompasses a period with a wealth of dramatic events. Titles that signal a profound rupture seem justified: it was a century of extremes and disastrous violence, consequently an age of betrayal. Reinhart Koselleck uses the title of the 'Age of the Total' (Koselleck, 2010, p. 229) – it was a time with symbolic power that reaches into the present. Among other things, the colonial wars of the British in South Africa were total, as were the extermination campaigns of the Germans on the African continent. But the political-military claims of the Americans, the rise of the Japanese or the uprising movements of the Chinese were also total. In East and West, political movements and military escalations could be observed that abruptly illuminated long-term developments. Totality became a characteristic feature in the social, political and military sense (Koselleck, 2010, p. 228–41).

At what point in the history of violence does one stand when placing this totality in the course of history? This question proves to be unavoidable. The twentieth century has not only left traces but has burned itself into memory. It represents a reality that can only be approached by stumbling. However, the highest point of view of social theory is, as shown, understanding.

The many meanings given to the twentieth century illustrate the power of narration. This is also to be demonstrated here. However, a minimum of *historical-philosophical expectations* is brought into play. For it is not simply a story that is told, which could also be told differently. Rather, a conception of the course of time is asserted that is in harmony with the basic human situation. This in no way means a romantic return to cultural, national or patriotic traditions. This would be a gross misunderstanding with far-reaching consequences. The proximity, for example, that Martin Heidegger's thinking had to ideas such as fate is pertinent; it famously led to a diffuse inability to distance oneself from violent politics (Farias 1989).

What is at stake here, however, is a philosophy of history that can be traced back to nothing other than the particular sense in the light of historical experience. The possibility of orienting oneself in the stories of the past is available for individual sociocultural entities as well as for larger state entities. Can it likewise be reconstructed in a horizon that goes beyond the particular?

The context spans the level of individual biographies to a collective whole. In the course of their lives, individuals acquire the ability to relate past and present to each other through narrative competences. In the best case, this leads to a historical consciousness that represents history as *my history*. This is integrated into a supporting world reference.

The bringing together of all these conceivable narrative achievements into an overarching horizon constitutes the difficulty from a methodological point of view. The history of humankind is difficult to tell, and if it is attempted, a subject must be assumed that simply resembles a phantasm. However, it is not a matter of conjuring up a unity that is simply not available, but rather of meaningfully integrating ideas about the course of time.

The peculiar sense we can assume for the twentieth century is multilayered. It is constructed retrospectively and at the same time it is received. In the moment of visualising the past, it becomes clear that human beings have their own culture and history. The past is not only a burden that one cannot get rid of but also a form of interpretation that is appropriated in a formative way (Rüsen 2020).

If one wants to narrate the twentieth century in a meaningful way, one has to consider the division into phases of experience, interpretation, orientation and motivation.

Experiences are external circumstances that have to be interpreted as events. If they can be brought into a narrative context, they can be integrated favourably into the cultural time frame.

Does this also apply to those events that radically elude the conventional creation of meaning? Which leave the human being peculiarly naked, deprive him of all motivation and give rise to a nothingness? This interpretation, made with the immeasurable violence of the twentieth century in mind – as a definitive rupture in history – forces reflection to walk a tightrope. This is precisely why not only historicising elements but also depth-psychological aspects are used in the present case. The historical meaning we take from the many violent moments is only fully grasped with the help of psychoanalytical criteria. The individual episodes touch on the depths of human experience, which do not appear definitively as rational and ordered. They require a sense of difference, the abysmal and inexplicable, the longing for death as well as all the unconscious forces that participate in the story. It is this ambivalence between formal interpretations, historical identity and the unfathomable depths of the soul that gives rise to the idea of the 'history'.

*

What is the space of meaning of the twentieth century? Posed in this way, the question seems unavoidable, however much one refuses easy answers. Everything depends on how one approaches the century and to what extent a distance is created to the events – without short-sighted conclusions. Everything depends – from the present point of view, which is in the hermeneutic tradition – on the attempt to *read correctly*. One could make it easy for oneself and capture the destruction and devastation in images and give them a moral language. Then wounds would become visible, historical wounds that would heal with time. In this case, a topography of violence unfolds before the eyes of those born later, which would be in a fatal continuity. Have spaces of violence not 'always' been a concomitant of human history? Have disastrous landscapes not 'always' clouded the view of history, because all the legacies in the earth bear witness to human furore and destruction? And in this respect, would one not be referred to a worldview of concern that 'finally' puts an end to such violence?

This interpretation, however, would be problematic because it would have fought the violence it addresses with the wrong means and thus literally understood 'nothing'. The worldview of concern that emerges from the twentieth century's space of meaning is relegated to a specific form of reading the world (Blumenberg, 1975; Liebsch, 2016).

This readability of the world is a claim that no philosophy can fully meet. Nor can the twentieth century be put into a readable form that suggests a lesson in history. Rather, it seems that the past century is an antinomy. Violence and meaning are in sharp contradiction and do not add up to a manageable meaning. But in this motif, too, one will recognise a productive reading.

What is the relationship between the event of violence and a respective meaning? The meaning attributed to the thing is by no means harmless, for it is not itself free of violence. Something is transferred into a rational discourse, rationalised, summarised and generalised. A historical determination, a salvation-historical meaning or a juridical measurement is laid over the singular experience like a shadow (Kapust, 2014, 51–74). The linking of violence with a general meaning is something completely ordinary, but what is forgotten is that the singularity of the violence suffered is thereby broken through. In a sense, it loses its claim to uniqueness, but is given to higher purposes.

This philosophical problematic, which relates to the relationship between the singular, unique and particular and the general, has been described at length. But the essence of the insight still remains as a memorable claim: that it is important not to sacrifice the singularity of sacrifices to a purpose (be it ever so sacred and significant). The mechanics of power are only broken when the connection back to the subject and the moment of violence suffered is found (Delhom, 2014).

If we find an initial orientation in these sentences, the task still remains: to ask what meaning we ascribe to the previous century and whether it cannot prove to be a readable and understandable one. The caveat that attribution is always also a bit violent must be kept in mind.

There are several criteria of meaning that allow us to interpret the space of meaning of the twentieth century. The first criterion is the aforementioned tension between the singularity of the victims and the violence of meaning. In connection with this, the question arises as to what images and what language we can transfer the past into in order to make it comprehensible.

The past century certainly cannot be captured in any of the familiar images that tell of *disastrous topographies* or of *Bloodlands* and thus contribute to a diffuse aesthetic of horror (Blanchot, 2005; Snyder, 2013). At the very least, this perspective is also exhausted when one realises that nature settles over every devastated landscape and that the signatures of violence as visible signs fade with time. Rather, the question is how to transfer the images of disaster into the present and present them to the following generations. So it remains with the original task that the century is read and understood, interpreted and must be 'deciphered'. The following reflections are under the sign of this hermeneutic motif. They show a certain parallelism to the movement of thought that sees itself as a philosophy of 'despite everything' (Didi-Huberman 2007). Images are to be shown, although they conceal so much; meaning is to be asked for 'despite everything', even if it is never free of violence. Despite *everything* means unfolding the contradictions mentioned, entirely in the understanding of critical theory.

Chapter Eight

THE VALORATIVE SPACE IN TIMES OF WAR

In these times: the sentence is difficult to digest. It refers to the presence of wars that are disturbing in their presence and irritating in their form. In February 2022, war moved onto the agenda of the international order; unlike other wars, Russia's attack on Ukrainian territory seemed to mark a turning point of which no one could say what options it opened up and in what direction it would point at all.

The present reflections must now distance themselves from current and time-bound events, if only because the overview of events cannot be assumed. The flood of publications and commentaries alone does not help to do justice to the dynamics of events, and only when this war, like many others before it, has been lost in the depths of history will it be possible to make more substantial statements.

Nevertheless, the fact that war enters the consciousness with all sharpness cannot be ignored. There is a need to deal with the phenomenon of war without being able to advance or influence the course of history. The reflections are thus again comparable to the flight of the eagle; they survey a wide field of violence and probe the violent events from a distance. The proximity to war, that is what affected people in contested zones have to endure, cannot trivially be produced; it cannot even be imagined or virtually generated.

The intrusion of violence into the present is remarkable in several respects. It is accompanied by a feeling of overwhelming and suddenness, as if a previously perfect world had been turned upside down and as if one had fallen back into the past. These are, however, 'feelings' that are understandable and plausible with increasing proximity. In view of this, is it necessary to emphasise that this war, too, must be placed in the context of the known history of war, and that the face of war is familiar in so many regions? Of course, this war is disturbing in the European consciousness – and this is probably also true when remembering the violence that was and is an equally oppressive historical fact in Southeastern Europe, in Bosnia, Kosovo, Georgia or Chechnya.

This war is as disturbing as wars are by their nature; there is no need for self-incrimination and accusations in this respect.

The basic idea that is to be unfolded in the following touches on precisely this contradiction at the highest level. The contradiction starts with the subject, who cannot escape the dilemma through any kind of escape from the category. 'We' live in a valorative space – a space that is 'now' filled with war, with images, feelings and with the horror that is only produced by wars. One must first consider the many levels that are included and excluded with this subjective sentence: levels of immediate concern of the victims, the fugitives, the dead and the injured.

Below that, the level of the combatants and war actors, mostly shown in casualty lists. Furthermore, the unspeakable misery, the suffering, for which no commentary can apply. It is only on the further levels that other aspects can and must come up: the presumably finite empathy of a host society as well as the conflicts within the community of states, squeezed between moral provisions and factual constraints. Finally, morality, which turns out to be both the morality of help and the unbroken morality of those fighting.

At the heart of the debate is the idea that the phenomenon of war is perceived in a particular space and can lead to shifts in boundaries in the long run. These shifts have long since taken on a concrete form: not only are categories being used again that have long been avoided: defense capability, resistance capability, defence readiness. Concrete measures are also being taken to be able to cope with violence in future situations, also to indicate a discrete willingness to use violence. These developments, which would have to be defined, quantified and assessed in more detail, are representative of contemporary historical revaluations, which are assumed here from the point of view of a Western European observer. But they also have general aspects of great significance.

Violence is up for debate in a specific space for which the philosophy of our time had other labels ready. War in the valorative, value-bound space of modernity is a dissonant relationship in every respect. Deciphering this relationship – between the human phenomenon of war and the normative space of the present – is the goal of the following discussion.

Modernity and Violence

Modern ways of life have an ambivalent relationship to violence. The existence of war puts pressure on modern society, because one has to establish a reference to a reality that contradicts the self-perception of modern society. The mistake that could be made at this point lies in the gross simplification. In such images, violence approaches a peace-loving society from the outside; in the life form of war, the affirmation of violence dominates, while the modern life form flees from violence, denies or conceals it. Such and similar insinuations impede a clear view of the conditions that deserve a more detailed sociological and philosophical inspection. This concerns not least the suspicion that the long period of non-violence of the 'West' is now over, and that after a period of renunciation of violence, a dramatic change in values will emerge – a change in values that now points in the direction of armament, militarism and bellicism.

To what extent such speculations will prove true remains to be seen. From a socio-theoretical perspective, the first question is the meaning of the renunciation of violence, its existential and cultural sources. In no way is it to be assumed that the 'West' is more peace-loving, even pacifist, in comparison to other cultures. Rather, things have to be looked at on different levels; the hope of being able to lead a life as far as possible without violence leads to existential–philosophical, sociological and political arguments. From an existentialist point of view, there is an indissoluble tension between violence and the claim to non-violence; sociologically, Western societies have practised forms of trust that distances them from violence. Finally, from a political perspective, there are numerous reasons to distance oneself from the worldview of heroism; in post-heroic times, violence is avoided or perhaps rather obscured. Whether violence can thus be mastered and whether one advances into the bright areas of enlightenment and humanity are not yet said.

First, it is advisable to admit a fundamental philosophical view of things. Human life forms are never completely free of violence; rather, violence is always already there; entering into human life also means entering a world of fragility, finiteness, suffering and negativity. This, of course, does not make a statement about the human being: the human being is not a being of violence, but a being that finds itself in a basic worldly situation – and makes sure of these determinations in cultural forms (Rentsch, 1999, 2000).

Philosophical thinking begins with introspection: to what extent can violence be recognised as part of life? To what extent is the moral outlawing of violence possible in the midst of this basic situation? In this context, phenomenology speaks rather of the determination of the negative, which is expressed in specific relations of violence. Thus, before a more detailed analysis of political violence, the possibility of a common world must be discussed. To enter into life is first to familiarise oneself with the basic features of a primary world. This primary world can be determined in practical sensory concepts; violence begins at the point where this precondition is disregarded – when a form of life is technocratically abridged or when lifeworld figures are reified; of course also when power tips over into powerlessness and suffering arises in the face of political relations of violence. In this respect, non-violence is a claim from the centre of a situation in which the possibility of evil, the reality of transgression and the disregard for the other are always already present. Only the consistent and systematic blinding of essential aspects of the totality of life then leads directly to a manifest situation of violence (Rentsch, 1999; p. 101 ff; p. 129 ff.).

Can we, however, accept the claim that modern society has found a distance to violence that leads to repression in times of war? At the very least, we must take into account that there are good reasons for the option of renouncing violence, which results from the 'essence' of modernity itself. Modern society certainly did not come into being without violence; the modern state in particular is founded on a special capacity for violence.

But practices of trust have emerged that have much to do with the self-image of modernity. We live in times of trust; in our daily dealings with each other, people are prepared to settle conflicts in a civil manner. The neighbour is not my enemy in every respect or even a threat. Practices of trust are exercised in the daily proximity of worldly actions that subconsciously create a sense of security. This trust is not trust in the neighbour (we know too little about him after all), but a trust in the 'always-on' of the modern way of life (Reemtsma, 2008).

Many developments go into this constellation: already in the first cities of man, violence was banished to the outside; violence on the inside was frowned upon or was transferred into cultural and religious rituals. The interest in cultural and material exchange is worth mentioning, as is the ability to communicate through language. These are significant aspects that lead to a feeling of self-evidence in the modern age. However, events are felt all the more harshly when violence intrudes into life or when war has to be realised as a real fact. The skin of civilisation then proves to be extremely thin; this violence, we think, does not belong to us, it originates from other times. Traumatised and overwhelmed by our own vulnerability, we perceive the violence as something that should not be.

Assaults on ourselves, our bodies, the bodies of others or on representations are met with a greater horror. In the ideal of civilisation there is a certain vulnerability, a disposition to trauma, which could be appreciated as an achievement, but also called a failure.

However, it is to be asked whether this characteristic of modernity must expose itself to the reproach: Do we as modern people completely avoid violence? As is well known, this hidden accusation is openly made in times of manifest violence. The pacifist quickly becomes a negative figure: not only does he shy away from violence, he is supposedly also unwilling to help his neighbour in need. He looks the other way, takes refuge in highly moral principles and slips into the role of the 'bystander'.

This accusation can be countered with more politologically precise analyses (without directly assessing the legitimacy of interventions in favour of third parties). The connection between modernity and trust is overlaid by a change in values that is tantamount to an ideal self-image. According to this, we are 'actually' in a period of the post-heroic (Münkler, 1999, 2006).

The renunciation of violence, basic trust and the 'post-heroic' are closely related. Trust means in principle: a trust in the whole. This whole 'works' because it confirms stable patterns of expectation. Social relations are legalised, for which the state's monopoly on the use of force acts as a guarantor. The disarming of certain groups is the responsibility of the forces with the corresponding licences. Because of this constellation, which is understood at an early age, we can trust each other – in a non-technical sense. Trust in the monopoly on the use of force ensures trust in one's neighbour.

In modern societies, therefore, there is no longer any room for the hero. The tightly woven network of trust relationships and expectations makes a specific social type who sacrifices himself for the whole through an outstanding deed superfluous.

Heroism is a multilayered concept. In the modern age, it seems to be common in everyday life alone; heroes are under special pressure, and they perform work that is perhaps bound to a particular professional ethic. The older concept of heroism, on the other hand, has become obsolete insofar as it was associated with the phenomenon of war.

Heroism was (and is) an attribution in bellicose cultures, an attribution that went hand in hand with victorious struggle and, above all, with the willingness to go to the extreme. The hero in a heroic community is willing to give himself with everything he possesses for the sake of the whole. He is prepared to sacrifice by transforming his own death into a symbolic victory. However, the meaningful-symbolic death had to be linked to an effective narrative. Heroic communities depend on 'narrative doublings'

(Münkler, 2006, p. 742). The hero and the heroic deed must be reported if this is to contribute to the cohesion of the community.

In contrast, we have good reasons to recognise social-moral progress in the post-heroic constellation. Heroic stories are written in the vicinity of civilisation, beyond violence. We have, one may generalise, lost sight and hearing of heroic stories because for the longest time they were understood as the religion of war. Notions of honour and sacrifice belonged to eras that produced the constant 'frenzy of strength and confidence in victory' (Münkler, 2006, p. 749). They were also societies that demanded the use of all forces to the point of self-sacrifice in order to serve the survival of the nation. This bellicose willingness to sacrifice was known to have special conjunctures; in the age of the first mass wars, in the Napoleonic Wars and in the First World War, this idea had contributed to the escalation of violence.

Today, the glorification of the victim has long been historicised; it originates from dark times. In fascism, as is well known, there was another attempt to instrumentalise the willingness to sacrifice and suffer. At present, however, urbanisation and technological advances, the development of weapons systems and the modern attitude to life have contributed to an erosion of the heroic. In the post-heroic situation, there is no need for the figure of the martial victim and it seems that the ideology of the heroic has passed its peak (Howard, 2001; Keegan, 1978; Münkler, 2006, pp. 310–38).

Understanding the Violence

It is easy to see that the renunciation of violence is fed by various historical sources. Societies that have developed spheres of trust do not live in a 'bubble' far removed from reality.

Rather, they are endowed with a sensitivity to all forms of martial violence. This constellation leads to moral self-descriptions of pacifism that can lead to misjudgements in certain situations. Cooperation and economic relations are cultivated and form the *ultima ratio of* all politics; the thought possibility of war is systematically avoided.

The talk of post-heroic societies, however, leads to simplification: as if these societies had ever managed without violence. However, an alternative approach is necessary in order to understand violence in all respects. Not only the renunciation of violence for reasons of decadence (as the latent accusation in Bohrer, 2007) must be addressed, but also the diversity of forms of violence, which also exists as a possibility in democratic societies. Various levels of observation are to be distinguished; in the overall view, they result in a broad spectrum that helps to understand the presence of violence. The first approach goes back to demography; the second discusses a specific cultural theory. Finally, the theory of democracy must also be question. All perspectives vary the question of the connection between specific orders and the tendency towards violence.

The conditions under which violence arises are self-evidently complex. They are closely linked to ideologies and patterns of legitimation that recognise violence in a specific resonance space. Behind these mechanisms, however, lie fundamental developments that some observers believe deserve greater attention (hereafter: Heinsohn, 2003; Heinsohn, 2007). Comparative genocide research lays the cards of knowledge on the table here: not learning processes, not even political ideologies are decisive in the context of violent events, but demographic factors first. The connection between the age structure and the intensity of violence is here translated into a ruthless diagnosis. How many young men remain in a given society without recognition as second- and third-born? How many young men are recruited for warlike purposes in these cultures, while sufficient career options are available in other welfare regions?

This form of cultural comparison draws semantically uncomfortable lines of enmity: here would be the 'shrinking West', there the observers would recognise an 'ascendant Islam' (Heinsohn, 2007, p. 771).

Numbers (supposedly) don't lie, empirical social research has to operate with uncomfortable truths in this respect. This reality states that the intensity of violence, war and even genocide increases when a mass of young men with no prospect of prestige 'explodes'. The so-called youth bulge claims that the proportion of mainly male youths is the decisive variable of violence. These second- and third-born, the argument goes, are without prospects for prestige or recognition in a culture and are seducible to the practice of war. However, it is not individual psychological categories that are being discussed here, but demographic ones alone. The figures in long-term observations lend these seemingly polemical statements a seriousness that leads to sceptical assessments (Urdal, 2006; Lam, 2014).

Let us draw a first conclusion. Violence arises with the greatest intensity when there is a disproportionate surplus of young men who do not find a proper place in a social order. Countries that follow the principle of primogeniture thus form a supposedly greater potential for conflict. Taking these considerations further, one gets into the contested zones of cultural comparison. This field is contested and not free of resentment. It is all the more important to emphasise that it is by no means a matter of establishing a specific aggressiveness in, for example, traditional or religiously influenced societies. A 'global' cultural theory recognises both universal patterns and certain distinguishing features (Mühlmann, 2011).

The cultural theoretical view recognises in principle in every culture a necessary potential of aggressiveness and the endeavour to assert oneself successfully in an environment.

Cultures are therefore aggressive in various ways. They wage ideological wars or economic wars, they thus follow different patterns of self-organisation.

But how far should these reflections be taken? Especially when it is a matter of factually relating the reality of a war not only to cultural factors, but applying the yardstick of the illegitimacy of violence alone? The decisive questions must therefore be answered last: not at the height of cultural theory, but in the valorative Ram of the present, which is of equally great importance.

Philosophy of History in the Face of Violence

What possibilities are there at all in the midst of our present to deal with forms of violence that cause so much suffering and at the same time feelings of powerlessness? What contribution, one should further ask, can democracies make in the field of violence? These questions lead directly to the unfinished chapters of the philosophy of history.

All hope is directed towards democracy. After all, this form of government is known to be the first instance that can ensure sustainable and reliable peace.

Accordingly, in terms of the philosophy of history, we are referred to a state that promotes the rationality of peace and links this to an order oriented towards the common good.

As is well known, it was none other than Immanuel Kant who recognised the possibility of lasting peace between states. A majority of citizens ideally orient their behaviour towards the greatest possible benefit in a republic. Interest in peace grows because this state is highly consensual: the destruction of cities and structures, the extent of suffering and the long-term costs – all these make war a great evil in a republican order (Kant, 2008).

For over 200 years, there has been a well-founded hope in the merits of democracy. There is a suspicion that civilising forces are unfolding between modern democracies that promote positive orders of peace. Such a triangle of peace is formed by the interplay of democracies, international organisations and economic relations (Russet/Oneal, 2001). The logic behind this in turn goes back to the insight of Kant, who was committed to maximising interests.

People live in peace-loving and peace-making orders because they have an interest in maintaining this very order – this story, however, is too beautiful to simply tell it again and again. The critical questions must not be left out: the interest in peace is already contradicted by the history of violence and war itself. Time and again war has been a guest in international relations, time and again war has been resorted to as a means. It is necessary to ask the right questions: democracies definitely wage fewer wars among themselves, but in mixed groups of states, democratic states are also capable of violence (Brock, 2006). Renouncing violence is not the answer to the question of violence in every case; at the very least, it requires a detailed discussion of the inherent logic of military interventions.

These questions lead into the past and the present without being able to merge the two perspectives. In the past, among other things, the dominant discourses on failing states and humanitarian interventions; in the present, questions of the defensibility of democratic orders are up for debate.

Which of these discourses can provide the helpful categories for the present is the question. At the level of real politics, a variety of organisations must be taken into account that lead to the internationalisation of governance. Denationalisation alone, however, cannot explain the order of the present; the international order is still considered 'under-institutionalised' (Habermas, 1999).

Modern democracies find themselves in a dilemma that manifests itself in various scenarios. In the worst case, the subjugation of individual states to international regulations leads to the endangerment of democracy or to the endangerment of the principle of democracy (Maus, 1999). In addition, a contradiction can be observed between legal self-binding and the preservation of autonomy, which gives rise to very different forms of politics. Either one seals oneself off from other states and refrains from any intervention, or one intervenes by force without worrying about the corresponding legitimisation. It seems to be the free play of forces in a hegemonic space. In this space legalisations, international organisations and self-binding of states become possible. At the same time, however, there is a political logic that observers call political irrationality (E. Krippendorff).

Recent history contains various episodes that cannot be imputed to any overall rationality: in 1991, a coalition of states intervened in Iraq in favour of a minority; in 1992, there was the failed UN intervention in Somalia; in Kosovo and Bosnia, there were breaches of law in 1999 as a result of atrocities that remain controversial (Merkel, 2000). Finally, the third Gulf War of 2003, headlined as the War on Terror, also demonstrated the difficulty of a coherent historiography of war. The return of the 'just war' to the agenda of international politics revealed not least how far modern orders have moved away from their goals. The prohibition of the use of force, the supreme principle in the legal space of the United Nations, is always undermined when self-interest prevails or a short-sighted morality is brought into play. The world of states follows its own preferences and it writes its own rules, as much as the observing global intelligentsia opposes these developments.

Recent events in February 2022 seem to confirm the dark forebodings of some contemporaries. The 'great regression', which began in a puzzling departure from liberal principles and democratic values, is now taking on a terrible momentum. Russia's invasion of Ukrainian territory seems to be plunging the world into a dark past. This war took its more frightening form when elderly Ukrainian refugees faced a situation they had already endured in their own childhood: destroyed houses and the violence of marauding troops, the misery in the barracks in which one has to endure or perish. For these people, history appears as an eternal return of violence.

In this respect, what remains of the historical-philosophical expectations directed at democracy, what remains of the achievements of civilisation? Does the history of the taming of violence end in a scenario of perpetual war, of which no one can say where it will lead?

There is no lack of political and socio-ethical interventions that oppose the dynamics of war. In this sense, the present reflection does not offer a substantial contribution, but is to be understood as an observation in the philosophy of history. However, as we will show in the end, the contradictions of the theory do correspond to current social contradictions.

One could claim, with a somewhat malicious undertone, that there is a flight and evasion from violence in both the political world and the intellectual sphere, the costs of which we are currently feeling. However, the mere enlightenment of these complex facts does not guarantee a better view; it merely confronts the crucial existential facts.

The accusation against social theory is that sociology, or social science perspectives, has never learned to see the existence of violence. Sociologies reflect categories in which violence as a phenomenon has been integrated into the mechanics of socialisation: Niklas Luhmann discusses acting under uncertainty in double contingency; Michel Foucault writes about the subtle strategies of power; Jürgen Habermas brings the logic of communicative action into view. In each case, violence is only subcutaneously in play or it is pushed completely into the background, as a latent threat, as something that is not thought through to the end and is only brought into play in exceptional cases. One can describe these preferences of sociologists as silence, which has many reasons and is by no means to be defamed as an escape from reality. But one can also go the decisive step further and dare to try to recognise violence as a social and communicative action. Violence as social action then becomes part of the 'coping strategy' of modernity, for which one needs the right theoretical means.

However, the real problem does not arise in an isolated space of theory production. Violence is indeed treated as a serious problem beyond the 'classics'. Violence appears as a constituent of anthropology (Sofsky, 1996), in the form of agency (Kapust, 2014) or, on the other hand, as violence suffered (Delhom, 2014). Violence can certainly be retold, at least partially recreated and reconstructed as a re-enactment of an event.

It is the circumstances before, during and after violence that cause difficulties. For if we accept the existence of violence and recognise its cruel effects, this says nothing about the conceivable forms of counter-violence. The merit of theory is to avoid hasty conclusions with good reasons and to refuse to make precise statements. The disadvantage of the theory is obvious: just thinking about war never ended any war, and trivially, you cannot put out a fire with ink.

Much is gained, however, by bringing theory as close as possible to reality. This reality forces us to also assume the existence of an unjust enemy from which a real danger emanates – danger in the form of a failing state and in the shape of rule that is hostile to law. In a space free of domination, the law binding all parties disappears. The quality of the state dwindles and makes way for a free, anarchic play of forces in which the warlord's capacity for violence prevails (Münkler, 2006).

The current developments of the year 2022 remind us of the other, seemingly suppressed possibility: the unjust enemy. This one shifts the lines of the republican order and enters a path hostile to the right. The question of how to bring the unjust enemy back into the existing legal order is philosophically incisive (Lutz-Bachmann, 1999). It leads into a thicket of trade-offs that reveal various alternatives of action, none of which remains free of danger. The difficulty, however, lies primarily in the perception of the figure of the enemy itself; it is a figure of which one does not want to know anything, from which one turns away. We cannot know anything about the enemy because he points us to the dark sides of human nature. He stands at odds with the basic assumptions of the philosophy of law and leads an accidental shadowy existence (Müller, 2006, p. 237).

In a realm where law is systematically established and citizens are reduced only to rational interests, the violence of the enemy must sooner or later disappear. Its existence touches on deep layers of the psyche that deny evil as the external.

What remains to be said, however, if one is prepared to understand the unjust enemy as a necessity of thought? This means inserting the category of enmity into the framework of liberal theory. This is not about specific images of the enemy that fall into line with the violence of attribution (Behnke, 2005). Rather, it is about the difficulty of appropriate reflection that directly relates to the repressed sides of human violent enmity. These sides can be described as dark areas for which a 'more' theoretical attention is to be demanded.

One can certainly claim that social theory has perceived too little of these aspects of the political. The conventional reading of the future referred to the probability of large-scale wars and the dissolution of regular warlike violence, that is, to the change of form of military logic.

The wars of the present would take place in the peripheries, in the zones beyond the state. For the longest time, they have been described as new wars (Kaldor, 2000; Münkler, 2002). War, according to the subterranean reading, is a problem of the others. It takes place in the geographies of vulnerability and receives little attention from a world public that has long since become accustomed to the permanence of violence.

The history of violence can be meaningfully told in this way, but it nevertheless requires an important addition. The existence of an enemy, in whatever form, goes hand in hand with the progressive ideological prohibition of enmity in modern times. This problem leads into the depths of that historical culture that we generally ascribe to Western civilisation. In this cultural context, enmity has been shifted below a threshold of articulability. Accordingly, modern culture saw itself as a haven of the civil: since the Enlightenment, the process of taming man has been advancing (Hölscher, 2003). In an eschatological perspective, the path leads to the ultimate reconciliation of man with himself – the way there is marked by the establishment of 'human parks' (Sloterdijk, 2000).

In another interpretation, however, enmity has never been completely eradicated from the social; real enmity has rather been shifted into a semantic underground. Enmity has not diminished, but has become more complex in an increasingly complex world. The category has many faces, but since the interventions of Carl Schmitt (Schmitt, 1942, 1950) we know that the radicalisation of enmities leads to an intensification of violence. Enemies of humanity need radical means to be fought. In the worst case, one no longer needs legal legitimacy, but only a moral conviction. In the horizon of historical enmity, this development is highly alarming: one thus becomes accustomed to a violence that simply strikes and does not care about the adequacy of the means. Enmities between states and groups have thus migrated into a darkness of inarticulateness (Hölscher, 2003, p. 256).

In this phenomenon there seems to be an occasion for learning from history: as a motive for a deeper understanding of political enmity, its function and handling. The dark spots of history would thus be illuminated less in the horizon of a theological reconciliation, but rather in a psychological framework. They lead us to basic anthropological questions that could best be clarified with the thought forms of depth psychology.

Chapter Nine

WHAT DOES 'LEARNING FROM HISTORY' MEAN? ON THE IMPLICIT PEDAGOGY OF HISTORY

Introduction

Of the many statements that can be made about modernity, Charles Taylor's idea stands out: that we live in a normative, value-bound space (Taylor, 1994). Life is, in the simplest terms, not mere physical behaviour, but qualified, location- and culture-mediated life. This very general statement is remarkable because it expresses a sense that in times of war and in the face of violence we have to face the value-bound dimensions. The history and present of war force us to come to an understanding with others about what still sounds very vague and indeterminate here as norm or value.

War has always been a reality in the midst of our everyday lives; some wars, however, receive special attention for obvious reasons, some forms of violence are disturbing and make us think. War is always not only the business of politicians and strategists, but also the subject and occasion for intense discourse. One step further, war is also an object of learning, of course as a 'subject', as educational content to be taught. But in an overarching sense, war as a historical phenomenon is even an occasion for implicit pedagogy. This is true even for contemporary wars, whose effects and scope no one can estimate.

Based on the idea that there is an implicit pedagogy of history and that this pedagogy is particularly directed towards the course of wars, the following reflections should be understood as follows. The central motif goes back to a philosophical figure of thought: How is human life, and more precisely its value, to be judged? The question aims at the way we perceive normative and empirical phenomena and how they find their way into our moral grammar. It is by no means trivial and self-evident.

This basic idea can be unfolded in simple sentences with lifeworld seriousness. People suffer from war. The sentence is seemingly trivial; it claims no originality. It could refer to the past, to a situation of the Thirty Years' War perhaps, or to a war of the present. Its ethical quality can be seen in a linguistic-theoretical perspective.

At first glance, we seem to be able to extract a moral statement from the facts. The cruel facticity of life in war suggests certain insights that we can 'acquire' in a cursory or complex analysis. Two worlds, in other words, are distinguished by our consciousness: a factual world, hard, inexorable, closely bracketed with our experience. And a world of moral propositions, in which ideals are far above reality. In the difference this distinction becomes concise; with reference to the aforementioned proposition, we can tie in further propositions: the facticity of war thus entails reflections on war. People who suffer from war should consequently receive help and the war should be ended if possible. These propositions would thus be the responsibility of ethical, moral–philosophical or utilitarian theories.

A challenge to thinking arises when we remain sceptical of this discriminating thinking and adopt a linguistic critical position that resists artificial separation. Does our world truly break down into being and ought? Do we necessarily have to separate 'values' from 'facts' in order to do justice to the reality of the human situation?

The alternative in thinking is as unusual as it is consistent. In the perspective of an inter-existential pragmatics, the talk of values turns out to be artificial; what we experience and know as the human world is characterised by an unbreakable wholeness. Human praxis, the first and last point of view of human world orientation, shows itself in the apriority of human forms of fulfilment (Rentsch, 1999, p. 192). The moral propositions with which we communicate do not go back to the individual worldviews of isolated subjects, but to the basic features of life that is always already common. In this holistic world, indivisible situations of guilt and powerlessness, indefensibility and blame open up. This orientation makes the dichotomy of facts and values seem invalid and artificial. In other words, we are never in a pure space of facts, nor in a sphere of higher moral insights. The orientation towards meaning in our life practice allows us to perceive forms of meaning and to carry out designs of meaning (Ibid., p. 196).

The value of this insight can first be seen in a philosophical analysis. In the context of the so-called "dianoia" (philosophical), an anthropological universalism can be justified. However, we will not stop at this point of a philosophical argument; rather, we will show that the position shown can be mediated with an implicit pedagogy of history. It is particularly in the context of the experience of war that the intrinsic value of this philosophical analysis becomes apparent. It leads us, as we shall see, to the categories of narrativity and cultural self-assurance.

But first to the status of dianoia in philosophical thought. Dianoia here means the interlocking of being and ought in the basic human situation. These insights go back to phenomenology and the philosophy of language; they refer to the simple fact that we do not receive our moral propositions from anyone outside and that only we ourselves are the subjects of our interpretations.

As self-evident as these considerations sound, they must be distinguished from a purely 'theoretical' starting point. The starting point is rather the immediate, non-delegable world reference of the human being. We stand directly in whole life situations and experience the world as practice, which we cannot cede to any formal semantics or to any other instance. The pragmatic existential situatedness is the human lifeworld that lies ahead of all theories and all instrumental procedures (Rentsch, 1999, p. 62). Because of this, we are not the 'executive recipients' of a prescription or the 'executors' of a theoretical will. Rather, all moral aspects of our lives are enacted and determined in a primary world. Consequently, a proposition that refers to the experience of war, to a suffering in the face of violent conditions, is immediately insightful and not 'applicable' to a 'case'.

In other words, we immediately understand what the speech about people in situations means, even if we do not know any closer contexts. In sentences like: This is human! or: This seems inhuman to me! we experience an emphatic basic understanding of a world reference in the midst of a humane situation.

This philosophical position is based on the foundations of a humane relation to the world and thus cannot be meaningfully translated into recipes for a better life. It has a philosophical- hermeneutical intrinsic value; but in relation to the moral grammar of common life, there are certainly practical insights to be mentioned here. For example, a predicative sentence denotes a factual insight, but implicitly it also determines a normative direction, a normative statement. *Dianoia* – the insight here does not mean the inferential reflection of a purely factual given, but the inseparable bracketing of a normative fact in the realm of facticity.

Accordingly, the world never breaks down into facts here and values there; rather, dianoetic judgements are implicit normative determinations. The aforementioned sentence at the beginning, that people suffer from war, is exemplary of this. It states what is the case (there 'is' human suffering) and it is at the same time normative – that is, morally substantial, meaningful, lifeworld related ('this suffering should not be'). It is not a sentence about a reality that only becomes moral in the horizon of an ideal world, but a practical insight about our existential and social identity.

What are these philosophical thoughts aiming at? It will be shown that we can relate this complex hermeneutic issue to pedagogical and historical contexts. The idea that people can learn from historical experiences – 'Historia Magistra vitae' – is unfolded here in an interdisciplinary constellation. The basic motif is comprehensible and understandable for everyone. The presence of violence in the form of contemporary wars is not only surprising for some observers (and, of course, shocking), it also offers an occasion for self-reflection on the anthropology of violence.

Do we understand the human being as a being who is capable of violence, but also as a being who is capable of insight and behavioural change? Then the obvious question would be what contribution can psychology, pedagogy and history make if they, to a certain extent, dedicate themselves to this task together. The task is not to show that twenty-first-century man has finally tamed violence (Pinker, 2011) or that violence falls at one with the end of history (Fukuyama, 1989, 1992). Nor does it aim at a ready-made moral theoretical concept that justifies the legitimacy of wars or military interventions (Hinsch/Janssen, 2006). The task is rather to be found in the field of hermeneutics, starting from the fact of the irrefutable normative determinations of our basic situation. The appropriate question is thus: How can we translate the fact of human violence and specifically the facticity of wars into a psychologically and historically informed pedagogy? Talk of an implicit pedagogy of history draws attention to a particular methodology that entails certain difficulties, as we shall see below.

Philosophy of History after the Illusion of Feasibility

In the context of the history of violence, we encounter events whose representation, perception and management are immensely challenging, if not overwhelming. Various things can be mentioned here, which in interaction make access difficult: some episodes of history are far away from us, they remain – despite all serious historical research – foreign and inaccessible to us. Other 'episodes', if we think of the totalitarian violence of the last century, are disturbing and overwhelming. Here too, access is difficult, at least access that goes beyond the mere reproduction of texts and formal sentences.

The difficulties go back to the human capacity of understanding, which is never automatic, but is accompanied by resistance and rejection, by immediate insight and by silent refusal.

Understanding is a presupposition-rich concept; in relation to the fact of the capacity for violence, it can only prove itself under special conditions.

The implicit pedagogy of history thus addresses a fundamental question of the human being that leads to sceptical conclusions. Has 'modern' man proven himself to be a being capable of learning? Is he, as it were, smarter, more reflective, more sensitive than people in earlier times? The focus here is not on the 'proof' of a decreasing actual violence or an increased sensitivity, but rather on the question of the conditions of a meaningfully reconstructable history of violence. It is not the omniscient, educated subject that guides these reflections, but the reconstruction of an educational process that ignites at the extreme of human violence.

What does 'implicit' mean here? An explicit approach is obvious when referring to the claim of learning. In simple sentences, this explicit form can be distinguished from the implicit form. The explicit sense of history is expressed in procedures of self-empowerment: diverse episodes of the past join together to form a lesson. History is transformed into exemplary forms; rules of dealing with present events are generated from the events of the past.

Since Cicero, the formula of history has been regarded as a teacher; history is not only opened up cognitively but also projected onto the field of the political. In the context of war history, however, the exemplary form leads to various unresolved contradictions. For trivially, no pure lesson can be taken from the past that could be used as a guideline for dealing with contemporary violence. Therefore, the exemplary form is to be mediated with the critical and the genetic theory of history. Given orders of life are to be viewed critically, their legitimacy is in question. Historical thinking only gains its appropriate form in view of the changes in human orders of life. Although the history of the twenty-first century is written within the horizon of the twentieth century, future perspectives always transcend the experiential space of past events (Rüsen, 2019, p. 42).

Explicitly, this means that we use history to some extent as an instrument, because we become wiser through cognitive access. What happened then is to serve as a lesson for the present; history is explicitly shaped and driven forward, it becomes plannable. The teleology of human history overcomes social and political boundaries.

The implicit form is by no means opposed to the explicit form. Rather, it is oriented towards the 'double contingency' of history (Rohbeck, 2019, p. 49). A distance must be found to the guiding idea that humans 'make' their history as active, shaping beings. As a grand plan, set in motion by people and generations and completed in the near future, history is misunderstood. It is burdened with a task that it categorically misses. The shapeability of history can currently no longer be seriously defended, the disappointments of the course of time are too great, the backward movements and relapses into times that one thought one had overcome are too dramatic. Today, the idea of feasible history is only whispered about or discarded altogether.

Feasibility is considered an illusion, but this does not absolve us of the responsibility to open history to human action despite all human limitations. Scepticism in the face of unavailable historicity is legitimate – nevertheless, a plea for the use of leeway is conceivable. Resigning oneself to one's own powerlessness is neither advisable in the private sphere nor in theory. As a historical and formative being, human beings are rather dependent on narratives that are useful for life and that adhere to the ethical dimension of historical responsibility (Rohbeck, 2019, p. 50; Rüsen, 2003; Angehrn, 2014, 2015).

Accordingly, the turn to the philosophy of history can be explicit or implicit. 'Explicit' would be, as indicated, the role of man, who no longer relies on divine effects. As is well known, the Enlightenment had presented man as a demiurge, a creator god, who now appears as the explicit guide of history. According to the guiding idea, the task of shaping the whole falls to him. The world would explicitly become a product of man.

Implicit, on the other hand, means that man has an ambivalent relationship to his history. This is not a product of his will; in his history, man does not stand as creator and guide, but as a broken and fragile being. In this, in the reference to fragility and finiteness, the cultural value of historical narratives, which reach back to the ancient myths, proves itself (Angehrn, 1996). Power is gained and lost again; empires are conquered and perish. It is the ability to capture both historical greatness and repeated failure, both a moral victory and terrifying violence, in narratives that contradict the axiom of feasibility.

In various dimensions, the claim of the implicit 'pedagogy of history' can be expressed. In the ability to grasp the past in narratives (The Power of Narration), and in an intercultural dimension of memory culture (Dialogical Culture of History). Only in mutual exchange does the intrinsic value of cultural constructs of meaning become apparent. Where this implicit dimension leads in the context of contemporary events is the last question to be asked. Can we draw conclusions from the previous discussions for morally guided action in the present (The Implicit Understanding of Hermeneutics)?

The Power of Narration

What is the basis, we can ask naively by way of introduction, for the hopes of human moral perfection? What is the basis of the expectation, which has proven to be deceptive time and again, that humanity will one day, near or far, finally leave violence behind? Human progress can be observed in individual spheres, in technical and scientific contexts. Artefacts are 'optimised', knowledge is replaced by new, different, supposedly higher knowledge. This progress touches on the knowledge of culture and yet cannot be reduced to it. But what about the spheres of morality and politics, democratic achievements and great ideas? Are they to be understood as a guarantee of the very progressiveness that we ascribe to humanity in every substantive field?

One can formulate the question in a deliberately simplistic way: Has humanity become wiser and has it helped the great ideas to come to fruition? If so, shouldn't politics become a great fulfilment figure and shouldn't individuals turn out to be splendid specimens presenting the course of humanity's development? Only with irony can these questions be answered today. They lead to the sceptical findings of postmodern and post-historical thinking, which would rather see man as a driven, powerless, vulnerable being.

Nevertheless, there are good reasons to ask what the course of human development is all about when one relates this course to the great political ideas of philosophy. As is well known, the first great drafts of the democratic form were drafted a good three thousand years ago. However, the practical course that this idea has taken in historical reality has been neither straightforward nor continuous. Progress and 'crashes' coincide in every epoch; the idea of a political unity encompassing all people took on different forms. But whenever the ideas came close to realisation, there was always the threat of a crash. Democratic as well as non-democratic forces have challenged each other in all cultures; in the process, the idea of democracy crashed again and again into brutality of authoritative rule (Oser, 2013, p. 333).

Only very cautiously, therefore, can formulations be made that, despite all setbacks, ask about the developmental progress in political judgements. This is less about the historical facts, which under certain circumstances reveal a primacy of power over all political wisdom; it is more about the value of political ideas, which would have to 'prove' themselves in the basic human situation.

Two approaches must be distinguished here, both of which relate to the implicit pedagogy of history. In the field of political judgement, one would have to assume progress in both phylogenesis and ontogenesis. The progress of an enlightened political consciousness would thus be reflected both in the psyche of humanity (Jüttemann, 2013, 2014, 2020) and in the individual persons who could be located at levels of political judgement. This approach asks about competencies at different developmental levels. Critical thinking in the pre-adolescent stage confronts the complex problems of law and state, constitution and responsibility and morality. Whether a positive cognitive finding, which could certainly be interpreted as progress in pedagogy, also contains a higher development of humanity is admittedly questionable (Oser, 2013, p. 239; Biedermann, Oser, Quesel, 2007).

The other approach of an implicit pedagogy proceeds in a different way and uses different means. In order to be able to act politically, the guiding ideas about history must be structured by strong images, symbols and narratives. Political action is thus only made possible in a divided horizon that is framed narratively. Narratives have a normative and political power; they enable, in psychological categories, strong self-images and a certain self-efficacy.

Michael Walzer's work can be used in this context. In his writings, let us think of *Exodus and Revolution* (1988), questions are asked about the conditions of collective action that exist in a historical situation. The book is about the interpretation of the biblical story of the Exodus from Egypt, but at the same time it is about aspects of Western political theory. The story of the Exodus is significant for the present in various ways. The bondage of the Israelites under Egyptian rule thematises an obvious injustice. As 'sojourners' the Israelites had come; as enslaved they had to free themselves from an unjust tyranny. However, the basic motif of liberation from unjust circumstances is primarily at the beginning of this story; the legitimate act of resistance is overlaid by other aspects as the narrative progresses. For the problems of the people of the Israelites only begin at the moment of their escape from bondage. The flight through the desert proves to be an experience of deprivation in which agonising doubts become apparent. The return to the original place appears in a different light in the desert; despite the humiliation and political oppression, Egypt becomes an unconscious place of longing. Anger and reluctance, longing and hunger thus form the deeper forces that emerge only after the one-off act of revolution.

It is about material deprivation, but also about a deeper existential self-determination. The morally legitimate counter-violence subsequently demands a comprehensive confrontation about what the present and the future hold in store. The world of the Israelites in this situation is characterised by polar tensions: in the house of bondage there was oppression and tyranny, but also enticements and securities. In the desert and the diaspora, the people find moral self-respect, but also extreme deprivation. The Exodus is thus not a pure symbol of liberation; the story does not serve a theology of the oppressed. Only in its paradoxical form can the Exodus be expressed as the unfolding of a great motif. The moment of a people's struggle for self-determination is thus the narrative core; for positive freedom is trivially not given, but must be laboriously won (Ibid., p. 83; Krause/Malowitz, 1998, pp. 84–98).

The exodus takes on a paradoxical form in this narrative. The journey through the desert leaves the people reluctant and broken; the willingness to resist is mixed uneasily with the unwillingness to bear the burden of liberation. Freedom shows itself in an undisguised light, in all the hardness and heaviness of existence.

Obedience to God forms the narrative core with political implications. After liberation, there is an arbitrary act of establishing a covenant; after negative freedom, positive freedom can be attained. The people are now in a position to form a moral and political history and to enter into a way of life together. The measure of freedom is now grasped in depth, with all its obligations and ties, with a sense of shared responsibility. Once set in motion, this covenant demands renewal throughout history by subsequent generations, not through ritual forms alone, but through moral acts (Ibid., pp. 85, 97).

Very fundamentally, we must now ask what exactly the value of such an exemplary narrative actually is, if it is to live up to the claim of an implicit pedagogy of history. These questions lead us to the basic forms of historical meaning formation. According to this, collectives communicate about themselves, about their past and present; the individuals involved see themselves enmeshed in the exemplary stories, as they were. Biographies become intertwined with events; self-thematisation is mixed with historical consciousness. History thus becomes a special world that is actively constructed and endowed with meanings. It is communicatively negotiated and symbolically represented. The effects that narratives have on the psychology of historical meaning in light of this are worth considering.

What are narratives 'good for'? Generally speaking, narratives organise pre-existing symbolic orders and deal with contingency. In this respect, they always work in more than one direction: they stabilise and destabilise, they create orientation or raise existential questions.

They promote insights and yet are a source of constant disquiet (Ricoeur, 1988; Straub, 1998a). The example of the Exodus shows the inner contradictoriness of freedom, just as the act of liberation from arbitrary rule must be accompanied by a positive act of a new covenant. So one can certainly claim that narratives orient actions and promote insights. In addition, however, they create an awareness of the ambivalence of any historical image. The desire for unambiguity and unreserved identification proves fragile and challenging. The historical understanding of what was set in motion in the past cannot be transformed into a compact judgement under the sign of reason. It remains bound up with inner contradictions and the burden of contingency.

The merit of narratives lies in the connection between the factual content, the 'res gestae' and the individual approach. Depth psychology fills those necessarily empty spaces of the past that make any historicising retrospective appear deficient. The historian's neutrality is allied with the narrator's partisanship. In this alliance lies the reasonableness of historical narration in the sense meant here.

The implicit reconstruction turns to the past in a dramatic staging. The factual information content remains secondary and incomplete; the narrator's wish world and fear world take centre stage (Booth, 1998, p. 338). Obviously, history in the conventional sense is 'deceived' here. The claim to objectivity and factual knowledge is given little credit here; the veto power of the sources (a term formed by R. Koselleck) gives way to the subjective experience of the contemporaries. Their expectations, experiences and hopes occupy the historical space.

Of course, this perspective cannot compete with historiography, because the initial question is already different. The question is under which conditions we can expect a historical narrative competence that we can bring into an analogy with moral consciousness. How far do concepts that conceive of the 'body of history' entirely as a subjective performance in a meaning-structured world carry the day? In the best case, the form of historical meaning-making complements conventional historiographical procedures: specific spaces of experience, but also individual voices and the overlooked articulations of the soul then step alongside the collections of data and chains of events.

The narrator thus forms a gateway to the historical world. He is first concerned with the fears, desires and hopes located in the present. The horror and beauty of the past, burned into the consciousness of those affected at the moment of crisis, require reorganisation. What has been suffered must be brought into a form of adequate memory, the psychological shock needs a form of support through life-serving stories (Rüsen, 2003).

The narratives of the past fulfil various psychological functions. When these stories tell of guilty involvement, they serve self-justification; when they tell of wrongdoing, they serve to unburden the conscience. When other subjects, 'fellow travellers', 'perpetrators' and 'accomplices', 'bystanders' or 'spectators' are viewed in historicising retrospect, mechanisms of accusation and indictment are used. But self-aggrandisement in the sense of hero and victim stories is also at the centre of such narratives. Not infrequently, collectives tend to project an aura of authenticity into these stories (Sabrow, 2014).

The ambivalence should not be ignored here. In view of violent events and historical injuries, narratives have a healing function; however, the specific dynamics must not be concealed.

The organising power of narration has narrow limits; the needs that are satisfied here remain harmless as long as they serve to process and integrate into a whole of meaning. All too easily, however, these needs are subjected to the clittering of history and instrumental action. Not only does the suffering subject not come to rest, but the entire collective may plunge into a frenzy of self-aggrandisement. What has been suffered is woven into a biography as a motif that gives meaning; on a higher social level, however, it can promote the actualisation of violence.

Identification with the past then leads to moral rearmament, and the collective seeks and finds a spiritual balm: self-assurance takes the place of insecurity and destabilisation.

Dialogical Culture of History

In summary, the implied power of narration can only be recognised within certain limits. The ambivalent psychology of narrative brings another problematic issue into focus. As soon as the suffering subject comes to the fore of the narrative, forces are brought into play that can assume a specific drift. It is therefore unavoidable to draw attention to the danger of closing particular discourses. In contrast, we need a dialogical culture of history in order to resist the self-referential tendencies of contemporary identification.

The indicated problematic arises simply from the experience that history cannot simply be understood as a neutral procedure of interlocking past, present and future. Furthermore, history serves a self-assurance and in this respect can become a hot procedure into which all good and bad human motives flow. From a neutral, distant point of view, the matter of history could be described as a mere 'incident', a chain of events that happens in a certain way. Accordingly, historical narratives bring up contingency and align it in a specific way. History thematises contingency and deals with it in a factual methodology, but it also creates an awareness of the respective meaning of the contingent (Ricouer, 1985).

Historical incidents do not remain external to one's own life; they are given a face and a form that mean something to someone. This simple and comprehensible insight, however, has consequences for every theory of history. What is decisive is who, under what circumstances, gives contingency a voice and to what extent history is given a face. History is not an abstract, anonymous process, but a qualified determination in narrative form. Various psychological motives flow into the narrative meaning: a story can disappoint or inspire an expectation, it can exaggerate a founding moment, but it can also thematise the rupture after which everything was perceived in a new and different way. In, with and through the story, a respective symbolic order is organised, but potentials are also released.

The difficulty hinted at results from this functional property. Historical narratives transform specific suffering into meaning; they connect the fates of happiness and unhappiness, fulfilment and failure into a collectively significant state of affairs. In doing so, these narratives are bound to normative standards, to normative images of the world and of humanity. In this respect, they are to be located on a level of generality, which they can, however, undermine under certain circumstances.

The specific intelligibility of stories in cultural contexts is thus in question – a question with great scope. Remembered history has to do with unease and a discomfort; put simply, because history cannot be stilled.

In various situations, we encounter this sensitive stubbornness of history with particular intensity. Superficially, the practice of remembering historical violations seems to have the greatest resonance. Here, for understandable reasons, the negative point of reference dominates. The violence suffered is articulated through the memories of the victims and their relatives; however, these memories are psychologically presuppositional. From the perspective of the 'victims', it is first about the withheld recognition. This has to be conquered, as it were, and fought for in a sometimes agonising process.

These are struggles for recognition that go hand in hand with discursive entanglements in various historical cultures, especially in Europe and the United States. Those who were denied recognition as a victim group were forced to make themselves heard, to raise their voices and to secure a place in the social hierarchy. This is only possible if one accepts the rules of victim competition. The need to compare oneself with others and to elevate the singularity of suffering to a level of 'equal-validity' results in the contemporary discomfort with the culture of memory (Assmann, 2013a; Maier, 1993).

A victim experience can become a privilege. It is perceived as a possession and defended like symbolic capital. Victim groups compete in the worst case in a hierarchy for status and recognition, but also for economic resources and political power (Assmann, 2013a, p. 143).

With the entanglement of history and memory, a wide gate is opened to the manipulation of history. The example of the current Russian politics of memory shows this problem in all its sharpness. It is all too easy to shift the dates of commemoration that create identity through political decisions. Since 2005, under the dictatorial government of V. Putin, the October Revolution of 1917 has no longer been commemorated. In contrast, an event dating back to November 1612 was reactivated by parliamentary resolution – the expulsion of the Poles from the Kremlin (Assmann, 2013a, p. 305).

The example may seem striking, as it suited the obvious strategy of the Russian government (and was surprisingly outdone by the neo-imperial incursions since February 2022 for the world public). Generally formulated, the case shows what the bracketing of memory and history entails: it is the selective and affirmative treatment of history that is 'savoured' in hot proceedings. The references to the history of violence and the glaring illumination of the image of history lead to a politics of blockade. Understanding with others can thus no longer succeed because the ethical horizon has long since been abandoned (Wevelsiep, 2022).

As haunting as the negative case of authoritarian power politics is, the positive aspects of modern historical procedures can always be defended. One can defend the implicit form of historical knowledge from the standpoint of humanities and cultural studies. This form of history is committed to recognised procedures, source orientation, truth reference and intersubjective rules. No historian and no single narrative thus stand above history. In each case, the binding to the ground of transcultural methodology is decisive (Assmann, 2013a, p. 306; Winter, 2010).

The conclusions for the theory of history thus point in a dialogical direction. Specific memory and formal history form two equally valid forms. Both sides – the personally coloured view and the formal reconstruction – are not only legitimate, but together they form the modern bond of history. As reciprocal correctors, they are extremely valuable; constructs of memory can meaningfully tie in with the results of scientific research. Only when the memoria leaves the boundaries of dialogical understanding does history become an illegitimate event. It is then only in the service of power and overrides historical knowledge.

How to avoid leaving the path of historiography, however, will be shown lastly. It is the theory of understanding that can be used against the dangerous trends of historical politics.

The Implicit Understanding of Hermeneutics

Let us finally try to transfer the previous considerations into a contemporary theory of hermeneutics. The demand on such a theory of historical understanding is by no means small; it should at least be able to free current trends in historical politics from their constrictions.

The danger of creating mythical self-images, for example by emphasising 'national honour' or the pathos of collective suffering, is immense. How can a narrative and hermeneutic approach to history avoid these constructions that focus exclusively on specific episodes?

How could the self-reference of memory constructions at least be weakened and brought into a transcultural reference?

The form of hermeneutics was elaborated especially by Hans-Georg Gadamer. It provides the decisive categories to redeem the claims mentioned before (hereafter: Gadamer, 1960, 1971). The basic features established by philosophical hermeneutics can be summarised in the concept of the horizon. Drawing on the work of E. Husserl and M. Heidegger, the human horizon denotes the possibility of human access to the world. Heidegger had located his understanding of reality in a horizon of possibilities of being (German: 'Dasein'); the existentialist form of thought in this respect focused on the moment of choice and decision.

Gadamer, however, is primarily concerned with the interpretativity of life.

Human understanding takes place within the horizon of a prior understanding. This horizon, however, is not a choice, but something that is predetermined and unavailable to the subject. Gadamer speaks of the sense that has become historical, which precedes all action and interpretation (Gadamer, 1960, p. 256). This is by no means prejudice in the strict sense, which one would simply have to brush off in an open encounter. The historical tradition therefore has precedence because, in principle, people let their explicit knowledge and actions be determined by an implicit pre-understanding. However, this pre-understanding cannot itself become definitively explicit. It remains subterranean, enigmatic, obscured, it eludes any attempt at explication.

This does not mean that we meet in no other way than in the structures of resentment. Rather, it means that history always continues and can only be transmitted in an implicit form. We are dealing here with a specific form of a sceptical theory of history. Implicit knowledge about us and about the world is at the centre of this hermeneutics, which can be described as a challenge to thinking. For, as Gadamer repeatedly points out, we overestimate ourselves in the project of radically questioning ourselves and freeing ourselves from all pretences; the ideal of the supreme subject of reason in the Enlightenment is at the same time a deluded ideal.

Subjectivity is never completely unbound, free or unhistorical. It is always embedded in contexts of tradition, which we can call an implicit form of historical knowledge.

Let us think of the introductory remarks on dianoia. Normative and factual findings do not form separate worlds that stand opposite each other in explicit forms. Rather, they are to be understood as implicit knowledge.

Gadamer has concluded that in this respect history does not 'belong' to us, but that we belong to history. The focus of subjectivity is only a distorting mirror (Gadamer, 1960, p. 262), a flicker in the closed stream of society.

Lastly, can we take from this position clues that enlighten us about contemporary discursive problems? In particular, the perception of current scenarios of violence could be analysed with this form of historical understanding. The questions in the field of tension between threatened human rights and legitimate counter-violence shape the discourses of the present – these not infrequently lead to eminent contradictions in the global politics of human rights.

Of course, there is no universally satisfactory solution in sight when it comes to the violation of fundamental rights. We have to retreat here to the position of one who views violence from a distanced standpoint and draws attention to the dangers of an 'explicit' theory of intervention. For how do current justifications of a politics of human rights proceed? Sceptical voices emphasise that current policies are gradually moving away from historically relevant peace positions and gradually undermining the legal principles of the Enlightenment (Maus, 2011). Domestic and international dimensions are known to be in stark contrast.

Enlightenment political philosophy had emphasised the close connection between sovereignty and liberties, which promotes peace in the long run. At present, however, this 'implicit' knowledge, if you will, is being abandoned. It is giving way to a new interventionism that does not care about the freedom of the individuals concerned, nor about democratic principles, nor about the ultimate purpose of legal doctrine. Global interventionism in favour of endangered rights is morally explicit, but it disregards the complex continuum of popular sovereignty, law and peace.

This explicit interventionist reason insulates human rights against their democratic context. Defensive rights in a state are reinterpreted under the table as a set of tasks in a global monopoly of force (Maus, 1999, p. 279). This position is not easy, because it attracts the criticism of ethics of mind – correctly understood, however, it can be formulated as criticism of a certain mood (German: 'Zeitgeist'). Human rights were originally founded as subjective claims, thus they do not serve an objective systemic purpose. In this respect, they should not be isolated against their democratic context.

This brief digression once again illustrates the difficult claim of an implicit pedagogy of history. We encounter the explicit meaning of history in the motif of self-empowerment.

As if one could simply combine various episodes of the past into a lesson and establish a higher order of morality. Self-empowerment in times of war thus appears as a diffuse but momentous danger.

In contrast, we can take a saving critique from the motif of implicit pedagogy, which is turned against its original historical-philosophical context. Thinking about history – which is not to be equated with conventional philosophy of history – proves its value in the face of violent relations. The unconditional progress of technical dispositions seduces one into thinking that everything humanly possible can be controlled through an act of self-empowerment. As we know, this includes the technical possibilities of disposal in the field of war. War is supposed to be technically controlled and finally relegated to a marginalised area. But it is precisely the human dispositions that stand in the way of this thought motif; as is well known, one of the basic ideas of critical theory is to take into account the imperfection and fallibility of human power of disposal. Thus, even in this older philosophical context, insights can be found that are highly topical.

Chapter Ten

WAR AGAIN? THE CONTRIBUTION OF PHILOSOPHY TO THE PHENOMENON OF WAR

Introduction

When talking about wars, the moral feelings evoked by them play a major role. This cannot be surprising – to the same extent that the intuitive historical evaluation of contemporary wars is also influenced by such strong feelings. War is rejected by the majority in modern times because it is morally unambiguous: it causes suffering and destroys the moral, social and economic foundations of societies. But when wars are waged in defiance of this insight, the question of consent becomes not only a moral question but also a historical self-questioning. In the sign of war, old and new lines of enmity are drawn, the capacity for violence is mobilised and present violence is related to past violence. Wars trivially take place against the backdrop of past wars, so that they sometimes seem like an endless succession of permanent confrontations.

An intellectual intervention from 2002 sounds correspondingly familiar. Karl Otto Hondrich wrote about the future and present of war from a Western European, or German, point of view with mixed feelings: for half a century here (in Western Europe) war was considered the greatest conceivable calamity. Memories of the world wars, Vietnam and the threat of nuclear war gave a deep seriousness to the fear of war. This condemnation of war has remained, but under the table the feelings and arguments are transforming: they are turning to war again (Hondrich, 2002, p. 7).

This consent to violence is ambivalent and reluctant; the new attitude towards war contained all the fears from the older wars. It was more like an acceptance of fate. One submitted to a development that was experienced as unstoppable.

The author wrote about the violence in Southeastern Europe, Bosnia and Kosovo; about the war in the Hindu Kush and the looming war in the Gulf at the beginning of the millennium. The participation of German society in these wars and interventions was, as we know, small; it had hardly affected everyday life. One participated in large coalitions and with only a small part of one's collective self; one left it to special troops and military specialists to enforce peace. The progress of military and technical systems offered a guarantee that this war, like all other 'small wars' in the periphery, posed no threats to world peace.

At that time, with a gap of a good two decades, from the perspective of the Western European intelligentsia, it was about discursive disputes; about questions of self-image and moral judgement (Habermas, 1999, 2004). In contrast, the current events of

2022 are to be assessed differently: once again, the legitimacy of wars is being disputed. Again polarisations and socio-moral trench warfare can be observed, again it is about the interplay of moral feelings and cool diagnoses about the present and future of war. But these aspects are now currently under the sign of an intrusiveness. The suffering of others can no longer simply be pushed away.

All intellectual disputes are under the sign of an obvious need for action. In this respect, moral feelings are in close contact with political judgements in an exceptional international situation.

No one can seriously say how the war in Ukraine of 2022 will develop. In general, however, the question arises as to the specific contribution of social theory to the practice of war. More specifically, what can be expected (or even demanded) in times of war from a philosophical or social theoretical position that naturally acts independently of politics? The interest in knowledge that is hidden in this question is by no means self-evident. What one can hope for from philosophical-theoretical reflections with a view to practice is not a question of cold calculation. Philosophy does not provide blueprints for a better approach to the world. It confronts the urgent and existential questions and thinks through the problems more deeply; it stands under different provisions than the sphere of action of politics, which is always about collective decisions under time pressure.

The interest in reflections on peace and war here is in a theoretical tradition, which raises some difficulties. The moral philosophical question in the background seems irrefutable, but answering it leads us into a thicket of paradoxes and antinomies. Let us think of the discussions around the 'just war' thesis. Can it be justified to wage war and what would the conditions of such a 'right' have to be? Proponents of just war emphasise the critical function that theories of morality carry with them for practice. However, this critique is negativistic in nature, pointing not only to the bright area of justice, but to de facto injustices and de facto illegitimacy. At best, just war theories could act like a corrective. They primarily show why and in what respect a military intervention can be unjustified (for the example of the NATO intervention in Kosovo: Merkel, 2000). At the same time, it must be borne in mind that under certain conditions a theory can have an affirmative function. The semantics of 'just wars' already suggest a proximity to ideology and no one can rule out that the title itself would be instrumentalised in a hegemonic situation. In the worst case, a morally explicit theory would even undermine the peace-securing function of international law (Habermas, 2004, p. 113 ff.).

The discussions on morality in war and on the right to war are to be conducted in the corresponding discursive public spheres. However, the expectation that one would open up a perspective for political action by singling out just reasons for the use of force would have to be judged sceptically. The chasms in the 'snake pit' of international politics are too great, as the actors are too entangled in the broad field of power and morality. It is probably only possible to designate the paradoxical provisions with which we are confronted in the case of a real war. In this case, the theory of just war developed underhand into a position of unjust war, because every even conceivable participation in a war is linked to violence (Iser, 2006). The suffering of innocent victims cannot be categorically excluded, as the means in war can presumably never guarantee the required integrity of those affected. In this sense, war remains an experience that happens to people in situations of powerlessness – no matter how well thought out the criteria of a higher morality provided by philosophy may be.

One could leave it at that and state the insolubility of moral conflicts, which is given in the case of real war. However, an alternative objective puts this statement in a different light. Without the expectation of being able to take a morally unambiguous position, violence in history and the present must be thought through. Rethinking war is a task of the utmost urgency. Social theoretical reflection has an intrinsic value especially in times of war; it creates a distance from the excitement of discourse, it cools down the overheated spaces of the public sphere. It enables a normative standpoint by exposing the criteria of meaning of violence that surround contemporary wars.

These criteria will be discussed in the following. In the background is a fundamental interest in the intrinsic value of philosophical reflection. Even if we cannot hope for instructions or recipes for a better life from philosophy, it does bring meaningful insights to light. And precisely because philosophy does not bow to any expectations of its political environment, because it is autonomous and *nobody's handmaiden*, it can provide life-serving criteria of meaning in the face of violence.

War is in the world, it is an unavoidable, cruel reality; but what access we have to this reality is a question of interpretation. In this respect, all talk about violence is dependent on the reference to the world that we adopt. This world reference goes back to cultural constructs that condense into specific temporal diagnostic judgements. The 'We', which underlies the following considerations, is to be understood here as a polemical self-description for which one should achieve sufficient awareness. At the centre of this specific knowledge of the world is a socio-moral force: the preference of one's own (1).

It is then up to philosophy to reduce the phenomenology of violence to its normative and social final elements. Philosophical reflection takes a distance from the understandable desire for normative purity. When we look for the causes and sources, the ultimate reasons for violence, from a philosophical point of view we are always referred to the interplay between violence and order. While this sceptical position needs the impulse of the Enlightenment and the orientation towards the concept of peace, it also needs the critical reflection of ethical violence (2).

Without being able to conclude these reflections once and for all, it will be shown that these philosophical determinations are by no means to be understood as self-referential exercises of science. The riddle of the divisiveness of man leads reflection to the boundary questions of science. How can we release the concept of enmity from all anthropological and social constrictions? Historicism and hermeneutics form here a productive alliance with which we can escape the entanglements of the violent present (3).

The Preference of the Own

Contemporary wars are a challenge to thinking. But every moral attitude takes place in a forecourt, in a predetermined, subconscious space of preconceptions, expectations and experiences. In this respect, talking about violence is always connected to the perception of this violence. Which constructions about the constitution of the world we take as a basis is decisive for all political and social concepts that we design in a supposedly unprejudiced attitude.

This 'world' is divided into different worlds. It is my world of experiences, of closeness, of familiarity. The experience that we can be at home anywhere, that we experience and grant hospitality, that we do not only remain bound to the 'homeland' but are also always connected to the distant and the foreign, does not contradict the reference to the living world at all. However, the ethos of cosmopolitanism comes up against a 'natural' limit, precisely at the point where we are confronted with violence in distant and foreign places.

Two motifs flow into each other and form a complex situation. Wars have to be interpreted and perceived; they need a heading, a title, so that we can place them in our perception of the world. At the same time, we need to find an attitude towards this violence, a normative equidistance that tells us where the boundaries between our own and other people's conflicts run. However, an interpretation of violence is complex. The talk of 'molecular civil war' was introduced by Hans Magnus Enzensberger (Enzensberger, 1993); it aimed at the insight that modern wars would be characterised by growing anomic conditions and by a loss of the political. In modern civil war, the signs of a disintegration of the state, increasing criminality, brutalisation and barbarisation are multiplying. This violence is no longer held together by any ideology; it 'proliferates' wildly and without restraint (Sloterdijk, 2006). The new wars are non-political wars because they are primarily aimed at acquiring power in a manageable space or because they serve the profit interests of the actors. The non-state character characterises the face of these new wars. The relevant variables of the 'trinitarian war' (v. Crefeld, 1998, p. 64; Schlichte, 2005) are dissolving. They form an inscrutable mixture of violent entrepreneurs and violent actors.

The boundaries between the civilian population and the fighting troops become blurred.

In global warfare, the classical attributes of interstate war become doubtful. However, this interpretation does not apply to all wars and it is especially not authoritative for the current discord. In a distanced view of the reality of violence, however, it is helpful in clarifying normative insinuations.

For these sociological observations become difficult when they expose themselves to normative questions. The relationship that one assumes as an outsider to a war is subject to socio-moral attitudes that would have to be made explicit. The short-sighted reference to the morality of human rights misses the point here; what is decisive is rather the extent to which the relationship to war reveals the tension between the own and the foreign unfold. These normative aspects require a deeper phenomenological examination.

In a normative view, we first encounter the language of human rights. This corresponds to our moral sensibilities, as they apply in a universal scope and open up a world of moral values. Life must be protected and preserved at all costs; this requires political entities that are committed to the responsibility to protect those affected. This moral language is 'not nothing'; it enters into the official preambles and the value catalogues of states. However, it must be related to a level of practical action, where it is drawn into a complex web of interests, embodiments and loyalties. This does not invalidate morality but makes it tense and contradictory.

Various aspects need to be considered here. On the one hand, there is the specific capacity for violence in cultural situations. The West, it is not infrequently argued, has worked towards the ideal of non-violence in the decades following the Second World War. Western societies are more precisely in the position of a hegemon, registering violence from afar and engaging in it only on a case-by-case and selective basis. Various aspects coincide here and form a contradictory situation. Technological advances make it possible to wage war from a distance; participation in battles thus tends to become disembodied. One intervenes from a distance, from the air, with the help of remote-controlled missile systems and ballistic weapons that make it possible to spare one's own troops. Moral progress also demands a civilisation and limitation of war, but the (assumed) morality of non-combatability evokes contradictory actions. The ability to use force from a distance leads to physical close combat being hemmed in, but this does not prevent blunders and devastating interventions.

As a consequence, this kind of warfare leads to serious normative constrictions. The morality of human rights dictates to the societies of the West a responsibility for which they cannot account. Some observers go so far as to deny these societies the capacity for armed defence. The West, they charge, is neither morally nor technologically capable of standing up to an enemy. A special form of decadence has long since established itself, which in the long run leads to shying away from any sacrifice (Bohrer, 2007).

In this situation, however, one has to recognise that this shyness before the victim is mixed with another basic force of social life: the orientation towards the 'own'. One's own – one's own values, one's own ties, closeness and familiarity – has a flip side: the exclusion of the foreign and the distant. One fights for one's own, one shows authentic interest and factual participation. The foreign becomes blurred and loses its relevance. It only has an artificial significance in discourses that speak of universalism but overlook the violence of the Other. Judith Butler speaks here of a disinterest in foreign suffering and thus continues an engaged literature in the sign of the Other (Butler, 2004, 2005; Sontag, 2003).

The answer to war is therefore: only when we are directly hit do we get involved with the necessary seriousness. Only when our own values, our own ties are endangered do we leave the cover of our moral values.

Violence and Order

The preference of one's own is the one great socio-moral force in common life to which one must turn with all seriousness. It is flanked by another force: order. In the broadest sense, order means a form of living together that is subject to a certain measure and specific regulations. Orders are political structures that bring both the human capacity for violence and structural power into balance, a balance that always remains bound to time and culture. When these orders are brought into a relationship with violence, phenomenological descriptions can be made.

An all-too-casual idiom dictates that we understand violence as a dependent variable of a particular order. Accordingly, violence is permitted or outlawed by orders, so it is always the order that determines the respective degree of violence. It is the Hobbesian scenario of primitive, raw violence that can only be controlled by a higher power – the order of the state. But this by no means represents the entire spectrum of violence in relation to order. For violence varies with the orders in which it occurs; violence takes on cultural and historical forms and always presents itself differently in relation to an order (hereafter Waldenfels, 2000, p. 21 ff.). These are rather parallel genealogies: violence and orders gain their contours in mutual reference: violence is used to install an order by force or to undermine it.

Violence is in the service of an order or in its shadow; in one case it serves the interests of power and in the other it can be addressed as a legitimate counter-power.

These varieties are familiar: violence becomes sacral because it promotes a value system; it is considered 'rational' because it maintains an established order. At the moment of a change of order, this violence takes on a higher meaning: it describes itself as just violence and the form of justification aims at a future order in which there should be supposedly less violence.

These hints remain vague and indeterminate. From a philosophical distance, one remains vague: violence is to be found in the shadow of orders; it can itself increase to excess and overshoot any goal, but it always remains bound to the contingency of an order in the background. The philosophical reflection on violence sees a hopelessness in this relationship: for orders that could always be different (more just, more benevolent, more responsible, etc.) can never be fully justified. They remain selective and exclusive.

It is a fundamental conviction of philosophy that every order contains a moment of violence. Violence proves to be the flip side of all orders. Of course, this is not a plea for indifference in the face of violent phenomena. Every speech and every action takes place in a space that already contains the traces of violence.

All actions that invoke the reason of non-violence are thus unintentionally 'infected' with an unavoidable violence (Derrida, 2000; Hirsch, 2004).

But one need not stop at this point, which inexorably confronts us with the antinomies of violence. The contradictions at the highest level of world politics (Who intervenes in whose name? Who lives up to their responsibilities? Who forms a self-proclaimed coalition of the 'righteous'?) cannot be resolved once and for all. Recognising them as contradictions and making them accessible to an unbiased critique can be the only goal. Therefore, an empirical example is helpful.

Let us think of the NATO intervention in Kosovo in 1999, which occupied the world's attention as a reaction to the mass murders in the area of the former Yugoslavia (on this Merkel, 2000). The background of the conflict itself is not to be clarified here; as is well known, these 'new wars' (Kaldor, 2000) in Southeastern Europe were serious violations of human rights to which countless people fell victim. The question of what means and in what form NATO troops should use to stop the escalation of violence is the only one to be discussed here.

Of course, the positions of international law experts, sociologists and philosophers cannot be lumped together. Characteristic, however, are individual voices that recognised in NATO's action an anticipation of a future world civil order (Habermas, 2004). On this point, however, opinions differed: some wanted to recognise in a morally motivated 'intervention' a half-hearted attempt to prevent worse war crimes and to stop the violence (Habermas, 1999).

Others saw in the action a more or less arbitrary force at work that disregarded the rights of the Serbian people and used the wrong means for moral ends (Merkel, 2000, Preface).

In this respect, it is difficult to identify a precise philosophical contribution that could pave the way to justice in the contested field of power, politics and threatened human rights. The insights one may hope for from a philosophical perspective can therefore only succeed in dialectical mediation: thinking about war is always integrated into the experience of war, and every war brings to light something new and surprising for which no previous experience can account.

If one is prepared to reject the imposition that philosophy should contribute to a spirited intervention in the field of violence, this does not say everything. Only in a long-term perspective can one ask for the principles that will serve the cause of peace. The conditions for such peaceful coexistence are well known: in functioning peace orders, a monopoly on the use of force exists alongside the supporting institutions of the rule of law. In every context of citizens' lives, the renunciation of violence is practised: in social intercourse, in legal procedures, but also in economic spheres. Social justice and a culture of conflict give such forms of life a contour of the civilisation (Senghaas, 1995).

The question, however, is where one stands in the development of international law. Can one simply transfer the expectations of domesticated, single-state entities to the international dimension? The presence of war speaks decidedly against it, but before making even a rudimentary social diagnosis, differentiating observations would have to be made. Modern democracy research has dealt intensively with the question of democratic peace – and the answers are as multilayered and complex as social reality allows. The very fact that democratic peace exists alongside democratic war provides sufficient reason for unbiased critical reflections.

The idea that democracies are willing to join international cooperation and adapt to the UN's set of rules is only one aspect among many. Democracies hardly ever go to war with each other. However, when an unjust enemy leaves the path of peace in the sense of Immanuel Kant, even liberal democracies use force (Geis, 2006; Hirsch/Delhom, 2019). The justifications lead deep into the thicket of moral–philosophical trade-offs that cannot be terminated from any Archimedean standpoint. The confrontation with dilemmatic situations remains as a challenge that is not 'sovereignly' mastered either in the field of decisions or at the height of philosophical reflection. It leads here as well as there to situations of hopelessness in which modest maxims set the tone.

However, this does not conclusively clarify what one can expect from philosophical reflection. As complex as the various wars of the present are, different lines can be traced that allow comparability to emerge. For example, the dilemmatic situation that the world community faced in the case of Kosovo is under different circumstances than the case of Ukraine. Jürgen Habermas had distinguished himself as a philosophically incisive voice in both cases. In the face of the violence in Ukraine, he reminded us of the dilemma 'that compels the West to weigh the risks between two evils' (Habermas,

2022). What is meant here is the looming (but not predictable) defeat of Ukraine on the one hand and the unleashing of a third world war on the other. However, this point of view is currently contradicted by a large number of public actors who want to see more in the violence of the Russian aggressor. According to Yermelenko, the world community is facing a struggle 'for the freedom of Europe and all humanity'. (Yermelenko, 2022, p. 11). The evil that must currently be fought leads back to the world of existential confrontation: totalitarianism and land grabbing, the unconditional will for expansion and escalation lead far beyond Ukraine. So, according to the author, it is not only about the defence of a state in an interstate conflict. But about the 'Whole' – freedom against despotism, brute, colonial violence in front against the civilised world.

The current situation leaves no room for complete objectivity and distance here. Because wars are by their nature boundless and sooner or later also affect the distant observer, there can also be no 'voice of reason' that could free itself from every partisanship and every affect. Such reflections can possibly only be made at a temporal and social distance.

The aim here can in no way be to build a bridge and achieve a harmonious understanding if at the same time countless victims have to be mourned. The actual decisive problems are aimed at the abstract criteria of enmity and partisanship. From a philosophical point of view, these criteria are to be brought into a context with the real political events.

We may have to roll back the particular expectations of philosophical reflection and focus solely on the heuristic value of ways of thinking about peace. The world of politics is the world of hard causality, of hard choices. This world cannot be directed from the philosophical high ground, as it is unavailable. This may be difficult to bear in times of war, which penetrates people's lives with unexpected harshness. The diversions via peace-theoretical reflection require time and space, but this does not mean that one has to be free of any partisanship.

The normative position is based on equal parts on the historical development of international law, the world of international relations and the moral expectations of existing institutional bodies. In this context, what can one hope for from the existing order?

From a long-term perspective, the history of international law can certainly be told as a story of progress (Brock/Simon, 2019, p. 31 ff.; Gleditsch, 2013; Fisch, 1984). The birth of international law was linked to civilisation by force. In the nineteenth century, a distinction was still made between civilised and uncivilised societies; the 'underdeveloped' states were the subject of colonial plans. The political world was divided into an inside and an outside – outside the civilised world there was the free right to wage war, land could be taken and peoples could be proselytised. It was not until the institutionalisation of peace and the sanctioning of interstate violence that this old order was broken (Brunkhorst, 2005). However, as is well known, it was a long way before the ideas of an Immanuel Kant could break through the frightening love of war. Waves of democratisation were and are always interrupted by political backsliding, as the mutual trust between states is always fragile and brittle. A violent act always breaks the peace once it has been established. However, the basic ideas of the law of peace can be defended against all sceptical objections: they go back to the universal commandment of reason and the monopoly on the use of force, which effectively puts a stop to belligerence (Koskenniemi, 2001; Knöbl/Schmidt, 2000; Koppe, 2001). Only in a cosmopolitan order in which there is mutual respect for the vital interests of others can peace be created in the long term. The irritating presence of war cannot shake these normative insights.

The history of international law reads as a history of change from the law of war to the law of peace. This change of perspective alone is telling and creative. The sceptical insight must be merged with the positive finding: the normative progress of the universal prohibition of the use of force and the duty of peace are to be understood as the *results of* two world wars (Brock/Simon, 2019, p. 41). The possibility of peace is closely tied to the reality of a war that has just been overcome. Hopes are thus directed towards learning progress, which encompasses a concrete level of interests and a general humanity dimension. Increasing interdependence, the expansion of international organisations and the progressive pacification of the world promote this progress for the better.

The sceptical objections are obvious: From where does this peace-philosophical reflection draw its optimism when the existing violence of war is viewed in unsparing openness? What can possibly give rise to a positive balance (Pinker, 2011), when these reflections seem to overlook the countless victims – in large parts of Africa or Asia, in Syria, Afghanistan or Ukraine?

Philosophical reflection obviously needs a corrective. It should enable us to open up the perspectives of peace in the horizon of enmities and thus to address the reality of evil.

The Challenge of Enmity

Establishing a peaceful order is like *building the Tower of Babel* (Brock/Simon, 2019). The search for peace leads through long and tough processes of understanding, in which a common language would first have to be found. The orientation towards the future is accompanied by historical awareness. Peace requires not only the will to renounce violence, but also the insight into one's own transgressions and one's own share in historical contexts. Consequently, it is not only a matter of thinking about the threat to one's own security but also of considering the historical context. War, colonialism and imperialism find a continuation in the present; the demand of philosophical peace research thus logically aims at the public discussion about the historical dimension of the formation of global order (Ibid., p. 43; Menzel, 2015). Violence is to be thematised in a respective order; it is misunderstood as something distant and foreign (Waldenfels, 2000).

One last point of view should be mentioned, which has been brought back into focus in the last weeks of 2022 (at least in the Western and European region). As is well known, the question of the capacity for violence is tied to the figure of the enemy.

That enmities can exist between historical cultures and societies, between nations and states, is a seemingly trivial insight. And yet this fact needs to be brought more strongly into consciousness because it stems from a rather repressed context. The societies of the West have successfully repressed this existential fact; in the face of a surprising renaissance of interstate war, they must come to terms with the existence of a concrete enemy. Cultures that see themselves as 'civilised' and 'non-violent' find this difficult.

However, various blinds would have to be cleared away to allow a more realistic self-image to emerge. The work for peace has always been entangled in the orders of war; and even the reference to law cannot guarantee non-violence. As is well known, even democratic societies have their share of organised violence in the age of globalisation (Knöbl/Schmidt, 2000; Geis/Brock/Müller, 2006; Geis/Müller/Wagner, 2007).

In this context, the criticism of the dark sides of democratic peace is obvious. It succeeds in different forms, sometimes as criticism of the West's feelings of superiority, sometimes as criticism of an advocatory attitude towards the Global South. Criticism of supposedly submissive or decadent tendencies of Western culture plays a role in this context (Bohrer, 2007). In summary, the accusation against Western culture is that, due to specific historical developments, the situation of an emergency has been forgotten. The emergency situation – when an enemy threatens one's own interests – would accordingly be overbearing for a decadent culture, because one would neither be 'mentally' ready to defend nor capable of defending oneself.

The emergency is notorious. For many, it is the decisive criterion for constituting political communities in a world of enemies. Yet the notorious distinction between friend and foe does not suffice for sophisticated moral–political reflection (Behnke, 2005). Enmities must be taken beyond a short-sighted ontology, for they do not stabilise sociality. As a final element in the world of politics, they are misleading and misunderstandable. For this very reason, however, a discussion of the reality of enmity is urgent and necessary. It is to take place here in two ways.

The first path leads via an existentialist interpretation, the other via the path of historicity. In interaction, possibilities for containing enmity are thus opened up; the basic idea being primarily how we can circumvent the mental escalation of existential enmity. Instead of the cardinal question of anthropology, whether man as a being is evil or good, we should first ask about the fundamental determinations of a human world. Only by looking at the basis of human world relations can we make statements about the forms of violence and the large-scale form of war. Constitutive for human life is the insight into the communicative forms of fulfilment and failure in the basic human situation (Rentsch, 1999, 2000). Only in a comprehensive horizon of inter-existence can we distinguish legitimate power and illegitimate violence, forms of recognition and disregard, and peace and war as forms of meaning. Such political inter-existentials are not properties or moral concepts that flow to us from a transcendent world; rather, they are deeply and inseparably embedded in our daily practice.

For the present discussions, the idea should be noted that the path via the anthropology of the human being capable of violence alone is not sufficient. As is well known, these perspectives of values lead to the justification of domination, but also to short-sighted justifications of a morality of violence. Because man becomes a threat to man and because he will never completely take off his wolf's clothing, reasons can always be provided for the willingness to use violence. However, these are discourses that will not be explored in depth here. The 'luxury' of philosophical reflection goes one step further: we must at the same time reflect on what results from the fact of human violence, which unfolds in all directions and takes on a life of its own. No human culture can sustain itself by fixating on the real or invented enemy.

Philosophical anthropology shows us another way of reasoning: human life forms are always already characterised by divisiveness and disruption. At the beginning of our lives, we do not enter a harmonious world to which all violence is only external. Rather, it is necessary to think more deeply about the possibility of enmity, the reality of evil and the vulnerability of the human being. Violence is not the other that threatens us from the outside, but an immanent component of all humane life.

Philosophy looks to this ground and finds here the first reason to 'work away' at divisiveness and alienation. But this is also connected with an implicit commandment: we must understand human forms of life in their pervasiveness of negativity (Rentsch, 2000, p. 85).

The questions of philosophy lead to a decisive difference. Enmity can be brought to an existential head or it can be transformed into living forms. From the standpoint of historicity, the historical fact of enmity must be realised, but first its possible distorted images and forms of fulfilment must be explored. This historically informed standpoint is primarily sceptical; it assumes that friendships and enmities stand as a formal difference behind all human histories of self-organisation (Koselleck, 2000, pp. 99–118). The historical world is thematised through enmities: Greeks rising above barbarians, Greeks fighting Greeks, Christians against pagans or Christians against Christians. In modern times, it was further semantic distinctions that intensified enmities: one fought in the name of a class or a nation; one recognised the enemy as a unit of action or one marginalised it by totalitarian means. Historicism recognises in these figurations a transcendental category of possible history (Ibid., p. 103). No matter how one relates to the conflicts of our time and on which side of the borders one stands, the opposition of friend and foe is the before and behind of all histories known to us.

But this does not necessarily mean that we have to tacitly accept enmity as a social phenomenon. Rather, from a sceptical standpoint, it becomes imperative to recognise ideological aberrations. For existential categories can be filled up existentially at any time. The formal distinction takes on a negative drift: the Other is no longer my counterpart, whom I meet at eye level and who is closer to me than all narratives prescribe. Rather, the Other becomes a darkened stranger, a threat to human life forms per se. Enemies of humanity are at the top of the theory of enmity; they become identifiable whenever modern societies come together in the name of humanity. The gain is obvious: morality binds the parties together and sharpens their perception of their own. The danger, on the other hand, lies in the absolutism of existential determinations: as an incarnation of evil to be eradicated, the enemy is deprived of all human dignity.

Let us summarise. The initial question about the specific performance of social theory for the reality of human violence leads to a hermeneutic and phenomenological description. From a philosophical point of view, it is first a matter of recognising the elementary basic forces that underlie all violence. The described preference for one's own is part of this, as is the inseparable intertwining of violence and order. Both insights do not speak against the possibility of solidary relationships, nor against morally motivated interventions. But they lead all talk about violence back to basic anthropological questions.

Hermeneutic and historical disciplines thereby enable a categorical framework that, from a certain theoretical 'altitude', can define the human capacity for violence as a transcendental determination. Historical facts have formal determinations at their back: the space of history unfolds between inside and outside, in the temporal span of earlier and later, between above and below and between generations. These formal oppositions, however, are further sharpened by the tension of friendship and enmity.

The philosophical tradition of phenomenology recognised in being-to-death perhaps the hardest of all possible distinctions. In a specific constellation of contemporary history, it led to an exaggeration of the categories of fate, of loyalty, Inheritance and being free to death (Heidegger, 1979; Grossheim, 2002; Farias, 1989; Faye, 2005). This German-style political existentialism finds its limit in political nihilist semantics. It is the merit of the humanities avant-garde after 1945 to open up free spaces of thinking against violence against these constrictions of philosophy. This task is by no means complete; more than ever we need the ideological critique of social theory. Here perhaps lies the hoped-for productive achievement of philosophical reflection: it would have to determine the categorical framework in which we recognise the abysses of human capacity for violence. And yet, with the help of philosophical categories, we can think across this abyss.

Chapter Eleven

FROM THE WORLDVIEW OF WAR TO THE WORLDVIEW OF CONCERN

Man is a being of conflict. Is he also necessarily a being of war? The confrontation with the world is constitutive for the deficient human being; however, confrontation does not only mean conflict but also self-assertion in an environment that appears violent, hostile and contrary to life. Man's confrontation with his world is not necessarily warlike, but it is also never free of any violence.

Brilliant metaphors are ready to point out the confrontation with the world. Let us think of the distinction between land and sea; man, wrote Carl Schmitt, is a being of solid ground (Schmitt, 1942). A firm standpoint is gained in space, on the earth, but the real admiration is nevertheless for the motif of taking the sea. The sea becomes the symbolic motif of reality; it is unpredictable, disorderly, shapeless and indeterminate. The dominion over the seas is, as it were, world dominion. The ocean reveals a defining facet of the human condition: if you venture too far out, you will be swallowed up by the elements; it is only on land that man wins the confrontation, when he opposes *his will to* the *arbitrariness of the powers that be*.

Another metaphor about realities in which we live is found in polar regions. The eternal ice confronts man with the experience of infinity. Under a mass of ice that stretches across the land masses like a gigantic carpet, life is, as it were, negated (Blumenberg, 1979, 1999). The human world threatens to suffocate under the rule of ice; everything that would be significant in the human world threatens to be shrouded by eternal silence.

The eternal ice threatens absolute insignificance and silence, but in the present, the ice becomes the object of a relationship of concern. In a global context, the melting of the ice becomes a metaphor of concern, both figuratively and literally. For beneath a thawed sheet of ice are the traces of a new kind of relationship of violence and world. Worry is not directed against the world, but is its own expression – henceforth, it no longer applies to the traditional reference to the world, which would simply be based on one's own survival. Categories have to be found for this world relation of concern. A language must be formed that can break free from the old orders.

Two titles are ready to indicate this change in the worldview: the *worldview of war* is being replaced by the *worldview of concern*. What exactly the categories of war and concern mean needs to be described in detail, for misunderstanding is obvious. It is not a matter of a teleology dedicated to the promotion of the good. In other words, it is not to be assumed that the idealistic projects of the past will finally be fulfilled because one now has a morally intact view of the world. Rather, what is at stake is a fundamental constellation in which the political and life are to be brought into a life-serving relationship with each other.

The following points should be considered in order to make the theses plausible. The topos of naked life should be placed in the centre at the beginning. It is about that life which, in its nakedness and unprotectedness, has always been the object of political thought. Critical theory has good reasons for opposing the fatal continuity of the state's political disposal of this life, which is done justice to by means of an ethics of the singular (Politics and Life). The alliance of politics and life, which was consolidated above all in the modern era, stands in the twilight of power. As soon as life begins to be reduced to its vegetative substance or to be dominated in favour of a supposedly objective order, the surrender of ethics is at stake. The politics of the state of exception, as we find it in Giorgio Agamben, is representative of this critical tradition.

The following reflections attempt to offer an alternative option to the critique of power. It is not the all-suffocating, totalitarian power that is in question, but the determinations of two worldviews. We are dealing with a shift in the longue dureé: the movement leads from a polemogenic to a caring worldview (The Logic of Worldviews and The Worldview of War).

Politics and Life

The Leviathan is the oldest of all creatures, which apparently does not belong to any human world. In the Old Testament, a figure is mentioned, gigantic but by no means monstrous, whose function was to represent the immense power of God. From the depths of the sea, this giant figure appeared to the doubting Job, terrifying by its very presence.

In the early modern era, the Leviathan has probably also been handed down as an image of terror, but with quite different references. Thomas Hobbes, the political doyen of methodical thought, chose the title to leave no doubt. Modern rule also cultivates the game of fear and terror; here is its essential element. The frontispiece of the body politic – the leviathan of state power – is the subject of art-theoretical and political considerations (Bredekamp, 2020). A closer examination is worthwhile even after centuries of learned research. To think the modern state is to form an image of it. The image corresponds with the textual theory of the state. Sword and crozier symbolise ecclesiastical and secular power; the sovereign spans a world landscape to illustrate the comprehensive claim of the Leviathan.

The monstrousness, of course, is not to be recognised in the sheer size, but it is revealed in the shadowy persons who are assembled in the body of the state. With their eyes fixed on the sovereign, they remain on the level of a mass, gathered in a zone of mute non-violence. Although the viewer of the picture can claim to reach eye level with the sovereign of the state, he simultaneously performs the same movement, which only makes sense as an operation of thought. In the face of this third party, the struggle becomes an order. Only by playing with fear and authority was it possible to prevent the divisiveness that was characterised by perpetual civil and religious wars.

It is the embodiment of a relationship of violence that has the worst possible reputation. This sovereign embraces life by virtue of its capacity for violence and its inviolability.

But it cannot be politics in the contemporary sense if one considers the positioning vis-à-vis a third party of which one is a part. Fear and terror form the core of this political image, whereby it is not the size of the sovereign alone that is decisive, but the gesture. The willingness to lay down one's arms and surrender them to the state is, as is well known, the great moment of Hobbesian state-building; the unconditional precedence is for order, into which all participants, without exception, submit.

Discourses on the birth of the totalitarian state have been conducted enough since then. What remains to be discussed, however, is to what extent the modern state has been able to free itself from the accusation of totalitarian drift or whether the basic problematic is not also found in the present, in view of the presence of a state that arguably unites all contradictions within itself. Long-gone, yet persistent, containing illegitimate violence, yet not itself free of violence.

Another crucial determination of the political is contained in the relationship between politics and life. Life here is bare life, a highly charged, morally compact concept. Politics and bare life are in a relationship of power – and already in this constellation all the fault lines of modern political philosophy can be found (Butler, 2005).

Giorgio Agamben, representative of many, draws sharp lines in the history of power from its ancient origins to the present. According to this, sovereign power is related to bare life in that it disposes of it completely. In the ancient Roman legal figure of *homines sacri*, life was excluded from the narrow sphere of law and released. In the state of exception, which grants this state entity the disposal of death and life, this political power is established (Agamben, 2002). According to Agamben, these political provisions can be traced back to the crisis debates of our day.

In this image, life is purely vegetative life, which would be deprived of all its spiritual, cultural and political capacities. The politics of exception, which thinks it can invoke the protection of that naked life as justification, becomes the signature of our time (Agamben, 2021).

In *Leviathan* and *homo sacer*, figurations of the political are named that prove to be contentious. Thomas Hobbes was concerned with the experience of war, with its horror, which could only be avoided through the establishment of legitimate rule. Violence and order are preserved as basic elements of this form of politics.

For Agamben, on the other hand, the violence of politics towards qualified life is always already present as soon as domination is established. Politics, in other words, becomes virulent whenever it positions itself vis-à-vis the fullness and potentiality of actual life – and curtails this potentiality.

In the image of the Leviathan, in other words, the *gain of* a political destiny is expressed; in the image of the state of exception, on the other hand, an unimaginable *loss of* ethics appears. Since in antiquity naked life was excluded in the polis, procedures of power have been able to prove themselves. The territorial state was able to emerge as the most prominent figure in the history of political ideas.

Techniques of governance created (and continue to create) docile bodies, a foundation and at the same time a threshold to modernity. The politicisation of naked life is of the deepest ambivalence, as long as it is claimed to protect life – while at the same time preserving the possibility of 'authorising the holocaust' (Agamben, 2002, p. 13).

Worldviews are known to be associated with fixed ideas; they are meant to set a course and focus interests of knowledge. But they also have to do with shifts and irritations. The outlined images of power, however, suggest the doubt whether the hardening of worldviews does not also lead to a hardening in thinking. In the traditional sense, the worldview of care would be synonymous with the technology of power that disposes over life. The state thus takes over the care of people's natural lives; it penetrates – to speak with Foucault – the bodies of the subjects and guides them to subjective techniques of self-care. The state thus consolidates the structure of power (Foucault, 1977).

The worldview of war, on the other hand, which can be identified in the giant-like appearance of Leviathan, is characterised by the repressive character of the monopolisation of violence. Admittedly, this is a problematic alternative.

Both worldviews, with which politics and bare life are inserted into an arrangement, are to be viewed from alternative angles.

In the political world of Thomas Hobbes, fear was a great, all-dominant theme that gripped both the author and the circumstances of the time itself. The fear of his peers was eminently justified: the civil wars had devastated the countryside, they had left an indelible impression of the destructive power of war. The political worldview, when looked at closely, was bound to presuppose a negative image of man. The justified fear of the capacity for violence pushed people under the shelter of the state. This state had the highest justification as long as it guaranteed protection and cared for order. It offered a solution in the face of the deep divisiveness that people had to experience in moral and religious conflicts.

For in the civil war, reason, language and insight failed. The desire for peace alone was no longer enough to stop the dynamics of attitudes. Morality, which can degenerate into self-righteousness and ignited the furore of holy war, only found an effective limit in the public state.

This fault line of fear continues into the present. The modern democratic state bears little resemblance to that state structure that was based primarily on people's fear of death. Fear alone drove people into the absolutist state, which in turn was overtaken by social forces of autonomy. Only the democratic state, which made the sovereignty of qualified political life possible, straightened out this line.

For now, as we know, it is the many political subjects who are subject to common laws whose purpose is the concern for vulnerability. The two-faced nature of the democratic body, according to Giorgio Agamben, lies in the formation of the sovereign subject (Agamben, 2002, p. 133). Bare life must become qualified life in order to satisfy the determination of the political. The body of Leviathan remains a brilliant metaphor for Agamben as well, insofar as it is formed from the individual bodies and now itself constitutes a sovereign body. The killable, vulnerable bodies take refuge in a state body that itself no longer has to fear violence. For it itself determines who is entitled to qualified life and which life is denied this attention.

The Logic of Worldviews

One of the advantages of such philosophical reflection is that it raises awareness of legitimate moral claims. The modern state is not solely obliged to defend against violence;

it is not only supposed to protect against the arbitrariness of rule. Subliminally, its tasks seem to be far greater. It should take care of the existing order, in which manifold expectations of the good life are gathered. In this respect, one could simplistically claim that the modern democratic state is not the child of war, for it is no longer in touch with the violent experiences of earlier times.

Only in the worldview of concern does its justification become clear.

From the *worldview of war* to the *worldview of care* – viewed in this way, a change has taken place from the state's absolute capacity for violence to the caring relationship in modernity. The following considerations are intended to show why these hints would have to be differentiated in order to produce a plausible theory. We are *not* dealing with a social change that replaces the old worldview with a new one. What is claimed, however, is that the worldview of concern is taking up more and more space and asserting itself more and more as a dominant narrative.

But what exactly are *worldviews*? The term deserves a more precise analysis, if only to clarify the subliminal semantic references. Worldviews are constructs about the nature of the world, and in this respect they belong to the natural sciences. However, they are, as it were, interpretations of life that hold an immeasurable abundance in store that no exact measurement can match.

Worldviews are known to arouse controversy because of their proximity to ideological constrictions. They make statements about the nature of the natural world, but also of the social world, and thus also statements about the nature of human beings. Worldviews become problematic the moment they claim an ultimate statement or an unquestionable truth. In this respect, one could conclude with good reason that worldviews are fluid entities, in a constant state of flux, without the legitimacy of ultimate knowledge. And one may add that this is a well-founded, historically saturated attitude that puts a stop to any rigorism of knowledge.

Worldviews tend to conflict, but that is precisely why their social potentials should be unfolded. Just as history itself does not follow a plan and it does not hold a higher meaning at the end of a path, the necessity of shaping history remains. The situation is similar with worldviews: they are the course set in the space of human history, bundle interests and enable positioning. Worldviews have subjective and objective faces that are closely interrelated. A worldview is both a private possession that no one can take away from you, but it is at the same time a concept of meaning that is available in a given time. In a broad arc of human history, one can speak in this sense of a fundamental change that led from the mythical worldview to the rationalisation of world religions – and finally culminated in the epoch of self-empowerment (Imhof/Romano, 1996).

In the worldview of myth, relationships of analogy and contrast prevailed in the midst of a naturalised society. Nature and culture were closely intertwined, things and people were in constant exchange, past and present indistinguishable. In this worldview, all that we take for granted today was not available. In the dense mirror play of relationships, language could not stand out as an independent medium. The social, objective and subjective worlds hung indiscriminately on each other. In the magical ritual of archaic societies, a wholeness was experienced that cannot be translated into modern categories. Only through the differentiation of a religious elite and the orientation towards individual suffering did the religious worldview replace the mythical one.

Religious worldviews arise at the bottom of a doubt that certainly touches on personal despair. Only when it is asked why happiness and unhappiness are unequally distributed and where the sufferings and passions come from, is religious thinking set in motion. The worldview of myth remained, as it were, unquestioningly in a horizon of history-less uniformity, in a 'magic garden of holistic thinking' (Ibid., 24). The *distribution of the goods of happiness* points the way out of the limits of this worldview.

Subjective orientations explode the old orders, they lead out of the garden of desirelessness; they challenge and they accuse. The further course of all salvation movements leads through the need for meaning that links individual suffering with religious symbolism.

As is well known, changing worldviews accompany further history. The question of where we currently stand and which worldview is available today is, of course, wrongly posed. For various preconditions must be clarified in order to be able to speak of a worldview that leads back to a specific worldview. Too many aspects remain unconsidered and many questions open if we simply speak of *the worldview of our time*. Nevertheless, it is doubtful that all worldviews, opinions and evaluations would be indifferent and thus arbitrary and that we would be standing on a fragile continent of knowledge.

Instead, it is to be shown that in the midst of all the noise of contingencies, the search for a supporting worldview is rational. We stand on the ground of an available knowledge that holds ready a worldview capable of insight and justification and that confronts our time with its own questions, challenges and consequences (Dux, 2017, p. 3). Anthropological, historical and social scientific insights have been formulated in this sense (Dux/Rüsen, 2014; Rüsen, 2013) – here it will be a matter of connecting these concepts of meaning with the title of concern.

Worldviews are not static and fixed. Their change is not linked to a single date, but is due to a development in thought and action. In this sense, the change from the worldview of war to the worldview of concern should not be understood in terms of replacement. While one worldview becomes porous and its folds already contain hints of other forms of meaning, this does not mean that the next image is already available. World pictures can become fragile without being able to rely on the superiority of the next narrative. Newly acquired knowledge is hinted at without already being a possession; questions are raised without answers already being able to be taken from the treasure of a culture. An older and a newer knowledge form a fluid transition, accompanied by contradictions and inconsistencies. One worldview no longer wants to fit so well into the other.

The worldview of concern, which receives the most attention here, is of course a system between meaning and knowledge 'beyond absolutist specifications' (Dux, 2017, p. 7). It establishes a new structure of justification for the human relationship to the self and the world. Previous interpretations by no means lose their relevance, nor are the grand narratives simply dismissed here. What is claimed, however, is that the category of concern (even if it resembles a long-processed philosophical theme of existence) enables a new justification of the world-relation that is already underway.

That the reflections resemble a tightrope walk becomes understandable from a philosophical point of view, because according to Heidegger, the theoretical reference to the world has long since been overcome. We live in lifeworld contexts and are factually embedded in existing situations (Heidegger, 1979). This means that worry, that comprehensive mode of relating to the world, is not properly understood as *worrying* about an abstract, objectified world. We stand in the world worrying, worrying is our access to all that is present. The language of Heidegger's analysis of existence demonstrates that life itself is a form of expression that transcends any artificial distancing.

Care as a category of the human means the inescapable situativity and facticity of life. In this worldview, it will thus again be about the position of the human being in the world, insofar as the oldest anthropological–philosophical aspects are addressed. Concern refers to a practical relationship to the world that belongs to each individual; whether it can be transformed beyond that into cultural meaning – this would have to be shown.

An open link to the theme of Dasein is of course ambivalent. The strict phenomenological basis cannot be translated into social, political and practical-ethical insights that would make the world better or more 'moral'. However, the category of concern in Being and Time offers further connections that have not yet been formulated. The factual acting and interpreting in the world establishes an inescapable ambivalence in the relation to the world.

The worldview of concern is an expression of the unavailable conditions of meaning of our existence. In it, a better humanity does not enter the stage, and the world does not become an object of a morally intact world reference. Rather, it is about the possibility of reconstructing the historical, which in fact goes hand in hand with the crossing of a threshold.

The spiritual–cultural way of being does not experience a triumph of ultimate self-empowerment, but it does resemble a significant return to what has always characterised human forms of meaning: life *as a* fundamental issue of concern.

The Worldview of War

An older worldview becomes fragile – and a new one appears on the horizon of history. Those who follow such motifs face justified reproaches. Is it a matter of historical–philosophical reveries, against which a mere reference to the realities of contemporary war was sufficient?

Rather, it seems advisable to ask at what point in the history of violence we actually stand 'today'. Are we – if one takes a subject of human history as a basis, against one's better judgement – at a vertex where previous violence would finally be dealt with? Are we really opening new chapters in the history of violence that will arouse curiosity? Because, in fact, violence is less and less damaging to life and the permanent renunciation of violence as a reality would have long since shaped modernity?

In the midst of all the decay of meaning and tradition, our time has brought forth a new measure of peaceful coexistence, Steven Pinker knows (Pinker, 2007). But all well-founded psychology of non-violence is countered, as is well known, by experiences of radical violence that could equally be described as modern. A unified diagnosis pointing to a final turn for the good is not in sight. Not only because violence as a phenomenon has an unavailable diversity, not only because violence is always present despite practised practices of trust, but because violence as a *fundamentum* permeates all areas of order and life. It is *in language, in practice, in past and present*, without being definitively disarmed.

Obviously, a narrative that aims at the disappearance of a reference to the world in the horizon of war is confronted with various difficulties. Such a thesis only becomes understandable if we take the philosophical interventions on the history of violence seriously. War becomes an abstractum, a challenge to thought and ethics. As a concrete experience translated into images, texts and narratives, it is of course a reality; but as a motif for social philosophy, war transcends the threshold of simple narrativity. War is representative of radicalised violence; it is a means and a measure in politics, but it is also a life force. Since everything is subject to war, writes Emmanuel Levinas, there is also no easy way out. Being is dominated by war, which is why ethics is always already confronted with the experience of violence, to which it sees itself unreservedly exposed. Such absolutism of reality does not dissolve in the disposal of violence; it cannot be mastered by rational means, but it makes possible the ethical reference to the world in the first place: by surrendering oneself and thinking of ethics from the point of view of the Other (Levinas, 1988).

Two levels must be considered in parallel here. On an ontological level, war is understood as the consummation of existence. The humanistic tradition of this motif goes back, as mentioned, to the dark Heraclitus of Ephesus. Thinking war became understood at the time as an exercise in humility – war is to be described not only as a means, but as the consummation of existence. The essence of things lies in becoming – and war, which aims just as ruthlessly at the becoming and passing of life, is to be thought through as the power of life. The universal paternity of war allows men and gods, slaves and free, victors and losers of history to emerge. In war, the logos is exposed – and people have no choice but to acknowledge its fearsome position in the social world.

An image of war could not be further removed from modern, reason-guided ideas – and yet trace elements of Bellicist metaphysics have been able to survive into modern times. We read Carl Schmitt – and hear about constellations of enemies that expose the alleged essence of the political. We follow Martin Heidegger's existential analytics – and are frightened by the themes of existence that seem to point us inevitably back to the deepest divisiveness.

Held in a nothingness, modern man – analogous to the ancient essence of war – is left to uncover being in the light of his own death?

A philosophy that interprets war as an expression of being promotes contradiction. The interpretations are not due to a totalitarian disproportion alone. Only in the mirror of the history of reason do they become bearable. For thinking through war without revering it as a fateful life force has always been an equally strong motif of the history of violence. Now war becomes a thing that should not be and is thus consigned to political limitation.

The worldview of the war shows cracks that did not appear overnight. Various lines of development are to be traced, resulting in a multilayered picture. By no means do these lines lead streamlined to the end point of non-violence. But they do indicate that the acceptance of a worldview that welcomes war as a basic element of existence no longer has the same interpretive power.

All that is needed are hints that point to the waning of a hardened consciousness. One line points to the state, which could never free itself from the logic of unreason and was always ready to sacrifice life on the altar of the state. The idea of raison d'état, according to Ekkehart Krippendorff (1985), was raison d'état of power for the longest time in history. It demanded marching to war as an abstract ideal that rulers and peoples had to serve. This state, which could expand on European soil, needed war to justify its existence. War and state were led into a holy alliance; in this respect, war was more than just a useful means, but the content, centre and axis of the state entity. This state was prepared to participate in any distortion of reality as long as the phantasm of unconditional violence was maintained. How deeply this state as a figure of fulfilment had penetrated the psyche of the rulers remains astonishing (Theweleit, 1994).

A worldview begins to fade when the façades peel away or when there are indentations that cannot be denied. The wars of the twentieth century indicated a threshold over which war had long since stepped. The loss of ethics and humanity could no longer be made good by a second façade of raison d'état. The wars against humanity had, as we know, burrowed deep into the world conscience and remained like an open wound. It was not the abstract state as a form of rule that had lost its credibility, but the totalitarian state that had unleashed the destructive forces that had been retained and yet preserved in the long nineteenth century. This is how one might describe the reproach that emanates from a comparatively peaceful nineteenth century.

In this respect, the worldview of war resembles an *anciem régime that* recognises the culmination of its fullness of power. War can no longer be written or spoken of in the way it was conceivable in earlier times. War has been outlawed and tamed without being imprisoned. It continues to be a phenomenon in the social world, but its shape and its 'image' are subject to change.

This change includes psychological and social, political and legal aspects. Peace is not a final product or a final state. It is quiet, fragile, but never powerless. With the language of law, it has found a backing in the long run. For in the present, it is international law that, while never achieving a resounding effect, shapes consciousness and embeds itself in minds. The language of human rights is familiar in a way that it seems to need no further justification when it comes to concrete violations.

Peacekeeping and peace-enforcing interventions may require the most sophisticated legal reflections – as to their legitimacy and feasibility – but they precisely evidence a shift in consciousness beyond the old war. This new world of concern, oriented towards nothing other than human rights, is of course problematic. A grounding in reality was only achieved by considering the concrete hegemony in the world of international relations and the constant ruptures in international law. So it is not a brave new world to which the talk of global concern could be oriented.

But the claim that Jürgen Habermas believed to recognise in the constitutionalisation of international law must be upheld (Habermas, 2004).

Wars continue to be fought, not as religious wars of earlier times, not as ideological wars that could mobilise the masses, not as purely state wars. The face of war today is opaque, a snake pit. The lines of conflict are tangled, the motives unclear, but the consequences are the same: war creates suffering. So what exactly would be the category of concern that would be able to defy this anciem regime?

Concern in the worldview does not mean that war would be removed from the social world. Nor can the development of international law be set in this sense on an end point that would result solely from outlawing all violence. That the new human law will break the old international law – this speculation is as memorable as it is inadmissible. For human law and international law remain in the tension in which they have always been. The abolition of war, pursued with seriousness as a serious intervention since Kant, has been an unavailable truth of interstate relations since the formulation of the UN Charter. A truth that is broken, denied and disregarded, but which no despot and no military logic can get around. It is the irreducible connection between fundamental rights and constitutional principles in the nation state framework and the establishment of a cosmopolitan constitutional state, which is to be emphasised here (Ibid., 160). The argumentation, no matter which aspects are brought into play, has its first and last reason here without any metaphysics.

The fact that the practised political observer points with good reason to the failure of war-preventing measures and enumerates the countless victims of war even in the twenty-first century is admittedly not an argument against the worldview of care. In a deeper sense, this scenario is rather the foundation on which the conditions of care relations are to be clarified.

The highest expression in that worldview of concern, which may still appear blurred and misleading here, is that violence which we experience and suffer has to thematise and cope with in modern orders. In the worldview of war, it was an unavoidable evil, a necessity.

It is only in the dialectical turn that the change in this image becomes clear; we have renounced the old wars and fear the new ones. The violence of war has been contained by means of morality, law and diplomacy, yet we must learn to deal with the new forms of war. In the worldview of concern, the old war lives on, but it does not have the former destructive power.

What has changed today, when asked unequivocally, compared to earlier times? Certainly many things that we take for granted. War is the greatest misfortune imaginable that societies can fall into. The willingness to go to war has diminished; the renunciation of violence has been able to establish itself as a basic idea in peace societies. A statement that may be true because it describes a principled attitude in concrete historical situations. But it cannot be carelessly applied to the state of the world as a whole. Next to the legally prescribed outlawing of war, war stands as a pure instrument of power; beyond the will to renounce violence, we experience an immediate willingness to use violence. The atavistic motives have been pushed into the background, but they still push forward from time to time.

Religiously motivated violence has not disappeared either, at least it acts as an accelerant in fragile conflict spaces. All this can hardly be included in a comprehensive diagnosis (Hondrich, 2002).

Nevertheless, war is insufficient as a category of meaning for the modern worldview. Its presence is undisputed, but other categories have emerged that change its meaning for the whole. Politically, one would speak of aspects of security and order in an international perspective, but in the same breath one must reclaim the position of those affected, whose suffering is multiplied with each new war. Even the most cruel and devastating war of the present in Syria seems to confirm this statement. Its origins and continuity are linked to a complexity that cannot be explained solely by the willingness of individual actors to use violence.

Efforts at the highest international level to break through the violence seem insufficient, but the concern is at the same time for the inhabitants of a country who have been forced to flee or have already perished in the ruins of war. The direction of vision alone shows that it is no longer about the old war and that a different worldview is on the rise.

The moral orientation towards humanitarian aspects is just as important as the apparent acceptance of violence that unleashes unspeakable suffering.

The worldview of concern is by no means autistic in the face of the reality of elementary violence. The ethics of an Emmanuel Levinas puts his finger on the wound: not the war that has been overcome, but the war that dominates everything is at the centre of common life (Levinas, 1987). In reality, literally everything falls to war; from the moment we are thrown into the world, we are at the mercy of violence, which can take many faces and forms. The morality that fights this ontological war has always already lost; only the insight into the irreducibility of violence could be understood as an ethical position in this respect. Possibly, this ethics between totality and infinity agrees with the present statements: for it is now about the caring self-relationship that describes itself as non-violent and at the same time has to acknowledge the entanglement in the totality of the relations of violence.

The Worldview of Concern

Coping with violence, which takes the form of war, is an 'eternal' motif of humanity. Even under prehistoric conditions, violence became an existential theme. The clumsy biped, which gradually refined its front limbs for hunting and became a specialised hunter, was a creature of ambivalence. Violent and vulnerable, endowed with social skills, though capable of manslaughter. The dichotomy in the way he related to the world showed itself in the fright in the face of threats, but also in the amazement at the beauty of the animal. At the same time, the dichotomy became apparent in the awareness that in the body of the killed animal is that life which belongs to the hunter himself. A human world thus emerges at the moment when one's own violence is linked with meaning.

As a being of violence, man has always stood between Cain and Prometheus. The possibility of killing accompanied the rise of man, but all Cain's deeds, which are supposed to testify to the warlike nature, ultimately remain in contradiction. For man, beyond violence, is capable of taming fire, taming animals, producing art, founding cities and confronting his own drives in discursive gatherings.

The following reflections are a venture and a challenge in that they play with obsolete concepts. The appearance of making history the final authority that could show the way for humanity should be avoided. But the basic idea is that history and the present are about the confrontation with the human relation to the world. The worldview of concern is one of the possible forms in which this confrontation is carried out.

The philosophical analysis of existence, however, does not start from one's own capacity for violence against other life, but from the insight into one's own mortality. Its basic ideas lead to essential insights. Worry is the basic element of the human relationship to the world and to the self (Heidegger, 1979, § 46–53). Death appears as the outermost limit of caring behaviour. This concern is the expression and core of the human self-understanding as an acting being.

The philosophical blueprint, not to be underestimated in its importance for twentieth-century philosophy, is to be unfolded in various directions.

The pragmatics of appropriating the world is what defines human beings as technical beings. At the same time, concern is a dimension of being able to be oneself, with which we shape our own existence as a historical design – as a life that is led and not just accepted. Both levels have a higher significance for the development of worldviews. The shaping and meaning-seeking human being is at the centre of philosophical consideration. He comes to terms with a reality that is recognised as objective and at the same time asks about his position in this world. The world is both a subject that the acting human being confronts; at the same time, it is the all-encompassing, unavailable reality of existence.

How can the title of concern be appropriately interpreted in the pragmatic world reference? The philosophical disputes are to be taken up. Let us read Heidegger with simple thought processes. Worry determines and assumes a single subject of orientation. *Someone* finds himself in the world and recognises himself as a *subject* in time. Worry arises from the pressures of the present and the demands of the future. The caring person is always already ahead of himself. Worrying behaviour arises from the certainty of death. This form of existence is to be described as a singular totality: it draws its meaning from the insight into one's own mortality. The world is the existential of existence, which proves to be unique, but always already lost. For the gradient towards death directs all further considerations of this philosophy, as is well known, onto a terrain full of conflict.

Is this an exhaustive treatment of care as a world relationship – or can't other aspects of the basic human situation be highlighted that condition the worldview of care? The title of totalitarian singularity conceals the unjustifiability of ourselves, and thus also the responsibility for our own lives. What is omitted here, however, is an examination of the facticity of common life. For the present reflection, the point of view of inter-existentiality is the decisive one (Rentsch, 1999, 1995).

Concern for the world – concern for one's own being – concern for others: these modes of being-in-the-world seem familiar. But which dimension is inscribed with a beginning and how do these dimensions relate to each other? We are always already in the world in a caring way and our thoughts are trivially always with us. But this does not mean that the reference to the world is from the summit of the autonomous, self-sufficient and yet solitary subject. In the older tradition, concern is conceived monologically in Heidegger. Concern for others is added as a possibility from outside. An ethics of care for the neighbour would be possible in this respect, but always only a derived, secondary form of care for others. The idea of coping with facticity in the horizon of one's own self dominates.

In contrast, contemporary philosophy is writing a new chapter that escapes the constrictions in the spirit of thanatos. Man lives in a basic situation in which the concern may always take the form of a monologue – as care within the limits of one's own existence. But prior to this, the possibility must be noted that all our senses have their seat in common life. This does not invoke an intimate alliance or a sacred commune in which individual life loses its value, but merely describes what it means to move and orient oneself in a human world. This structure of concern, which is not irrelevant to everything else, is embedded in the communicative and social horizon of fragile beings. Accordingly, the human situation is inter-existentially constituted – and can only be understood inter-existentially.

However, it would be misleading to conclude from this the ethos of an era. In the worldview of care, the essence of the human being remains bound to that stubbornness that can never be finally translated into pedagogical meaning. Only in the delimitation and redefinition of the social can we recognise the value of an inter-existential perspective.

The social, that genuinely human category, polarises the knowledge of human possibilities. Living in a human world, some say, has always had to do with the possibility of being with. That we bury our neighbours and hold them in honour; that we feel sorrow and pain for the other – this alone could be described as evidence of social resonance in a human lifeworld. According to this narrative of origins, human beings have always been referred to other human beings: in cooperation and opposition, in relationships of solidarity and enmity, as equals, unequals, members or strangers, or as excluded life.

The other narrative directs the gaze to the modern era and thus to a determination of the relationship between the political and the social that had only found its form here. The social is not a property of being, but an invention (Liebsch, 2018, pp. 41–99).

The social, which is now at stake, has to do with increased attention to the vulnerability of the human being, which is only made possible in political conditions. The *social* – it becomes the object of moral language and the object of politics. As is well known, social questions have been asked since the nineteenth century and have been raised again and again in many variations ever since. Since then, the social has been a problem area of modernity, politicised or instrumentalised, fought over or forgotten.

The beautiful idea that under a worldview of concern, it is precisely this area of the social that becomes an ultimately justifying motive must, of course, be rejected here. Concern, which is reflected in the inter-existential dimension, emphasises the fragility of the basic interpersonal situation without claims to socio-political programming. Its ethics draw from insights of connectedness in the form of life, for which primary distance, concealment, denial and alienation are characteristic. Only in the perspective of failing beings does the concern meant here become authentic. In it, strangeness and unavailability, alterity and the non-identical are distinguished as the motifs that spell out the actual reference to care in the world relationship.

Philosophy and History

The narratives that run towards the development of a worldview stand at the intersection of psychology and history (Jüttemann, 2013; Ders., 2014). All history, as we know, has to do with human intentions, so the connection is not surprising. But to what extent psychological conditions are reflected historically is the real question. It is answered differently, depending on the contexts of scientific theory. Here, of course, we are dealing with a very specific interpretation of what happens between psychological motives and historical developments. The basic thesis aims at an impact event that unfolds in a particular worldview. A worldview cannot be aligned with an epoch or a mood of the times; it claims to represent something else. In the worldview of care, horizons of experience, meaning and language come together. And to get close to this happening, psychology is particularly called upon. It is not enough to describe all events, expectations and experiences as mental dispositions. That which is to be assessed as 'psychological' in the history of events must be considered in depth.

Psychoanalysis must thus be questioned in the first place in order to substantiate the thesis (Rüsen/Straub, 1998a).

To understand an age, the emergence of historical consciousness must be explained. But the difficulties cannot be dismissed: for history cannot be mapped psychologically; or if it is attempted, the findings are manageable. We live, for example, in risky circumstances, in an age of anger or under the impact of a crisis. However, the fear or furore that particularly affects single individuals cannot simply be subsumed and lead to a general statement.

So why psychoanalysis as a counsellor? As we shall see, the view of historical self-understanding is to be opened to a historical event that eludes rational analysis. In history we find: fractures that have not been understood, dark spots that remain enigmatic. We reconstruct events and come across a void that is not filled linguistically. Admittedly, everything that takes place in human history can be explained logically. But turning to the past requires the depth of psychology in order to integrate the affective distance, the unconscious affects, the intentional non-understanding and the repression. History is only fully understood when these elements are taken into account.

There are various reasons for this approach to history, which will only become apparent in the course. However, the basic idea is defensible: the history of genres is parallel to individual history. Many motifs that are alluded to in this context are misleading. These include, for example, the custom of presenting history as something that was produced by great men.

Likewise, the psychological analysis of the circumstances underlying certain events is difficult. It perhaps directs interest to the hidden world reference of the agents and to their unconscious driving forces that were not apparent to them (Wehler, 1974).

This reading of history is to be understood, so to speak, as a procedure in which actors are subsequently subjected to an analysis that reveals their behaviour, their decisions, their misconduct or even their willingness to use violence. It is then about the motives of historical actors that determine their actions under certain cultural, political and social conditions.

The basic idea at hand is to be formulated differently. What do we understand by history? It is neither a sum of events nor a product. It can be represented and interpreted: then it is our history and thus helpful for our orientation needs. Beyond that, however, it is a historical achievement of meaning formation that is narratively structured.

History is primarily a product of meaning. It is a performance that elevates meaning above the everyday world of experience and enables a representation of the course of time. This representation is circumscribed here as the worldview of care, a narrative that configures reality in a specific way. Worry is a response to the experience of violence. It is to be understood as a way of coming to terms with the past that is equivalent to a historical narrative competence. The way in which history is told is admittedly a special one.

The basic idea of a worldview of concern goes back to a motive that is certainly arguable. World society is on a level of reflexive possibilities that were not there before. This does not refer to a unity of reason in the sense of idealistic philosophy, but rather to a communicative competence: a consciousness of history that has emerged from a historical event of impact (Straub, 1998a, pp. 12–33). For this consciousness, the passage through painful processes of insight into the human capacity for violence was unavoidable.

The question is how one can theoretically approach the history of violence and the motif of concern. Looking back, the experience of violence is usually transferred into a common horizon of meaning; looking to the future, on the other hand, one tries to counter the threat of violence. The suspicion that we do not understand the ways of acting and the attributions of meaning of the past is, however, an indication of the immanent difficulties.

The conventional understanding often emphasises a 'humanity' that in retrospect realises its fallibility and thus draws the right conclusions. Therein lies a profound deception about a 'subject' in the philosophy of history. But if this image does not satisfy – in what image does such a narrative succeed?

The reflection accepts the risk of creating another image that is just as misleading. But the attempt is worthwhile because it meets the demands of interdisciplinary thinking and makes a grand narrative possible. In the medium of language, actions are mapped meaningfully in the course of time. Here this means: *humanity* has thus freed itself from archaic conditions and attained a new level of consciousness. It has reached a level where many things seem possible. But at the same time, it is referred to its weakness, for which intensified efforts are necessary – to 'its' violence, which continues to be the silent companion of all stories. For this weakness, the title of the worldview of concern is decisive here: it suggests that it is not in the simplest sense about the conscious action of a collective, but rather about coping with adversity. In order to come close to concern in this sense, the fractures and dark spots must also be considered.

Concern is to be understood both as historical consciousness directed towards past suffering, but at the same time towards the horizons of meaning that is not understood.

Concern means the conscious reconstruction of the past, but at the same time the understanding of the seemingly meaningless. The unexplained dark and abysmal belong to this historical consciousness just as much as historiographical clarity. The opening to psychoanalytical levels is thus indispensable for the approach (Rauschenbach, 1998).

In this sense, the history of violence in the twentieth century was reconstructed and sharpened towards a conception of time. In question is whether humanity continues to be embraced by violence or whether it has set a limit to the renunciation of violence. In question, however, is more than this: namely, whether one can gather under a worldview that meaningfully unites past and present. Since doubt has the upper hand here, the conclusion is obvious. This worldview of worry is only properly understood when one includes the mechanisms of the unconscious, the dark driving forces, defence and repression.

One can sharpen the thesis defended here even more. The violence of the twentieth century created a space of meaning that is groundbreaking for all subsequent epochs. In this, a relationship of care is expressed, which of course is always connected with forms of failure. More precisely, we need to ask in depth how we can grasp this space of meaning and translate it for later generations. We need to ask what actions this space of history opens up, what moral options it offers and what orders are associated with it.

At the centre of this space is the experience of violence. However, it is too simplistic to understand this violence as one that needs to be conditioned and contained. This would probably only add another one to the established philosophies of peace. What is to be attempted here, on the other hand, can be described using a thought experiment by Jean F. Lyotard. Repression, wrote the author of postmodern thought, is a form of preservation. The genocide of the Jews, which is considered the prototype of an unrepresentable, incomprehensible experience of violence, is only properly understood as a form of repression of a traumatic event. Only if its unavailable form were accepted in the absence of a record or in the unreality of a place would one be close to the event (Lyotard, 1988).

It is easy to misunderstand such philosophical thoughts. Memory in writing and language, in monuments and places of remembrance, is seen as a means against forgetting. Only in this way, through writing and text, through the voices and records of those affected, is this history of violence protected from oblivion. But, according to Lyotard, only the insight into the paradoxical structure of memory leads beyond this interpretation. What has been recorded can be erased. That which 'for lack of a place or a duration' (Ibid., 38) was not recorded, is the actual tradition. It directs interest to contexts that do not fit together in a meaningful way, to contexts that do not synthesise and stand transversely in space, time, geography and diachrony.

So has the space of meaning of the past century never been properly understood – and consequently can never be adequately represented? At the very least, the means that have been used since then to depict past realities are negativistic in character. The unconceptualised, the unheroic memory, the damaged self – these are consistently negative determinations that remain in the face of traumatic experiences. The possibilities of an integrative conception are shattered. The meaning that one wants to transmit would thus be antinomic, dissonant and directed against any desire for meaning.

This can be used to justify strategies that counteract the disproportion between violence and historical narrativity.

This abstract thought is of eminent importance for the understanding of history. We cannot resolve the contradictions of the past century and translate them into manageable recipes. There are no lessons of history that are unbreakably perpetuated and translated into plans of action. In this respect, the caveat of *posthistoire* is right. The basic mood of the following narrative corresponds to the sceptical experience that has failed because of the resistance of the world.

History and action are characterised by a distance that no political imperative can eliminate. It is only in the limits of constructability and agency that this form of history is expressed. In the events that we simplistically call *our history*, the finitude in the human condition is revealed (Angehrn, 2014).

The present narrative is understood as a form of re-experience. History has often been misunderstood as a practice of making, but this scepticism is not to be confused with impotence. Rather, it is that we need to make sense of the open futurity in a context. This reading emerges if we do not inappropriately shorten history: history is not an object of technical feasibility, but an event that precedes all conscious action.

The worldview of concern has the claim to be a qualified narrative. History was told in a way as if there were a linear history in which a context could be seen that we could grasp with subject-theoretical means. This approach will rightly be called daring. It results from an attitude of resistance: although the plurality of history cannot be dissolved, although the many particular spaces of experience cannot be put together like a jigsaw puzzle, a process of transmission must be observed. So we *write history in* a way as if a unity of event, experience and action that structures meaning and significance could be grasped. Even if we know that there is currently no unity that is represented as humanity in one person, such a narrative with a reference to the world can be justified. This opens up spaces of action and experience that are captured with psychological criteria.

Within this narrative horizon, there is room for interpretations, for acts of meaning-making that do not merge into a grand narrative. What is crucial, however, is the assumption of a subjectivity that underlies the worldview of concern.

A subject suffers something and draws conclusions for future situations. A knowledge of the world is formed that is deficient and incomplete, but remains connected to the claim of meaningfulness, linked to an implicit pedagogy in a moral and valorative space (Taylor, 1994; Straub, 1998a).

But what about this subject when it finds itself in a context of action that is experienced above all as violence? Does such a subject of humanity recognise itself as an acting subject? Or does it remain relegated to a historicity whose meaning and order remain elusive to it? Is this subjectivity simply embedded in a series of experiences that leave it sometimes powerless, sometimes traumatised?

It is possible that the narrative form that entangles itself in such speculative sentences proves to be helpful and therapeutic. At least the claim should be recognisable that it is primarily about the healing function of narrative in the face of traumatic events. The narrative, which is guided by the past experience of violence, does not allow the imagined subject to come to rest. It is forced to absorb what it has suffered into the experience and to accept it as part of its history. This space of meaning, which actualises the pain and the repressed, produces a new image of the world.

BIBLIOGRAPHY

Adorno, T. W.: *Negative Dialektik*. Frankfurt am Main: Suhrkamp, 1980, (1st edition 1966)
Agamben, G.: *Homo sacer*. Frankfurt am Main: Suhrkamp, 2002
———: *Was von Auschwitz übrig bleibt. Das Archiv und der Zeuge (Homo sacer III.)*. Translated from the Italian by Stefan Monhardt. Frankfurt am Main: Suhrkamp, 2003
———: *At What Point Are We? The Epidemic as Politics*. Vienna: Turia and Kant, 2021
Althusser, L.: *The Solitude of Machiavelli*. Part 2, Berlin: Argument, 1987
Anders, G.: *Der Blick vom Mond*. Munich: C. H. Beck, 1994
Angehrn, E.: Ursprungsmythos und Geschichtsdenken. In: Herta Nagl-Docekal (ed.): *Der Sinn des Historischen*. Frankfurt am Main: Fischer, 1996, pp. 305–333
———: Konstruktion und Grenzen der Konstruierbarkeit. In: Günther Dux/Jörn Rüsen (eds.): *Strukturen des Denkens. Studien zur Geschichte des Geistes*. Wiesbaden: Springer VS, 2014, pp. 219–235
———: *Die Herausforderung des Negativen. Zwischen Sinnverlangen und Sinnverlust*. Basel: Schwabe Reflexe, 2015
———: Die zweifache Geschichte der Psyche. In: Gerd Jüttemann (ed.): *Psychologie der Geschichte*. Lengerich: Pabst Science Publishers, 2020, pp. 56–64
Arbeitsgemeinschaft für Religions- und Weltanschauungsfragen (ed.): *Jörg Lanz v. Liebenfels: Praktische Einführung in die arisch-christliche Mystik*. Munich, 1980
Arendt, H.: Konzentrationslager. In: *Die Wandlung. Eine Monatsschrift*. Nr. 4 (3. Jahrgang). Hg. von Dolf Sternberger. 1948, pp. 309–330
———: *Eichmann in Jerusalem. A Report on the Banality of Evil*. New York: Viking Press, 1963
———: *The Origins of Totalitarianism*. New York: Penguin Classics, 1951
———: *Vita activa*. Munich: Piper, 2002
———: *What is Politics? Fragments from the Bequest*. Edited by Ursula Ludz. Munich/Zurich: Piper, 2003
Aron, R.: *Frieden und Krieg. Eine Theorie der Staatenwelt*. Frankfurt: Fischer, 2016
Aron, R./Ionescu, V.: *Democracy and Totalitarianism*. London: Weidenfeld and Nicolson, 1968
Assmann, A.: Einheit und Verschiedenheit der Geschichte: Jasper's Koncept der Achsenzeit. In: S. N. Eisenstadt (ed.): *Kulturen der Achsenzeit II*. Frankfurt am Main: Suhrkamp, 1992, pp. 330–341
———: *Das neue Unbehagen an der Erinnerungskultur. Eine Intervention*. München: C. H. Beck, 2013a
———: *Ist die Zeit aus den Fugen? Aufstieg und Fall des Zeitregimes der Moderne*. Munich: Hanser, 2013b
———: *Der europäische Traum. Vier Lektionen aus der Geschichte*. Munich: C. H. Beck, 2018
Assmann, J.: *Herrschaft und Heil. Politische Theologie in Ägypten, Israel und Europa*. Munich: Hanser, 2000
———: *Die Mosaische Unterscheidung oder der Preis des Monotheismus*. Munich: Hanser, 2003
———: *Achsenzeit. Eine Archäologie der Moderne*. Munich: C. H. Beck, 2018
Baberowski, J.: *Der Rote Terror*. Munich: Beck, 2003 (2nd ed. Munich, 2004)
——— (ed.): *Moderne Zeiten? Krieg, Revolution und Gewalt im 20. Jahrhundert*, Göttingen, 2006
Baberowski, J./Metzler, G. (eds.): *Gewalträume. Soziale Ordnungen im Ausnahmezustand*. Frankfurt/New York: Campus, 2012
Baecker, D./Krieg, P./Simon, Fritz B. (eds.): *Terror im System. Der 11. September und die Folgen*. Heidelberg: Carl Auer, 2002

Baer, U. (ed.): *Niemand zeugt für die Zeugen. Erinnerungskultur nach der Shoa.* Frankfurt am Main: Suhrkamp, 2000

Baumann, Z.: *Modernity and the Holocaust.* Ithaca, New York: Cornell University Press, 2001

Bayertz, K./Hoesch, M. (eds.): *Die Gestaltbarkeit der Geschichte.* Hamburg: Felix Meiner, 2019

Beck, U.: *Was ist Globalisierung? Irrtümer des Globalismus – Antworten auf die Globalisierung.* Frankfurt am Main: Suhrkamp, 1997

———: (Hrsg.): *Perspektiven der Weltgesellschaft.* Frankfurt a. M. Suhrkamp, 1998a

——— (Hrsg.): *Politik der Globalisierung.* Frankfurt a. M. Suhrkamp, 1998b

———: Über den postnationalen Krieg. In: *Blätter für deutsche und internationale Politik.* 8/1999, pp. 984–990

Beck, U./Poferl, A. (eds.): *Große Armut, großer Reichtum. Zur Transnationalisierung sozialer Ungleichheit.* Frankfurt am Main: Suhrkamp, 2010

Bedorf, T./Röttgers, K. (eds.): *Das Politische und die Politik.* Frankfurt am Main: Suhrkamp, 2010

Beevor, A.: *D-Day. The Battle for Normandy.* London: Viking, Penguin, 2009

Behnke, A.: 9/11 und die Grenzen des Poltischen. In: *ZIB 12. Jg.,* 2005, Heft 1, S. 117–140

v. Below. N.: *Als Hitlers Adjutant 1937–1945.* Mainz, 1980

Belting, H.: *Faces. Eine Geschichte des Gesichts.* München Beck, 2014

Benjamin, W.: *Gesammelte Schriften.* Edited by R. Tiedemann and H. Schweppenhäuser, Frankfurt a. M.: Suhrkamp, 1974

———: *Das Kunstwerk im Zeitalter seiner technischen Reproduzierbarkeit. Drei Studien zur Kunstsoziologie.* Frankfurt am Main: Suhrkamp, 1996 (22. Ed.)

Bertillon, A.: *Die Gerichtliche Photografie. Mit einem Anhange über die anthropometrische Classification und Identification.* Halle a. d. Saale, 1895

Biedermann, H./Oser, F./Quesel, C. *Vom Gelingen und Scheitern politischer Bildung.* Zürich: Ruegger, 2007

Binding, K./Hoche, A.: *Die Freigabe der Vernichtung lebensunwerten Lebens. Ihr Maß und ihre Form.* Leipzig, 1920

Blanchot, M.: *The Writing of Disaster.* Translated from the French by Gerhard Poppenberg and Hinrich Weidemann. University of Nebraska Press, 1995

Blumenberg, H.: *Die Genesis der kopernikanischen Welt.* Frankfurt am Main: Suhrkamp, 1975

———: *Schiffbruch mit Zuschauer.* Frankfurt am Main: Suhrkamp, 1979

———: *Lebenszeit und Weltzeit.* Frankfurt am Main: Suhrkamp, 2001

Böhme, H.: *Fetischismus und Kultur. Eine andere Theorie der Moderne.* Berlin: Rowohlt, 2006

———: *Aussichten der Natur. Naturästhetik in Wechselwirkung von Natur und Kultur.* Berlin: Matthes und Seitz, 2017

Bohrer, K. H.: Kein Wille zur Macht. In: Bohrer, K. H./Scheel, K. (Hrsg.): *Kein Wille zur Macht. Dekadenz.* Sonderheft Merkur. (61), 2007, pp. 659–668

Booth, B.: Die Biographie – ein Traum? Selbsthistorisierung im Zeitalter der Psychoanalyse. In: Straub, J. (ed.): *Erzählung, Identität und historisches Bewusstsein.* Frankfurt am Main: Suhrkamp, 1998, pp. 338–362

Bredekamp, H.: *Der Leviathan. The Archetype of the Modern State and its Counter-Images. 1651–2001.* Berlin/Boston: W. de Gruyter, 2020 (5th ed.)

v. Bredow, W./Neitzel, S.: *Lehren des Abgrunds. Politische Theorie für das 19. Jahrhundert.* Berlin: Daedalus, 1992

Brock, L.: Kriege der Demokratien. Eine Variante des demokratischen Friedens. In Geis, A. (ed.): *Den Krieg überdenken. Kriegsbegriffe und Kriegstheorien in der Diskussion.* Baden Baden: Nomos, 2006, pp. 203–233

Browning, C.: *Ordinary Men. The Reserve Police Battalion 101 and the Final Solution in Poland.* New York: Harper Perennial, 2017

Bruner, J. S.: *Acts of Meaning.* Cambridge, 1990

Brunkhorst, H.: *Solidarity: From Civic Friendship to a Global Legal Community (Studies in Contemporary German Social Thought).* MIT Press, 2005

Buc, P.: *Holy War. Violence in the Name of Christianity*. Darmstadt: Wiss. Buchgesellschaft, 2015
Buchholtz, E.: *Geländerundgang „Topographie des Terrors". Geschichte des Historischen Orts*. Berlin: Stiftung: Topographie des Terrors, 2010
Bujak, A./Swiebocki, H.: *Auschwitz. Residenz des Todes*. Staatliches Museum Auschwitz Birkenau. Oswiecim, 2003
Bultmann, R.: *Geschichte und Eschatologie*. Tübingen, 1964
Butler, J.: *Precarious Life: The Power of Mourning and Violence*. London/New York: Verso, 2004
———: *Giving an Account of Oneself*. Fordham, 2005
Capra, F.: *Wendezeit. Bausteine für ein neues Weltbild*. Translated from the American by E. Schuhmacher. Bern/Munich: Scherz, 1982
Chamayou, G.: *Drone Theory*. London: Penguin, 2015
Churchill, W.: *The River War*. London, 1899
Conrad, S.: *Deutsche Kolonialgeschichte*. Munich: C. H. Beck, 2008
Dabag, M.: Katastrophe und Identität. In: Hanno Loewy/Bernhard Moltmann (eds.): *Erlebnis-Gedächtnis-Sinn. Authentische und konstruierte Erinnerung*. Frankfurt am Main, 1996, pp. 177–235
———: Jungtürkische Visionen und der Völkermord an den Armeniern. In: Mihran Dabag/Kristin Platt (eds.): *Genozid und Moderne. Strukturen kollektiver Gewalt im 20. Jahrhundert*. Opladen: Leske und Budrich, 1998, pp. 152–206
———: Gewalt und Genozid. Annäherungen und Distanzierungen. In Mihran Dabag/Antje Kapust/Bernhard Waldenfels (eds.): 2000, pp. 170–186
———: Der Genozid an den Armeniern im Osmanischen Reich. In: Volkhard Knigge/Norbert Frei (eds.): *Verbrechen erinnern*. Munich, 2002, pp. 33–56
———: National-Koloniale Konstruktionen in politischen Entwürfen des deutschen Reiches um 1900. In: Mihran Dabag/Horst Gründer/Uwe-K. Ketelsen (eds.): *Kolonialismus. Kolonialdiskurs und Genozid*. Munich: Fink, 2004, pp. 19–67
Dabag, M./Platt, K.: *Identität in der Fremde*. Bochum: Universitätsverlag Brockmeyer, 1993
Dabag, M./Kapust, A./Waldenfels, B. (eds.): *Gewalt. Strukturen, Formen, Repräsentationen*. Munich: W. Fink, 2000
Dabag, M./Gründer, H./Ketelsen, U. K. (eds.): *Kolonialismus. Kolonialdiskurs und Genozid*. Munich: Fink, 2004
Därmann, I.: *Undienlichkeit. Gewaltgeschichte und Politische Philosophie*. Berlin: Matthes und Seitz, 2020
Deitelhoff, N.: *Überzeugung in der Politik. Grundzüge einer Theorie internationalen Regierens*. Frankfurt am Main: Suhrkamp, 2006
Delhom, P.: Phänomenologie der erlittenen Gewalt. In: Michael Staudigl (ed.): *Gesichter der Gewalt*. Paderborn: W. Fink, 2014, pp. 155–175
———: Die Zeitlichkeit des Friedens als Herausforderung. In: Christina Schues/Pascal Delhom (eds.): *Zeit und Frieden*. Freiburg/Munich: Karl Alber, 2016, pp. 131–156
Derrida, J.: *Die Schrift und die Differenz*. Frankfurt am Main: Suhrkamp, 1967
———: *Politik der Freundschaft*. Frankfurt am Main: Suhrkamp, 2000
Descartes, R.: *Meditations on the Foundations of Philosophy*. Edited and translated by L. Gäbe. Hamburg, 1960 (first 1641)
Descola, P.: *Jenseits von Kultur und Natur*. Frankfurt am Main: Suhrkamp, 2011
Didi-Huberman, G.: *Bilder trotz allem*. Translated from the French by Peter Geimer. Munich: Fink, 2007
———: *Trying to See*. Translated from the French by Horst Brühmann. Konstanz University Press, 2017
Diner, D.: Zwischen Aporie und Apologie. Über die Limitierungen der Historisierbarkeit der Massen-Extermination. In: *Babylon 2*, 1987, pp. 30–44
———: *Zivilisationsbruch. Denken nach Auschwitz*. Frankfurt am Main, 1988
———: Konfliktachsen – zum historischen Profil des 20. Jahrhunderts. In: *Gedächtniszeiten. Über jüdische und andere Geschichten*. Munich: C. H. Beck, 2003, pp. 16–32

———: Zivilisationsbruch oder der Verfall ontologischer Gewissheit. In: Ulrich Bielefeld/Heinz Bude/Bernd Greiner (Hrsg.): *Gesellschaft-Gewalt-Vertrauen. J. P. Reemtsma zum 60 Geburtstag.* Hamburg: Hamburger edition, 2012, pp. 458–471

———: *Das Jahrhundert verstehen. 1917–1989. Eine universalhistorische Interpretation.* Munich: Pantheon Verlag, 2015

Dörner, K.: Die institutionelle Umwandlung von Menschen in Sachen. Behinderte und Behinderung in der Moderne. In: Michael Emmrich (Hrsg.): *Im Zeitalter der Biomacht. 25 Jahre Gentechnik – eine kritische Bilanz.* Frankfurt am Main: Mabuse, 1999, pp. 15–45

Droysen, J. G.: *Historik.* Edited by Peter Leyh. Stuttgart/Bad Cannstatt: Frommann-Holzboog, 1977

Dux, G.: *Die Logik der Weltbilder. Strukturen der Bedeutung im Wandel der Geschichte.* Wiesbaden: Springer VS, 2017

Dux, G./Rüsen, J. (eds.): *Strukturen des Denkens.* Wiesbaden: Springer VS, 2014

Eisenstadt, S. N.: *Die Vielfalt der Moderne.* Weilerswist: Velbrück, 2000

Engelking, B./Hirsch, H. (eds.): *Unbequeme Wahrheiten. Polen und sein Verhältnis zu den Juden.* Frankfurt am Main: Suhrkamp, 2008

Enzensberger, H. M.: *Aussichten auf den Bürgerkrieg.* Frankfurt am Main: Suhrkamp, 1993

Farias, V.: *Heidegger und der Nationalsozialismus.* Frankfurt a. M.: Suhrkamp, 1989

Faye, E.: *Heidegger, l'introduction du nazisme dans la philosophie.* Paris: Albin Michel, 2005

Fest, J.: *Hitler. Eine Biographie.* Frankfurt/Berlin/Wien: Propyläen, 1980

Finkielkraut, A.: *Verlust der Menschlichkeit. Versuch über das 20. Jahrhundert.* Stuttgart: Klett-Cotta, 2000

Fisch, J.: *Die europäische Expansion und das Völkerrecht.* Stuttgart: Steiner, 1984

Foucault, M.: *Power: Essential Works of Foucault, 1954–1984*, Vol. 3. Edited by James D. Faubion. New York: New Press, 2000

Frankopan, P.: *The First Crusade. The Call from the East.* London: Bodley Head, 2012

Franzen, W.: Die Sehnsucht nach Härte und Schwere. Über ein zum NS-Engagement disponierenden Motiv in Heideggers Vorlesung: "Die Grundbegriffe der Metaphysik" von 1928/39. In: Gethmann-Siefert, A./Pöggeler, O. (eds.): *Heidegger und die praktische Philosophie.* Frankfurt a. M.: Suhrkamp, 1988, pp. 78–92

Freud, S.: *Zeitgemäßes über Krieg und Tod.* Leipzig: Internationaler psychoanalytischer Verlag, 1924

Frühwald, W.: Hannah Arendts Bericht von der Banalität des Bösen. In: Richard Riess (ed.): *Dem Entsetzen täglich in die Fratze sehen. On the Dark Side of Man.* Darmstadt: Wiss. Buchgesellschaft, 2019

Fukuyama, F.: The End of History? In: *The National Interest.* Summer, New York, 1989

———: *The end of History and the Last Men.* Free Press, 1992

Gadamer, H. G.: *Wahrheit und Methode. Gesammelte Werke Band I.* Tübingen: Mohr, 1960

———: *Hermeneutik und Ideologiekritik.* Frankfurt am Main, 1971

Geis, A. (ed.): *Den Krieg überdenken. Kriegsbegriffe und Kriegstheorien in der Diskussion.* Baden-Baden: Nomos, 2006

Geis, A./Müller, H./Brock, L. (eds.): *Democratic Wars. Looking at the Dark Side of Democratic Peace.* Houndmills: Palgrave Macmillan, 2006

Geis, A./Müller, H./Wagner, W.: *Schattenseiten des demokratischen Friedens. Zur Kritik einer liberalen Außen- und Sicherheitspolitik.* Frankfurt am Main: Campus, 2007

Gentile, E.: Die Sakralisierung der Politik. In: Maier, H. (ed.): *Wege in die Gewalt. Die modernen politischen Religionen.* Frankfurt: Fischer, 2002, pp. 166–183

Gilbert, M.: *Final Solution. The Expulsion and Extermination of the Jews. An Atlas.* Reinbek near Hamburg, 1982

Girard, R.: *Violence and the sacred.* Baltimore: J. Hopkins University Press, 1987

Gleditsch, N. P. The Decline of War – The Main Issues. *International Studies Review* 15, 2013, pp. 397–399

Glucksmann, A.: *Hass. Die Rückkehr einer elementaren Gewalt.* München/Wien: Carl Hanser, 2004. Original: "Le discours de la haine"

Goldhagen, D. J: *Hitlers willige Vollstrecker.* Ordinary Germans and the Holocaust. Berlin: Fischer, 1996
———: *Worse Than War. How Genocide Occurs and How it Can Be Prevented.* Munich: Goldmann, 2009
Graeber, D./Wengrow, D.: *The Dawn of Everything. A New History of Humanity.* London: Allen Lain, 2021
Graf, F. W./Meier, H. (eds.): *Politik und Religion. Zur Diagnose der Gegenwart.* Munich: C. H. Beck, 2013
Grice-Hutchinson, M.: *The School of Salamanca. Readings in Spanish Monetary Theory, 1554–1605.* Oxford: Clarendon Press, 1952
Gross, J. T.: *Nachbarn. Die Ermordung der Juden von Jedwabne.* Translated from the English by Friedrich Griese. Frankfurt: Suhrkamp, 2001
Grossheim, M.: *Politischer Existentialismus. Subjektivität zwischen Entfremdung und Engagement.* Tübingen: Mohr Siebeck, 2002
Grotius, H.: *Über das Recht des Krieges und des Friedens,* Edited by J. H: Kirchmann. Boston: Elibron, 2003 (1869)
Gruchmann, L.: *Total War. From Blitzkrieg to Unconditional Surrender.* Munich dtv, 1991
Günther, K.: Liberale und diskurstheoretische Deutungen der Menschenrechte. In: Wilfried Brugger/Ulfried Neumann/Stephan Kirste (eds.): *Rechtsphilosophie im 21. Jahrhundert.* Frankfurt am Main: Suhrkamp, 2008, pp. 338–360
Habermas, J.: *Eine Art Schadensabwicklung.* Frankfurt am Main: Suhrkamp, 1987
———: *Theorie des kommunikativen Handelns.* 2 volumes, Frankfurt am Main: Suhrkamp, 1988
———: *Die Einbeziehung des Anderen.* Frankfurt am Main: Suhrkamp, 1996
———: Humanität und Bestialität. In: Die Zeit, Nr. 18, 2. 04. 1999
———: *Der gespaltene Westen. Kleine politische Schriften X.* Frankfurt am Main: Suhrkamp, 2004
———: *Krieg und Empörung.* https://www.süddeutsche.de/projekte/artikel/kultur/das-dilemma-des-westens-juregen-haberams-zum-kreig-in-der-ukraine-e068321/?reduced-true
Hall, S.: The West and the Rest. Discourse and Power. In: Stuart Hall/Bram Gieben (eds.): *Formations of Modernity.* Cambridge: Cambridge Polity Press, 1992, pp. 275–320
Hardt, M./Negri, A.: *Empire – Globalization as a new Roman Order, Awaiting its Early Christians.* Frankfurt: Campus, 2000
Heidegger, M.: *Sein und Zeit.* Tübingen: Mohr Siebeck, 1979 (15th edition, first 1927)
———: *Einführung in die Metaphysik.* Tübingen: Niemeyer, 1987
———: Grundprobleme der Phänomenologie. In: *Gesamtausgabe,* Vol. 63, Frankfurt am Main, 1988
Heilbronn, C./Rabinovici, D./Sznaider, N. (Hrsg.): *Neuer Antisemitismus?, Fortsetzung einer globalen Debatte,* 2. Aufl., Berlin: Suhrkamp, 2019
Heinsohn, G.: *Söhne und Weltmacht.* Zürich: Orrell Füssli, 2003
———: Schrumpfender Westen, aufsteigender Islam. In: Bohrer, K.H./Scheel, K. (eds.): *Kein Wille zur Macht. Dekadenz.* Merkur: Deutsche Zeitschrift für europäisches Denken, Heft 8/9, (61) 2007, pp. 771–780
Heraclitus of Ephesus: *Fragments. Greek and German.* Edited by Bruno Snell. Zurich: Artemis und Winkler. 2007
Hillmann, J.: *Die erschreckende Liebe zum Krieg.* Kösel, 2005
Himmler, H.: *Geheimreden 1933 bis 1945.* Frankfurt/Berlin/Wien, 1974
Hinsch, W./Janssen, D.: *Menschenrechte militärisch schützen. Ein Plädoyer für humanitäre Interventionen.* München: C. H. Beck, 2006
Hirsch, A.: *Recht auf Gewalt? Spuren der philosophischen Rechtfertigung der Gewalt nach Hobbes.* Munich: Fink, 2004
Hobbes, T.: *Leviathan oder Stoff, Form und Gewalt eines kirchlichen und bürgerlichen Staates.* Frankfurt am Main, 1984 (zuerst 1651). Original: Leviathan. Or the Matter, Forme, & Power of a Common-Wealth Ecclesiasticall and Civill. Hg. v. I. Shapiro. New Haven: Yale, 2010

Höffe, O.: *Ethics and Politics. Basic Models and Problems of Practical Philosophy.* Frankfurt am Main: Suhrkamp, 1985
———: *Demokratie im Zeitalter der Globalisierung.* Munich: C. H. Beck, 1999
Hölscher, L.: *Die Entdeckung der Zukunft.* Frankfurt a. M., 1999
———: Feindschaft als politisch-soziale Beziehung. In: Medardus Brehl/Kristin Platt (Hrsg): *Feindschaft.* München: W. Fink, 2003, pp. 255–272
———: *Semantik der Leere. Grenzfragen der Geschichtswissenschaften.* Munich: Wallstein, 2009
Hondrich, K. O.: *Wieder Krieg.* Frankfurt am Main: Suhrkamp, 2002
Horkheimer, M./Adorno, T. W.: *Dialektik der Aufklärung. Philosophische Fragmente.* Frankfurt am Main: Fischer, 1997 (1969)
Howard, M.: *Die Erfindung des Friedens. Über den Krieg und die Ordnung der Welt.* Lüneburg: zu Klampen, 2001
Huntington, S.: *The Clash of Civilizations and the Remaking of the World Order.* New York: Simon & Schuster, 1996
Hüppauf, B.: Der entleerte Blick: Gewalt im Visier. In: Baer, U. (ed.): *Niemand zeugt für den Zeugen. Erinnerungskultur nach der Shoa.* Frankfurt am Main: Suhrkamp, 2000, pp. 219–236
———: *Fotografie im Krieg.* Paderborn: Fink, 2015
Imhof, K./Romano, G.: *Die Diskontinuität der Moderne. Eine Theorie des sozialen Wandels.* Frankfurt/New York: Campus, 1996
Iser, M.: Paradoxien des (un)gerechten Krieges. In: Geis, 2006, pp. 179–203
Jaeger, F./Rüsen, J. (eds.) *Handbuch der Kulturwissenschaften, Vol. 3, Themen und Tendenzen.* Stuttgart/Weimar: Metzler, 2004
Jäger, F.: Historische Kulturwissenschaft. In: Friedrich Jäger/Jürgen Straub (eds.): *Handbuch der Kulturwissenschaften. Paradigmen and Disciplinen.* Vol. 2, Stuttgart/Weimar: J. B. Metzler, 2011, pp. 518–546
Jäger, F./Straub, J. (eds.): *Handbuch der Kulturwissenschaften. Paradigms and Disciplines.* Vol. 2, Stuttgart/Weimar: J. B. Metzler, 2011
Janecki, S./Mac, S.: Unsere Schuld. In: Engelking/Hirsch, 2008, pp. 206–217
Jaspers, K.: *Vom Ursprung und Ziel der Geschichte.* Munich, 1949
Joas, H.: *Braucht der Mensch Religion? Über Erfahrungen der Selbsttranszendenz.* Freiburg i. Br. 2004
———: Sakralisierung und Entsakralisierung. In: Graf/Meier, 2013, 259–287
———: *Die Sakralität der Person. Eine neue Genealogie der Menschenrechte.* Frankfurt am Main: Suhrkamp, 2015
Joas, H./Vogt, P. (eds.): *Begriffene Geschichte. Contributions to the Work of Reinhart Koselleck.* Frankfurt am Main: Suhrkamp, 2011
Jünger, E.: Tagebücher. In: Ders.: Werke, Vol. 2, Stuttgart, 1962
Jüttemann, G. (ed.): *Die Entwicklung der Psyche in der Geschichte der Menschheit.* Lengerich: Pabst Science Publishers, 2013
———. (ed.): *Entwicklungen der Menschheit. Humanwissenschaften in der Perspektive der Integration.* Lengerich: Pabst Science Publishers, 2014
———: *Psychologie der Geschichte.* Lengerich: Pabst Science Publishers, 2020
Kaldor, M.: *Neue und alter Kriege: organisierte Gewalt im Zeitalter der Globalisierung.* Frankfurt am Main: Suhrkamp, 2000
Kant, I.: *Kritik der Urteilskraft.* Werkausgabe, ed.: W. Weischedel. Bd. X. Frankfurt a. M.: Suhrkamp, 2005
———: *Zum Ewigen Frieden. Ein philosophischer Entwurf.* Frankfurt: Fischer, 2008 (zuerst 1795)
Kapust, A.: "Languages" of Peace. In: Alfred Hirsch/Pascal Delhom (eds.): *Denkwege des Friedens. Aporias and Kaszinski, A.: The Burnt Offering.* In Engelking/Hirsch: Unbequeme Wahrheiten, 2008, pp. 150–164
———: Die Bedeutung der Gewalt und die Gewalt der Bedeutung. In: Michael Staudigl (ed.): *GEsichter der Gewalt. Beiträge aus phänomenologischer Perspektive.* Paderborn: W. Fink, 2014, pp. 51–74
Keegan, J.: *The Face of Battle.* London: Jonathan Cape Ltd, 1978

Kersting, W. (ed.): *Gerechtigkeit als Tausch? Auseinandersetzungen mit der Politischen Philosophie Otfried Höffe*. Frankfurt am Main: Suhrkamp, 1997

Knigge, V./Frei, N. (eds.): *Verbrechen erinnern. Coming to terms with the Holocaust and genocide*. Munich: C. H. Beck, 2002

Knöbl, W./Schmidt, G. (eds.): *Die Gegenwart des Krieges. Staatliche Gewalt in der Moderne*. Frankfurt am Main: Fischer, 2000

Knopp, G.: *Weltenbrand. The Wars of the Germans in the 20th Century*. Munich/Zurich: Pendo Verlag, 2000

Koppe, K.: *Der vergessene Friede: Friedensvorstellungen von der Antike bis zur Gegenwart*. Opladen: Leske und Budrich, 2001

Koselleck, R.: *Geschichtliche Grundbegriffe*. Frankfurt a. M.: Suhrkamp, 1984

———: *Vergangene Zukunft. Zur Semantik historischer Zeiten*. Frankfurt a. M.: Suhrkamp, 1985 (1979)

———: Sprachwandel und Ereignisgeschichte. In: Merkur 43, 1989, 657–673

———: *Zeitschichten. Studien zur Historik*. Frankfurt a. M.: Suhrkamp, 2000

———: Formen und Traditionen des negativen Gedächtnisses. In: Volkhard Knigge/Norbert Frei (eds.): *Verbrechen erinnern. Vom Umgang mit Holocaust und Genozid*. Munich: C. H. Beck, 2002, pp. 21–33

———: *Begriffsgeschichten*. Frankfurt a. M. Suhrkamp, 2006

———: *Vom Sinn und Unsinn der Geschichte. Essays and Schriften aus vier Jahrzehnten*. Edited by C. Dutt. Frankfurt a. M. Suhrkamp, 2010

———: *Kritik und Krise. Eine Studie der Pathogenese der bürgerlichen Welt*. Frankfurt am Main: Suhrkamp, 2013 (12th ed.)

Koskenniemi, M.: *The Gentle Civilizer of Nations. The Rise and Fall of International Law 1870–1960*, Cambridge: Cambridge University Press, 2001

Krause, J.: Multilateral Kooperation in the Face of Old and New Security Challenges. In: William Wallace/Young Soogil (eds.): *Asia and Europe. Global Governance as a Challenge for Cooperation*. Washington/DC: Council for Asia-Europe Cooperation, 2004

Krause, S./Malowitz, K.: *Michael Walzer zur Einführung*. Hamburg: Junius, 1998

Krippendorff, E.: *Staat und Krieg. Die historische Logik politischer Unvernunft*. Frankfurt am Main: Suhrkamp, 1992

Kristeva, J.: *Fremde sind wir uns selbst*. Übersetzt von X. Rajewsky, Frankfurt am Main: Suhrkamp, 1990

Kufi, F.: *Only a Daughter. A Woman Changes Afghanistan*. (Translation: Anne Emmert). Munich: Goldmann, 2020

Lam, D.: *Jugendüberschuss und Jugendarbeitslosigkeit*. IZA World of Labor, 2014

Langewiesche, D.: *Der gewaltsame Lehrer. Europas Kriege in der Moderne*. Munich: C. H. Beck, 2019

Latour, B.: *Battle for Gaia. Eight Lectures on the Climate Regime*. Berlin: Suhrkamp, 2017

Leimgruber, U.: Das Malum als Mysterium. In: Richard Riess (ed.): *Dem Entsetzen täglich in die Fratze sehen. On the Dark Side of Man*. Darmstadt: Wiss. Buchgesellschaft, 2019, 257–265

Levene, M.: *Genocide in the Age of the Nation-State*. Volume I. The meaning of Genocide. London, 2005

Levi, P.: *I sommersi e i salvati. (Die Untergegangenen und die Geretteten)*. Übersetzt von Moshe Kahn. München: Hanser, 1993

Levinas, E.: *Wenn Gott in das Denken einfällt*. Freiburg/Munich: Alber, 1988

———: *Totality and Infinity. An Essay on Exteriority*. Translated by Alphonso Lingis. Pittsburgh: Duquesne University Press, 2007

———: *Ethik als erste Philosophie*. Translation: G. Weinberger. Wien: Sonderzahl Verlag, 2022

Liebsch, L.: Lebensformen zwischen Widerstreit und Gewalt. In: Burkhard Liebsch/Jürgen Straub (eds.): *Lebensformen im Widerstreit. Integration and Identitätskonflikte in pluralen Gesellschaften*. Frankfurt/NewYork: Campus, 2003, pp. 13–47

———: Was (nicht) als Gewalt zählt. Zum Stand des philosophischen Gewaltdiskurses heute. In: Staudigl, M. (ed.): *Gesichter der Gewalt*. Paderborn: W. Fink, 2014, pp. 355–383

———: Landschaften der Verlassenheit – Bilder des Desasters. Maurice Blanchot and Georges Didi-Huberman. In: Marco Gutjahr/Maria Jarmer (eds.): *Von Ähnlichkeit zu Ähnlichkeit. Maurice Blanchot and the Passion of the Image*. Vienna: Turia and Kant, 2016, pp. 237–269

———: *Einander ausgesetzt – der Andere und das Soziale. Elemente einer Topologie des Zusammenlebens*. 2 Vol., Freiburg/Munich: Karl Alber, 2018

Lovelock, James: *Die Erde ist ein Lebewesen*. Translated from English by J. Eggert and M. Würmli. Bern/Munich/Vienna: Scherz Verlag, 1992

Löw, M.: *Raumsoziologie*. Frankfurt am Main: Suhrkamp, 2001

Löwith, K.: *Weltgeschichte und Heilsgeschehen: die theologischen Voraussetzungen der Geschichtsphilosophie*. Stuttgart: Reclam, 1953

Lübbe, H.: *Geschichtsbegriff und Geschichtsinteresse. Analyse und Pragmatik der Geschichte*. Basel: Schwabe, 2012

Lüdtke, A.: Gewalt und Alltag im 20. Jahrhundert. In: W. Bergsdorf u. a. (ed.): *Gewalt und Terror*. Weimar: Rhino, 2003

Luhmann, N.: *Die Gesellschaft der Gesellschaft*. Frankfurt am Main: Suhrkamp, 2000

Lutz-Bachmann, M.: Weltstaatlichkeit und Menschenrechte nach dem Ende des überlieferten Nationalstaats. In: Brunkhorst, H./Köhler, W./Lutz-Bachmann, M. (eds.): *Recht auf Menschenrechte. Demokratie und internationale Politik*. Frankfurt a. M.: Suhrkamp, 1999, pp. 199–216

———: Weltweiter Frieden durch eine Weltrepublik? Probleme internationaler Friedenssicherung. In: Lutz-Bachmann, M./Bohman, J. (eds.): *Weltstaat oder Staatenwelt? Für und wider die Idee einer Weltrepublik*. Frankfurt a. M.: Suhrkamp, 2002, pp. 32–46

Lyotard, J. F.: *The Differend. Phrases in Dispute*. Minneapolis, 1988

Machiavelli, N.: *The Art of War*. New York: Da Capo, 1965 (1521)

———: *Gesammelte Werke in einem Band*. Hg. v. A. Ulfig. Frankfurt am Main, 2006

Mäder, D.: The Psychologisierung des Fortschritts. In: Gerd Jüttemann (ed.): *Psychologie der Geschichte*. Lengerich: Pabst Science Publishers, 2020, pp. 134–141

Maier, C. S.: A Surfeit of Memory? Reflections on History, Melancholy and Denial. *History and Memory* 5, no. 2, 1993, pp. 135–151

Makropoulos, M.: Historische Semantik und Positivität der Kontingenz. In: Hans Joas/Peter Vogt (eds.): *Begriffene Geschichte. Beiträge zum Werk von Reinhart Koselleck*. Frankfurt am Main: Suhrkamp, 2011, 481–511

Mann, M.: *The Sources of Social Power. Volume 1. A History of Power from the Beginning to A.D.1760*. Cambridge: Cambridge University Press, 1986

———: *The Sources of Social Power, Volume 2. The Rise of Classes and Nation-States 1760–1914*. Cambridge: Cambridge University Press, 1993

———: Das Gewaltdispositiv des Modernen Kolonialismus. In: Dabag et al. 2004, pp. 111–136

Marquard, O.: *Abschied vom Prinzipiellen*. Stuttgart: Reclam, 1981

Marshall, T.: *Prisoners of Geography*. London: Elliott & Thompson Ltd, 2015

Maus, I.: Menschenrechte als Ermächtigungsnormen internationaler Politik oder: der zerstörte Zusammenhang von Menschenrechten und Demokratie. In: Hauke Brunkhorst (ed.): *Recht auf Menschenrechte*. Frankfurt am Main: Suhrkamp, 1999, pp. 276–292

———: *Über Volkssouveränität. Elemente einer Demokratietheorie*. Frankfurt am Main: Suhrkamp, 2011

Mbembe, A.: *Exit from the Long Night. An Attempt at a Decolonised Africa*. Frankfurt am Main: Suhrkamp, 2016

McCarthy, T.: *Race, Empire and the Idea of Human Development*. Cambridge: Cambridge University Press, 2009

Meier, C.: *Die Entstehung des Politischen bei den Griechen*. Frankfurt a. M.: Suhrkamp, 1983

———: *Kultur, um der Freiheit willen. Griechische Anfänge – Anfänge Europas?* Munich: Siedler, 2009

———: *Das Gebot zu vergessen und die Unabweisbarkeit des Erinnerns. Über den öffentlichen Umgang mit schlimmer Vergangenheit.* Munich: Siedler, 2010
Meier, Hans (Ed.): *Wege in die Gewalt. Die modernen politischen Religionen.* Frankfurt: Fischer, 2002
Meier, Heinrich: Epilog. Politik, Religion und Philosophie. In: Graf, F. W./Meier, H. (eds.): *Politik und Religion. Zur Diagnose der Gegenwart.* München: C. H. Beck, 2013, pp. 1–315
Menninghaus, W.: *Wozu Kunst? Ästhetik nach Darwin.* Berlin: Suhrkamp, 2011
Merkel, R.: *Der Kosovo Krieg und das Völkerrecht.* Frankfurt a. M.: Suhrkamp, 2000
Merleau-Ponty, M.: *Phenomenology of Perception.* Berlin: W. de Gruyter, 1966
———: *Keime der Vernunft.* Translated by A. Kapust. München: Fink, 1994
Mettler, M.: Ehrkultur und Weiblichkeit. On the Role of Women in the Reproduction of the Authoritarian Personality in Islam. In: Katrin Henkelmann/Christina Jäckel/Andreas Stahl/Niklas Wünsch/Benedikt Zopes (eds.): *Konformistische Rebellen. Über die Aktualität des autoritären Charakters.* Berlin: Verbrecher Verlag, 2020, pp. 333–348
Metz, K. H.: *Geschichte der Gewalt. War. Revolution. Terror.* Darmstadt: Wiss. Buchgesellschaft, 2010
———: *Von der Erinnerung zur Erkenntnis. Eine neue Theorie der Geschichte.* Darmstadt: WBG, 2012
———: Geschichte und Psychologie. Über die Möglichkeit einer Begegnung. In: Jüttemann, 2020, pp. 87–94
Mishra, P.: *Das Zeitalter des Zorns. Eine Geschichte der Gegenwart.* Frankfurt am Main: Fischer, 2017a
———: Politik im Zeitalter des Zorns. In: Heinrich Geiselberger (ed.): *Die große Regression. Eine internationale Debatte über die intellektuelle Situation unserer Zeit.* Berlin: Suhrkamp, 2017b, pp. 175–197
Morris, I.: *War. What it is Good For.* New York: Farrar, Straus & Giroux, 2013, Translation: Frankfurt am Main: Campus
Morsink, J.: *The Universal Declaration of Human Rights. Origins, Drafting, and Intent.* Pennsylvania: Pennsylvania University Press, 1999
Mouffe, C.: *The Return of the Political.* London: Verso, 1993
Mühlmann, H.: *Die Natur der arabischen Kultur.* München: W. Fink, 2011
Müller, F.: *Sonderbehandlung. German Adaptation by Helmut Freitag.* Munich: Bertelsmann, 1979
Müller, H.: Kants Schurkenstaat: Der ungerechte Feind und die Ermächtigung zum Kriege. In: Geis, A. (ed.): *Den Krieg überdenken. Kriegsbegriffe und Kriegstheorien in der Diskussion.* Baden Baden: Nomos, 2006, pp. 229–251
Münkler, H.: Den Krieg wieder denken. Clausewitz, Kosovo und die Kriege des 21. Jahrhunderts, In: *Blätter für deutsche und internationale Politik*, Heft 6, 1999, pp. 678–688
———: *Die neuen Kriege.* Hamburg: Reinbek, 2002
———: *Imperien. Die Logik der Weltherrschaft – vom Alten Rom bis zu den Vereinigten Staaten.* Berlin: Rowohlt, 2005
———: *Der Wandel des Krieges. Von der Symmetrie zur Asymmetrie.* Weilerswist: Velbrück, 2006
Nagl-Docekal, H. (ed.): *Der Sinn des Historischen. Debatten über Geschichtsphilosophie.* Frankfurt am Main: Fischer, 1996
Neitzel, S./Welzer, H.: *Soldaten. Protokolle vom Kämpfen, Töten und Sterben.* Frankfurt am Main: Suhrkamp, 2011
Nietzsche, F.: *Zwischen gut und böse.Über die Entwicklung der Moral. Kritische Studienausgabe*, Vol. 5. Edited by Giorgio Colli and Mazzino Montinari. Munich: C. H. Beck, 1988a
———: Morgenröthe. In: G. Colli and M. Montinari (eds.): *Friedrich Nietzsche.* Critical Study Edition. Vol. 3. Munich: C. H. Beck, 1988b
Oeser, E.: *Die Angst vor dem Fremden. Die Wurzeln der Xenophobie.* Darmstadt: Wiss. Buchgesellschaft, 2015
Ogilvie, S./Miller, S.: *Refuge Denied. The St. Louis Passengers and the Holocaust.* Madison: University of Wisconsin Press, 2006
Onfray, M.: *Décadence. Vie et mort du judéo-christianisme.* Flammarion: Paris, 2017
Ortmann, G.: *Regel und Ausnahme.* Frankfurt am Main: Suhrkamp, 2002

Oser, F.: Politisches Urteilen: Aufstieg und Fall großer Ideen. In: Gerd Jüttemann (ed.): *Die Entwicklung der Psyche in der Menschlichen Geschichte.* Lengerich: Pabst Science Publishers, 2013, pp. 313–342

Osterhammel, J.: *Die Flughöhe der Adler. Historische Essays zur globalen Gegenwart.* München: C. H. Beck, 2017

Otto, R.: *Das Heilige. Über das Irrationale in der Idee des Göttlichen und sein Verhältnis zum Rationalen.* Munich: C. H. Beck, 1979

Pettitt, P.: *The Paleolithical Origins of Human Burial.* Oxford: Oxford University Press, 2011

Pinker, S.: *The Stuff of Thought: Language as a Window into Human Nature.* New York: Viking, 2007

———: *The Better Angels of Our Nature. Why Violence Has Declined.* New York: Pengiun, 2011

———: *Enlightenment now: The Case for Reason, Science, Humanism and Progress.* New York: Viking, 2018

Ranciere, J.: *Das Unvernehmen. Politik und Philosophie.* Frankfurt am Main: Suhrkamp, 2002

Randeria, S./Eckert, A.: *Vom Imperialismus zum Empire.* Frankfurt am Main: Suhrkamp, 2009

Reemtsma, J. P.: *Vertrauen und Gewalt. Ein Versuch über eine besondere Konstellation der Moderne.* Hamburg: sigma, 2008

Reid, R. J.: *A History of Modern Africa 1800 to the Present.* Chichester: Wiley, 2009

Reinartz, D./v. Krockow, C.: *Tödliche Stille. Bilder aus den ehemaligen deutschen Konzentrationslagern.* Göttingen, 1994

Renfrew, C. (ed.): *Death Rituals and Social Order in the Ancient World. "Dath shall have no Dominion".* Cambridge: Cambridge University Press, 2016

Rentsch, T.: Wie ist eine menschliche Welt überhaupt möglich? Philosophische Anthropologie als Konstitutionsanalyse in einer humanen Welt. In: Christoph Demmerling/Gottfried Gabriel/Thomas Rentsch (eds.): *Vernunft und Lebenspraxis.* Frankfurt am Main: Suhrkamp, 1995, pp. 320–350

———: *Die Konstitution der Moralität. Transzendentale Anthropologie and Praktische Philosophie.* Frankfurt am Main: Suhrkamp, 1999

———: *Negativität und praktische Vernunft.* Frankfurt am Main: Suhrkamp, 2000

Reuber, P.: *Politische Geographie.* Paderborn: Ferdinand Schöningh, 2012

Ricoeur, P.: *Geschichte und Wahrheit.* Munich: List, 1975

———: *Zufall und Vernunft in der Geschichte.* Tübingen: Mohr Siebeck, 1985

———: *Zeit und Erzählung, I-III.* Munich: List, 1988–1991

———: *Anders. Eine Lektüre von Jenseits des Seins oder anders als Sein geschieht von Emmanuel Levinas.* Vienna/Berlin: Turia and Kant, 2015

Rohbeck, J.: *Geschichtsphilosophie zur Einführung.* Hamburg: Junius, 2004

———: *Zukunft der Geschichte. Geschichtsphilosophie und Zukunftsethik.* Berlin: Akademie Verlag, 2013

———: Machbarkeit oder Unverfügbarkeit der Geschichte? Zur doppelten Bedeutung historischer Kontingenz. In: Bayertz, K./Hoesch, M. (eds.): *Die Gestaltbarkeit der Geschichte.* Hamburg: Felix Meiner, 2019, pp. 49–67

Rorty, R.: *Kontingenz, Ironie und Solidarität.* Frankfurt am Main: Suhrkamp, 1992

Rosenthal, G.: *Erzählte und erlebte Lebensgeschichte. Gestalt und Struktur biographischer Selbstbeschreibungen.* Frankfurt am Main: Suhrkamp, 1995

Rosling, H./Rönnlund, A. R./Rösling, O.: *Factfulness. Wie wir lernen, die Welt so zu sehen, wie sie wirklich ist.* Berlin: Ullstein, 2019; (Original: New York: Flatiron, 2018)

Röttgers, K.: Flexionen des Politischen. In: Thomas Bedorf/Kurt Röttgers (eds.): *Das Politische und die Politik.* Frankfurt am Main: Suhrkamp, 2010, 38–68

Ruggie, J. G.: Multilateralism. The Anatomy of an Institution. *International Organisation* 46, 1992, pp. 561–598

Rüsen, J.: *Kann gestern besser werden? Über die Bedenklichkeit der Geschichte.* Berlin: Kadmos, 2003

———: Sinnverlust und Transzendenz – Kultur und Kulturwissenschaft am Anfang des 21. Jahrhunderts. In: Friedrich Jaeger/Jörn Rüsen (eds.): *Handbuch der Kulturwissenschaften, vol. 3, Themen und Tendenzen.* Stuttgart/Weimar: Metzler, 2004, pp. 533–544

———: *Zeit und Sinn. Strategien historischen Denkens.* Frankfurt am Main: Humanities Online, 2013

———: Universalgeschichte als Sinnkonzept. In: Günther Dux/Jörn Rüsen (eds.): *Strukturen des Denkens. Studien zur Geschichte des Geistes.* Wiesbaden: Springer VS, 2018, pp. 235–250

———: Psychologie des Geschichtsbewusstseins – eine Skizze. In: Gerd Jüttemann (ed.): *Psychologie der Geschichte.* Lengerich: Pabst Publishers, 2020, pp. 35–42

———: Warum sich die Geschichte nur historiographisch gestalten lässt und was das für die Zukunft bedeutet. In: Bayertz, K./Hoesch, M. (eds.): *Die Gestaltbarkeit der Geschichte.* Hamburg: Felix Meiner, 2019, pp. 39–49

Rüsen, J./Jürgen Straub, J. (eds.): *Die dunkle Spur der Vergangenheit. Psychoanalytische Zugänge zum historischen Bewusstsein. Erinnerung. Geschichte, Identität 2.* Frankfurt am Main: Suhrkamp, 1998

Russett, B./Oneal, J. R.: *Triangulating Peace.* New York: W. W. Norton & Company, 2001

Sabrow, M.: *Zeitgeschichte schreiben. Von der Verständigung über die Vergangenheit in der Gegenwart.* Munich: Wallstein, 2014

Sartre, J. P.: *L'Etre et le Neant. Essai D'ontologie phènoméménologique.* First 1943, Reinbek: bei Hamburg, 1993

Schlichte, K.: *Der Staat in der Weltgesellschaft. Politische Herrschaft in Asien, Afrika und Lateinamerika.* Frankfurt/New York: P. Lang, 2005

Schlögel, K.: *Im Raume lesen wir die Zeit. Über Zivilisationsgeschichte und Geopolitik.* Munich/Vienna: Carl Hanser, 2003

Schmitt, C.: *Politische Theologie. Vier Kapitel zur Lehre von der Souveränität.* Berlin: Duncker & Humblot, 1922

———: *Die geschichtliche Lage des heutigen Parlamentarismus.* Berlin: Duncker & Humblot, 1923

———: *Politische Romantik.* Berlin: Duncker & Humblot, 1925

———: *Verfassungslehre.* Berlin: Duncker & Humblot, 1928

———: *Land und See.* Stuttgart: Klett-Cotta, 1942

———: *Der Nomos der Erde.* Berlin: Duncker & Humblot, 1950

———: *Theorie des Partisanen.* Berlin: Duncker & Humblot, 1963

Schnell, F.: *Räume des Schreckens. Gewalt und Gruppenmilitanz in der Ukraine 1905–1933* Hamburg: Hamburger Edition, 2012

Schott, H.: Die Stigmen des Bösen – kulturgeschichtliche Wurzeln der Ausmerzideologie. In: Peter Propping/Heinz Schott (eds.): *Wissenschaft auf Irrwegen. Biologismus – Rassenhygiene – Eugenik.* Bonn: Bouvier, 1992, pp. 9–23

Schues, C.: Trauen oder Misstrauen vertrauen? In: Alfred Hirsch/Pascal Delhom (eds.): *Friedensgesellschaften zwischen Verantwortung und Vertrauen.* Freiburg/Munich: Karl Alber, 2015, pp. 156–185

Schues, C./Delhom, P. (eds.): *Zeit und Frieden.* Freiburg/Munich: Karl Alber, 2016

Schwartz, R. M.: *The Curse of Cain. The Violent Legacy of Monotheism.* Chicago: Chicago University Press, 1997

Schwarz-Friesel, M.: Educated Anti-Semitism in the Middle of German Society. Empirical Findings. In: Haim Fireberg/Olaf Glöckner (eds.): *Being Jewish in 21st Century-Germany.* Oldenburg: de Gruyter, 2015, pp. 165–187

Senghaas, D.: *Den Frieden denken.* Frankfurt am Main: Suhrkamp, 1995

Sheehan, J.: *Where have all the Soldiers Gone? The Transformation of Modern Europe.* Boston: Houghton Mifflin Harcourt, 2008

Sloterdijk, P.: *Regeln für den Menschenpark.* Frankfurt am Main: Suhrkamp, 2000

———: *Zorn und Zeit.* Frankfurt am Main: Suhrkamp, 2006

———: *Was geschah im 20 Jahrhundert?* Berlin: Suhrkamp, 2016

Snyder, T.: *Bloodlands: Europe Between Hitler and Stalin.* New York, 2013

Sofsky, W.: *Die Ordnung des Terrors. Das Konzentrationslager.* Frankfurt a. M: Fischer, 1993

———: *Traktat über die Gewalt.* Frankfurt a. M.: Fischer, 1996

Sombart, N.: Nachrichten aus Ascona. Auf dem Weg zu einer kulturwissenschaftlichen Hermeneutik. In: Prigge, W. (eds.): *Städtische Intellektuelle. Urbane Milieus im 20. Jahrhundert.* Frankfurt am Main: Suhrkamp, 1992, pp. 107–119

Sontag, S.: *Looking at the Suffering of Others.* Munich: Hanser, 2003
Stadler, C.: *Krieg.* Vienna: Facultas WUV, 2009
Stark, R.: *One True God. Historical Consequences of Monotheism.* Princeton: Princeton University Press, 2001
Stockhammer, R.: *Ruanda. Über einen anderen Genozid schreiben.* Frankfurt am Main: Suhrkamp, 2005
Straub, J.: Geschichten erzählen, Geschichte bilden. Grundzüge einer narrativen Psychologie historischer Sinnbildung. In: *Erzählung, Identität und historisches Bewusstsein. Die psychologische Konstruktion von Zeit und Geschichte.* Frankfurt am Main: Suhrkamp, 1998a, pp. 81–170
———: Psychoanalyse, Geschichte und Geschichtswissenschaft. In: Jörn Rüsen/Jürgen Straub (eds.): *Die dunkle Spur der Vergangenheit. Psychoanalytische Zugänge zum historischen Bewusstsein.* Erinnerung, Geschichte, Identität 2. Frankfurt am Main: Suhrkamp, 1998b, pp. 12–33
———: *Die Macht negativer Affekte. Identität, kulturelle Unterschiede, interkulturelle Kompetenz.* Gießen: Psychosozial Verlag, 2019
v. Suttner, B.: *Die Waffen nieder.* First print, Edgar Pierson, 1889
Taylor, C.: *Sources of the Self. The Making of the Modern Identity.* Cambridge, MA: Harvard University Press, 1994
Ther, P.: *Die Außenseiter. Flucht und Integration im Modernen Europa.* Frankfurt am Main: Suhrkamp, 2018
Theweleit, K.: *Männerphantasien.* 2 Vols. Berlin: Rowohlt, 1994
Todorov, T.: *Angesichts des Äußersten.* München: Fink, 1993
———: *Abenteuer des Zusammenlebens. Versuch einer allgemeinen Anthropologie.* Berlin: Wagenbach, 1996
Trojanow, I./Hoskote, R.: *Kampfabsage. Kulturen kämpfen nicht, sie fließen ineinander.* Frankfurt am Main: Suhrkamp, 2013
Urdal, H.: A Clash of Generations? Youth Bulges and Political Violence. *International Studies Quarterly* 50, no. 3, 2006, pp. 607–627
v. Crefeld, M.: *Die Zukunft des Krieges.* München: Akademia, 1998
Waldenfels, B.: *Topographie des Fremden. Studien zur Phänomenologie des Fremden I.* Frankfurt a. M.: Suhrkamp, 1997
———: Aporien der Gewalt. In: Mihran Dabag/Antje Kapust/Bernhard Waldenfels (eds.): *Gewalt. Strukturen. Formen. Repräsentationen.* Munich: Wilhelm Fink, 2000, pp. 9–25
———: Metamorphosen der Gewalt. In: Michael Staudigl (ed.): *Gesichter der Gewalt.* Paderborn: W. Fink, 2014, pp. 135–155
———: Friedenskräfte und Friedenszeichen. In: Alfred Hirsch/Pascal Delhom (eds.): *Denkwege des Friedens. Aporien and Perspektiven.* Freiburg/Munich: Karl Alber, 2019, pp. 256–280
Walzer, M.: *Exodus und Revolution.* Berlin: de Gruyter, 1988
———: *Just and Unjust Wars.* New York: Penguin, 1992
Weber, M.: *Wirtschaftsethik der Weltreligionen. Gesammelte Aufsätze zur Religionssoziologie I.* Tübingen: Mohr Siebeck, 1922
Wehler, H. U. (ed.): *Geschichte und Psychoanalyse.* Cologne: De Gruyter, 1974
Weinfurter, St.: *Karl der Große. Der heilige Barbar.* München/Zürich: Pieper, 2005
Welzer, H.: *Täter – wie aus ganz normalen Menschen Massenmörder werden.* Frankfurt a. M.: Fischer, 2005
———: Gewalt Braucht kein Motiv. In: Bielefeld, U./Bude, H./Greiner, B. (eds.): *Gesellschaft-Gewalt-Vertrauen.* J. P. Reemtsma zum 60. Geburtstag. Hamburg: Hamburger edition, 2012, pp. 504–524
Wetz, F. J./Timm, H. (eds.): *Die Kunst des Überlebens. Nachdenken über Hans Blumenberg.* Frankfurt am Main: Suhrkamp, 1999
Wevelsiep, C.: *Im Horizont des Allgemeinen.* Baden Baden: Nomos, 2022
White, H.: *Metahistory.* Frankfurt a. M.: Suhrkamp, 1991
———: Literaturtheorie und Geschichtsschreibung. In: Nagl-Docekal, H. (ed.): *Der Sinn des Historischen. Debatten zur Geschichtsphilosophie.* Frankfurt am Main: Fischer, 1997, pp. 67–106

Will, W.: *Die Perserkriege*. München: C. H. Beck, 2010

Wingert, L.: Unpathetisches Ideal. Über den Begriff des bürgerschaftlichen Wir. In: Brunkhorst, H. (ed.): *Demokratischer Experimentalismus*. Frankfurt am Main: Suhrkamp, 1998, pp. 33–44

Winter, J.: Introduction. The Performance of the Past: Memory, History, Identity. In: Tilman, K./van Vree, F./Winter, J. (eds.): *Performing the Past, Memory, History, and Identity in Modern Europe*. Amsterdam: Amsterdam University Press, 2010, pp. 11–34

Wood, D.: Die Philosophie der Gewalt. Die Gewalt der Philosophie. In: Mihran Dabag/Antje Kapust/Bernhard Waldenfels (eds.): *Gewalt. Strukturen, Formen, Repräsentationen*. Munich: W. Fink, 2000, pp. 25–55

Yermelenko, A.: Widerstand Statt Verhandlung. In: *Frankfurter Allgemeine Zeitung vom 20*. Mai, 2022, p. 11

Young, J.: *Beschreiben des Holocaust. Darstellung und Folgen der Interpretation*. Frankfurt am Main: Suhrkamp, 1992

Zantop, S.: *Colonial Fantasies. Conquest, Family and Nation in Precolonial Germany, 1770–1870*. Durham, 1997

Zbikowski, A.: Es gab keinen Befehl. In: Engelking/Hirsch, 2008, pp. 181–191

Zimmermann, R.: *Moral als Macht. Eine Philosophie der historischen Erfahrung*. Reinbek: Rowohlt, 2008

Zurawski, N. (Hrsg.): *Sicherheitsdiskurse. Angst, Kontrolle und Sicherheit in einer "gefährlichen Welt"*. Frankfurt: Peter Lang, 2007

INDEX

A
abolition of war 162
Agamben, Giorgio 44, 154–56
'Age of the Total' 113
aloof, strange and uncomfortable phenomena 67
ambivalent psychology of narrative 135
ancient Persian Achaemenid Empire 3
Angel of History ix
antinomian impulse 35
anti-Semitic ideology 80
anti-semitism 50–51, 70
Arendt, H. xx, xvi, 20, 60, 65, 74, 106, 109
Armenian genocide 40–44
Auschwitz camp xviii, 28, 53, 56–57, 59–60, 63, 107

B
banality of evil concept 55
Battle of Thermopylae 72
Being and Time 73, 97
Bellicist metaphysics 160
Benjamin, Walter ix, 26, 100
Bertillon, Alphonse 59
Binding, Alfred 77
Birkenau camp 78
Blumenberg, Hans 65
Brute force xii, 21, 85, 95
Butler, Judith 50, 145

C
Carl Schmitt's political theory 75
Charlemagne's rule xiii
Christ-killers 85
Churchill, Winston 45
colonialism 8–9, 36, 38–39, 46, 111
colonial violence 33; Armenian genocide 40–44; cultural psychology reflections 44–48; in 'German Southwest Africa' 37–40
comprehended violence xx
concern xvi, xxi, xxiii, xxiv, 3, 6, 27, 43, 93, 97–98, 110, 153, 156, 159, 162, 165, 168
Congo Conference of 1884/1885 8, 10
Constantine's victory in 324 85
constellations of enmity 5
contemporary social theory 63

coping strategy 111, 125
cosmic fatalism xiv
cosmopolitanism xxi
critical theory 7, 26, 116, 139, 154
cultural guiding concepts 69
cultural memory 34–35
cultural theory 47, 121–22
cynicism 56

D
daring 169
Darwinism 65
de facto violence xiv, 49, 110
defensive rights 138
democratic peace 147, 150
demythification process 65
depth psychology 134
Derrida, Jacques 50
development of international law 147
dianoia 128–129
digital cultures 51
dignity xvii, xxii, xxiii, 15, 90–91, 93, 99, 151
Diner, Dan 41, 54
disastrous violence 113; *aloof, strange and uncomfortable* phenomena 67; anthropological fragility 68; concept of banality 64–66; metaphysical connotation 63; paradoxical morality 66; transformation morality 67
distribution of the goods of happiness 158

E
Egypt 133
Eichmann, A. 55, 64–66
emancipatory universalism 46
emotional participation 34–35
empty seeing 57
enemies of humanity 126
Enlightenment ix, xvi, xvii, xix, xx, 17, 52, 64, 72, 87, 119, 124, 126, 131, 138
enmity 4–5, 23, 39–40, 45, 51–52, 63, 74–78, 84, 122, 125–26, 141, 143, 148–52, 165
Enzensberger, Hans Magnus 144
eternal silence 153
ethnification of religion 41

Eurocentrism/European centrism 32, 46
European geopolitics 10
European 'Theatrum Belli' 99
European war 17, 38
evil 56
Exodus 133–134
Exodus and Revolution (1988) 132
explicit theory 138, 142

F
fanaticism 65
fascism 63, 68–69, 91, 121
Fascist movements 74
Federal Republic of Germany 54
Fest, Joachim 70
Finkielkraut, Alain 77
First World War 33, 41, 53, 106, 108, 121
Foucault, Michel 43–44, 124
French Revolution 88–89
Frenssen, Gustav 44
Freud, Sigmund 106

G
Gadamer, Hans-Georg 137–138
genocide in Armenia 33
geopolitical determinism 12
Georg Ritter v. Schönerer 70
German colonial history 46
German-style political existentialism 152
German war 39
'global' cultural theory 122
global interventionism 138
Glucksmann, André x
God warriors 81
Greek-Turkish conflicts 41
'Großer Brockhaus' of 1931 44
third Gulf War 2003 124

H
Habermas, Jürgen 124, 147, 162
Heidegger, M. 4–5, 64, 68, 70–73, 96, 100, 105, 114, 137, 159–60, 164–65
Heraclitus of Ephesus 3, 6, 64, 72, 160
hermeneutics viii, xvii, 42–43, 48, 56–57, 95, 98, 115, 129, 137–39, 143
heroism 120–21
Himmler, Heinrich 55, 66
'Historia Magistra Vitae' 98, 129
historical competences 33
historical consciousness xxiv, 31–33, 35, 43, 114, 133, 166, 168
historical-philosophical expectations 114, 124
historical reality 32, 33, 35, 42, 52, 132
historical violations xxii, 46, 49, 136
historicism ix, 6, 70, 143, 151
Hitler, A. 40, 65–66, 69, 70

Hobbes, Thomas 6, 154, 156
Hobbesian scenario of primitive 146
Hoche, Karl 77
holy violence 22
holy war 85, 90, 156
homines sacri 155
homo sacer 155
Hondrich, Karl Otto 141
human authenticity 42
human existence 5, 70, 100
human history xv, xxi, 7, 12–13, 16–17, 19, 50, 71, 112, 115, 130, 157, 159, 166
humanity viii, xxiv, ix, xv, xviii, xxi, 5–6, 17, 40, 46, 50, 65–67, 75–76, 83, 91, 95, 106, 119, 126, 131–32, 135, 148–49, 151, 159, 161, 163–64, 167–69
humankind 114
human moral self-interpretation 113
human praxis 128
human rights xxii, xvii, 17, 59, 91–93, 138, 144–47, 161
Hüppauf, Bernd 57
Husserl, E. 137

I
illegitimate violence 150, 155
implicit pedagogy 127, 169; contemporary theory of hermeneutics 137–39; critical thinking 132; cultural value of historical narratives 131; dialogical culture of history 135–37; dianoia 128–29, 138; double contingency of history 130; feasibility 131; historical thinking 130; ontogenesis 132; philosophical-hermeneutical intrinsic value 129; phylogenesis 132; power of narration 131–35; presupposition-rich concept 130; scepticism 131; self-empowerment 130, 138–39
instrumental point of view of care 97
intercultural psychology 47, 48
international law 8, 11, 76, 142, 146–49, 161–62

J
'just war' thesis 142

K
Kant, I. xi, xxi, 106, 123, 147–48, 162
Kapust, Antje 78
Koselleck, R. 4–5, 26–27, 39, 55, 70–71, 74–75, 80, 97, 113
Krippendorff, Ekkehart 161

L
language of modernity 86
Lanz v. Liebenfels and 69

Levene, Mark 40
Leviathan 154–56
Levinas, E. xxiii, 6, 50, 63, 107, 160, 163
liberal theory 125
life-serving constellation 47
Lueger, Karl 70
Luhmann, Niklas 124
Lyotard, Jean F. 168

M
Machiavelli, N. 105
Machiavellianism xiv
Mann, Michael 43–44
Marshall, Tim 11
martial violence 121
Marxism ix
Massacres of Armenians 41
mass murders 39, 41, 43, 57, 65, 146
materialism 19
Mbembe, Achille 46
Melians xii
The Merchant of Venice 77
metaphysical politics 82
metaphysics 3, 4, 81, 87, 97, 160
millenarianism 81
modernity xi, 12, 15, 18, 37, 43, 53, 58, 82, 86–88, 90, 95, 118–21, 127, 155, 157, 165
molecular civil war 144
monotheism 83–84, 86
moral feelings 141–42
morality xix, xxii, xxiii, 3, 29, 38, 42, 45, 52, 63–67, 75, 78–80, 88–90, 101, 105, 108, 118, 124, 131–32, 142–45, 150–51, 156, 162–63
moral universalism 91, 112
Morris, Ian xv, 6
Münkler, Herfried 95

N
Napoleonic Wars 121
narrative competence 31–35, 114, 134, 167
National Socialism 68, 72, 77–78, 91
National Socialist ideology 56–57, 80
National Socialist violence 40, 75
NATO intervention, Kosovo in 1999 146
Nazi death camps 59
Nazi ideology 76, 80
Nazi regime threat, May 1939 25
Nazism 66, 76–77
Nicolaus v. Brelow 65
Nietzsche, Friedrich ix, 26–27, 67, 76, 96, 105
nihilism 53, 71, 103
non-Aryan 77
non-political wars 144
non-violence 17, 18, 20–21, 23, 43, 85, 88, 96, 100–101, 107–10, 112, 118–19, 145–46, 150, 154, 159–61

nuclear war 141
number tattooing 60

O
October Revolution of 1917 136
odyssey of St Louis, passenger ship 25, 34
One-God-Will 84
online hate communication 51
Ottoman rule in 1908 41

P
pacifism 121
peace viii, xi, xiv, xv, xxi, xxiii, 4–5, 7, 11, 18, 21, 39–40, 74, 85, 93, 96, 107, 109, 112, 118, 123, 138, 141–43, 147–50, 156, 161–62, 168
peace-theoretical reflection 148
Peloponnesian War 4, 95
Persian Wars 3–4
Peter Moor's Journey to the Southwest 44
phantasm 9, 21, 114, 161
phatic function 34–35
phenomenological social theory 22
philosophical anthropology 10, 14, 16, 98, 100, 151
philosophical existentialism 71, 73
philosophical thinking 100, 119
philosophy of history viii–x, 122–26, 166–70
Pinker, S. xix, 49, 159
polemogenic reflection 64
political existentialism 5, 71, 73–74, 152
political kinetics xxii
political-military claims of Americans 114
political psychology 11
political religions 88–89
political thanatology 97
political violence 82, 119
Posen, Himmler 79
principle of primogeniture 122
prisoners of Auschwitz 28
protection treaties, indigenous rulers 39
psychic effects 111
psychoanalytical criteria 115
purification process 65
Putin, V. 136

R
radical violence 6, 160
Red Army 60
religious dark spots: ambivalence of 90; Christ-killers 85; concept of time 87; Constantine's victory in 324 85; democratic consensus 87; democratic-theoretical conviction 88; dialectical paths 87; divine justice 87; faith 87; holy war 85, 90; human rights 91; intolerance and negation 84;

legitimisation 85; loyalty and devotion 89; massacre of 1099 85; monotheism 83–84; morality 89; myths and rites 84; One-God-Will 84; political religions 88–89; promises of salvation 82; religious 'nature' of humans 83; revolutionary movement 89; secularisation 88; theocratic temptation 82; and theological traditions 90; universalisable rights 92; and violence 81–93
religious legitimacy x
religious worldviews 158
renouncing violence 52, 98, 119, 123
repression 40, 42, 57–58, 119, 166, 168
rethinking war 143
Russian politics of memory 136
Russia's invasion of Ukrainian territory 124

S
Sartre, Jean-Paul 52
Saxon wars xii
sceptical reflections 27
scepticism 131
Schlögel, Karl 12
Schmitt, Carl 73, 75–76, 126, 153, 160
School of Salamanca 105
Second World War 51, 108, 145
secularisation 86–87
'Sein und Zeit' 5
self-aggrandisement 112, 134–35
self-empowerment 130, 138–39
silencing 58, 109
social theoretical reflection 143
social theory xix, xx, xxi, 20, 22, 44, 49–50, 63, 75, 96–97, 101, 105, 114, 124, 126, 142, 151–52
socio-moral force 143
space 27, 29, 35, 38–39, 44, 47–48, 88, 103, 107, 112, 115–16, 128, 134, 143–44, 146, 148, 152–53, 157, 163, 168–69; aesthetic and cultural dimension 13–16; alterity 13; cataclysms 13; communicative space 113; disillusioning 16; epistemology of 12; historical-political claims 15; historical studies 10; history of violence 10; horrors 13; intrinsic value 13; modern contemporaneity 15; normative space 36; phenomenology of 23; political psychology 11; ruptures 13; temporal space 35; valorative space (*see* valorative space); world politics 11
Szklarek, Moshe 51

T
Taylor, Charles 127
the terrifying love of war 33

thanato politics 51
theory of power 43
thesis of Egyptology 83
threat of enemy invaders 12
Thucydides xii, 95
totalitarianism xviii, 25, 79, 89, 148
totalitarian system 53
totalitarian violence 130
traumatic violence 92
triangle of peace 123
tribal wars 39
trinitarian war 144
Tripolitan War of 1911 41
Trojan War 11
trust 119, 120
Turkish-Armenian conflicts 41
Turkish national homogenisation 41

U
Ukraine war of 2022 142
unified substance of responsibility 113
universalisable rights 92
universal paternity of war 160
untamed violence 44

V
valorative space 35, 117–18, 169
violence 45; action and performance 28; annihilation 29; antinomies of 146; anti-semitism 50, 51; archaic violence x; in Auschwitz 28; awareness of 6; blatant sadism 57; in 'bloodlands' 108; bloody alliance xii; body functions 19; Charlemagne's rule xiii; colonial violence 33 (*see* colonial violence); comprehended violence xx; constitutional law xiv; contemporary discourses 50; in context of Holocaust 28; critical theories 44; cultural and religious rituals 120; dark forces of xi; death-dealing systems 28; de facto violence 49, 110; dehumanisation acts 29; disastrous violence 32 (*see* disastrous violence); discursive approach 50; dispositive of 44; and domination x–xvi, 37; of empty gaze 58; endemic conditions 18; enmity 74–78; ethical reflection 7; extra-state zones 22; faces of violence 12; forlornness of 106; fragility 100–101; genocidal violence 43; ghettos 55; Hate existence 50–53; heroism 120–21; historical-theoretical approach 79; historical violence 98, 136; history of viii–x, 8–10, 31, 57, 126, 168; holy violence 22; human affairs 18; in human existence 100; humanity 17; ideological doctrines 79; ideologies of 68–71; illegitimate violence 155; intercultural psychology 48;

inter-existential form 8; inter-existential tensions xi; interpretation of 144; language 109; and language 8, 49, 109; and linguisticity 110; martial violence 121; mass murders 43; materialism 19; meaning of 58–61; memory of terror 26; mistrust 55; modernity xi, 12, 120; morality 78–80, 101, 156; narrative competence 31–34; natural history 12; between nature and culture 20–23; against nature and living conditions 16; non-understanding 54; number tattoo 28, 29; objective history 27; in the Old World 28; online hate communication 51; and order 145–49; personification 8; phenomenology of xv, 8, 18–19, 23, 42, 143; philosophical reflection 102, 146; and philosophy 96–98; physical constitution 19; political violence 82, 119; post-metaphysical conditions 106; preoccupation 58; principle of primogeniture 122; prisoners of Auschwitz 28; psychological dispositions 102; psychology 16–18; racism 57; radical violence 6; reflection of violence xviii–xxiv; rehabilitation 55; and religious dark spots 79, 81–93; renouncing violence 119, 123; renunciation of 16, 118, 120–21, 147, 162; rule is based on violence xii; rupture of civilisation 53; sense and sensibility 19–20; senselessness 29; signatures and metamorphoses xxi; silencing 109; sober analysis 49; in space 10–16; spaces of transparency 55; threats and vulnerabilities 7; threshold of conceptualisation 58; topography of 115; totalitarian system 53; traces of gnosis 21; transcendental violence 50; triviality 14; trust 119–20; in Ukraine 147; untamed violence 44; and violation 102; youth bulge 122

W
Wagener, Richard 70
Waldenfels, Bernhard 21
Walzer, Michael 6, 132

war: adventures 45; on African continent 38; anthropological tensions 106; ballast existences 77; Battle of Thermopylae 72; *Being and Time* 73; condemnation of 6; cruel facticity of life 127; cultural self-assertion 105; dark language 73; despotism 4; enemies of humanity 76; ethical ontology of 6; European war 17; First World War 33, 41, 53, 108, 121; German war 39; third Gulf War 2003 124; holy humility 6; law and morality 64; legalisation of 105; moment of polemic 72; moral claim 3; moral condemnation of 104; moral dissolution 76; morality 142; Napoleonic Wars 121; non-Aryan 77; nuclear war 141; occidental culture 73; past war 72; Peloponnesian War 4, 95; Persian Wars 3, 4; philosophy of history 166–70; photographs of 57; polemogenic reflection 64, 73; political existentialism 73, 74; reality of the bios 73; reasonableness of the logos 73; rethinking war 143; Second World War 51, 108, 145; state-building wars 104; teaching and ordering function 98–101; totalitarian linguistic politics 77; tribal wars 39; Tripolitan War of 1911 41; Trojan War 11; truthfulness of the polemos 73
war-preventing measures 162
'Weimar' mood 76
Welzer, Harald 79–80
Wertman, Gal 60
Western civilisation 126
The West 145
Widukind xii
worldview of care 157
worldview of concern 159, 163–66
worldview of myth 157–58
worldview of our time 158
worldview of war 157, 159–63
worry 164, 167

Y
Yermelenko, Anatoly 148
Young Turks 41
youth bulge 122

www.ingramcontent.com/pod-product-compliance
Lightning Source LLC
Chambersburg PA
CBHW021828300426
44114CB00009BA/361